SELF-LOVE, EGOISM AND THE SELFISH HYPOTHESIS

Key Debates from Eighteenth-Century British Moral Philosophy

Christian Maurer

EDINBURGH
University Press

Edinburgh University Press is one of the leading university presses in the UK.
We publish academic books and journals in our selected subject areas across the
humanities and social sciences, combining cutting-edge scholarship with high editorial
and production values to produce academic works of lasting importance. For more
information visit our website: edinburghuniversitypress.com

Edinburgh University Press Ltd
The Tun – Holyrood Road, 12(2f) Jackson's Entry, Edinburgh EH8 8PJ

First published in hardback by Edinburgh University Press 2019

Typeset in 10.5/13pt Sabon
IDSUK (DataConnection) Ltd, and
printed and bound by CPI Group (UK) Ltd,
Croydon, CR0 4YY

A CIP record for this book is available from the British Library

ISBN 978 1 4744 1337 4 (hardback)
ISBN 978 1 4744 7797 0 (paperback)
ISBN 978 1 4744 1338 1 (webready PDF)
ISBN 978 1 4744 1339 8 (epub)

Contents

Tables

Acknowledgements

This book is short. It was with me for a long time and had an inherent tendency to be much longer, but restrictions on space and the non-native speaker's limited eloquence have kept it within narrow boundaries. In various ways, it is connected to my (much longer) *Thèse de doctorat*, entitled 'Self-love in Early Eighteenth-century British Moral Philosophy: Shaftesbury, Mandeville, Hutcheson, Butler and Campbell', which I wrote as an *Assistant doctorant* in the Philosophy Department of the Université de Neuchâtel, and as a visiting doctoral student in philosophy and history at the University of Glasgow. With Richard Glauser as a supervisor, and Alexander Broadie, James Harris and Laurent Jaffro as members of the *Jury de thèse*, I was lucky to get most inspiring feedback. In some way or other, I continued to explore the theme in various circumstances – as a post-doc in the research centre Philosophies et rationalités (PHIER) at the Université Blaise Pascal, Clermont-Ferrand II (now 'Université Clermont Auvergne'), as an *Assistant docteur* in the Philosophy Department at the University of Fribourg, and as a Visiting Research Fellow at the University of Glasgow (in history), at the University of St Andrews (in philosophy and intellectual history) and at the University of Edinburgh at the Institute for Advanced Studies in the Humanities (IASH).

During these last years, this book has benefited directly and indirectly from countless inspiring discussions in, around and outside conferences, workshops and seminars with numerous colleagues, many of whom I am lucky enough to consider my friends. Exchanging and debating ideas with them has always been one of the most beloved parts of the academic enterprise, and I am deeply grateful for the encouragement, benevolent interest, patience and, sometimes, endurance my spoken and written contributions have met. I wish to mention particularly Thomas Ahnert, David Allan, Michèle Amacker, Marina Barabas, Bihotz Barrenechea, Michele Bee, Ondřej Beran, Laura Berchielli, Donna Bezat, Michel Bourban, Ian Bradley, Alexander Broadie, Chris Brooke, Lisa Broussois, Dan Carey,

Christine Clavien, Remy Debes, Abigail Dehart, William Duba, Elisabeth Dutton, Mark Elliot, Claire Etchegaray, Delphine Faivre-Carron, James Foster, Aaron Garrett, Giovanni Gellera, Julie Giangiobbe, Richard Glauser, Andreas Graeser, Gordon Graham, Christian Grosse, Simon Grote, Béatrice Guion, Knud Haakonssen, Ryan Hanley, James Harris, Eugene Heath, Tomáš Hejduk, Colin Heydt, Sarah Hutton, Laurent Jaffro, Tom Jones, Béla Kapossy, Filip Karfík, Richard King, Ester Kroeker, Neven Leddy, Eléonore Le Jallé, Wim Lemmens, Susan Manning, Cheryl Mendelson, Anne Meylan, Tony Milligan, Jim Moore, Elena Muceni, Tarek Naguib, Fritz Osterwalder, Martin Otero-Knott, Kamila Pacovská, Alain Petit, Pauline Phemister, Nick Phillipson, Eva Pibiri, Maria-Cristina Pitassi, Wolfgang Pross, John Purser, Sophie Ramsay, Stephen Reid, Justine Roulin, Paul Sagar, Eric Schliesser, Daniel Schulthess, John Sellars, Sandy Stewart, Sarah Stewart-Kroeker, Charles-Olivier Stiker-Métral, Jan Swearingen, Jackie Taylor, Spiros Tegos, Angélique Thébert, Mikko Tolonen, Lena Wånggren, Richard Whatmore, Jean-Claude Wolf and Simone Zurbuchen. I should name many others. I am especially grateful for my students' interest, curiosity and critical company – they have always been, and continue to be, a source of inspiration. Staff at numerous libraries and archives have helped and impressed me with their patience and gentle guidance. The National Library of Scotland and the National Records of Scotland in particular have become parts of a second home. At Edinburgh University Press, Carol Macdonald, Kirsty Woods and Ersev Ersoy have very gently helped me through the various stages of the publishing process.

On many occasions, I would have wished to spend more time and words on the description of intellectual contexts and biographies, on more profound assessments of arguments, and on more critical discussion of secondary literature. Trying to cover a full century of a rich debate with so many participants, and giving enough attention to rather unknown, but in themselves important figures, is difficult. Having no female philosophers to discuss makes me uneasy and is hopefully not the result of inattention. Trying to cope with very different disciplinary expectations and norms has proven especially challenging. Over these last years I have been given the opportunity to work in very diverse research environments, and I have made my best efforts to blend some facets of these in a stimulating manner. Hopefully, the combination of methods and perspectives I have chosen to present the debates on self-love brings into conversation diverging understandings of the enterprise called the 'history of philosophy'. I also hope that the comparisons between the chosen authors, both so-called 'major' and 'minor' figures, and the discussion of their connections will help render more visible the fascinating diversity of early modern debates on self-love.

Several passages of this book formed part of my *Thèse de doctorat*, or have been sections of journal articles or book chapters, in which cases I have benefited from the careful guidance of editors and reviewers. Excerpts from the following published pieces are included in this book, and I want to thank the publishing houses for their permission: 'Self-interest and Sociability', in J. Harris (ed.), *The Oxford Handbook of British Philosophy in the Eighteenth Century* (Oxford: Oxford University Press, 2013), 291–314, reproduced by permission of Oxford University Press, https://global.oup.com/academic; 'What Can an Egoist Say Against an Egoist? On Archibald Campbell's Criticisms of Bernard Mandeville', *Journal of Scottish Philosophy* 12:1 (2014), 1–18, reproduced by permission of Edinburgh University Press, https://www.euppublishing.com; 'Doctrinal Issues Concerning Human Nature and Self-love, and the Case of Archibald Campbell's *Enquiry*', *Intellectual History Review* 26:3 (2016), 355–69, © International Society for Intellectual History, reprinted by permission of Taylor & Francis Ltd, www.tandfonline.com on behalf of International Society for Intellectual History.

I furthermore want to acknowledge the Swiss National Science Foundation (SNSF), and the Conseil Régional d'Auvergne for their support on several occasions over the last years. Directly and indirectly this helped to develop the book. In 2006–07 I had the chance to be in Glasgow with a 'Young Researcher Grant' bestowed by the SNSF (grant number PBNE1–114683). In 2009–10 I spent a most inspiring year in Clermont-Ferrand as 'Chercheur invité' of the Conseil Régional d'Auvergne. In July and August 2012 I translated seventeenth-century Scottish Latin material with Alexander Broadie and Giovanni Gellera in Glasgow with a 'Short Visit' grant from the SNSF (grant number IZK0Z1_144942), and in 2013–14 I explored the libraries and archives in Edinburgh and St Andrews thanks to an 'Advanced Post-Doc Mobility' grant from the SNSF (grant number P300P1_147813).

The most important people to thank for their encouragement and support are close friends and family – especially in Berne and in other places in Switzerland, in France, in the Netherlands, in Scotland and elsewhere. I do not want to compile a list of names here, but I wish to express my deep gratitude to those who know how much they are concerned. I also want to thank Fausta Benini and, especially, Elisabeth, for their patience during the completion of this book.

Abbreviations

Butler, *Sermons* – Joseph Butler, *Fifteen Sermons Preached at the Rolls Chapel.*

Campbell, *Enquiry* – Archibald Campbell, *An Enquiry into the Original of Moral Virtue.*

Campbell, *Further Explications* – Campbell, *Professor Campbell's Further Explications.*

Campbell, *Remarks* – Campbell, *Remarks upon some Passages in Books Publish'd by Mr. Archibald Campbell.*

Campbell, *Report* – Campbell, *The Report of the Committee for Purity of Doctrine.*

Hume, *Enquiry* – David Hume, *An Enquiry Concerning the Principles of Morals.*

Hume, *Essays* – Hume, *Essays Moral, Political, and Literary.*

Hume, *Treatise* – Hume, *A Treatise of Human Nature.*

Hutcheson, *Essay* – Francis Hutcheson, *An Essay on the Nature and Conduct of the Passions and Affections.*

Hutcheson, *Inquiry* – Hutcheson, *An Inquiry into the Original of Our Ideas of Beauty and Virtue.*

Hutcheson, *Remarks* – Hutcheson, *Reflections upon Laughter and Remarks upon the Fable of the Bees.*

Hutcheson, *System* – Hutcheson, *A System of Moral Philosophy.*

Mandeville, *Charity* – Bernard Mandeville, 'An Essay on Charity, and Charity-Schools', in *The Fable of the Bees, or Private Vices, Publick Benefits.*

Mandeville, *Enquiry* – Mandeville, 'An Enquiry Into the Origin of Moral Virtue', in *The Fable of the Bees.*

Mandeville, *Fable I* – Mandeville, *The Fable of the Bees, or Private Vices, Publick Benefits.*

Mandeville, *Fable II* – Mandeville, *The Fable of the Bees. Part II.*

Mandeville, *Honour* – Mandeville, *An Enquiry Into the Origin of Honour, and the Usefulness of Christianity in War.*

Mandeville, *Remarks* – Mandeville, 'Remarks', in *The Fable of the Bees.*

Mandeville, *Search* – Mandeville, 'A Search Into the Nature of Society', in *The Fable of the Bees.*

Shaftesbury, *Inquiry* – Anthony Ashley Cooper, 3rd Earl of Shaftesbury, 'An Inquiry Concerning Virtue or Merit', in *Characteristics of Men, Manners, Opinions, Times.*

Shaftesbury, *Miscellanies* – Shaftesbury, 'Miscellaneous Reflections on the Preceding Treatises and Other Critical Subjects', in *Characteristics.*

Shaftesbury, *Moralists* – Shaftesbury, 'The Moralists, a Philosophical Rhapsody, being a Recital of Certain Conversations on Natural and Moral Subjects', in *Characteristics.*

Shaftesbury, *Sensus Communis* – Shaftesbury, 'Sensus Communis, an Essay on the Freedom of Wit and Humour in a Letter to a Friend', in *Characteristics.*

Shaftesbury, *Pathologia* – Shaftesbury, *Pathologia, A Theory of the Passions.*

Smith, *TMS* – Adam Smith, *The Theory of Moral Sentiments.*

1. Introduction

The Self-love of Mankind in their present Circumstances is corrupted and depraved, [. . .] a most vitious and inordinate Passion, and cannot possibly be the Principle of any virtuous Action whatsoever.

Alexander Moncrieff, secessionist minister, 1735

Neither does there appear any reason to wish self-love were weaker in the generality of the world, than it is.

Joseph Butler, Anglican bishop, 1726[1]

1.1 THE QUESTIONS OF SELF-LOVE

The first term in the title of this book, and the key notion for the present study, is *self-love*. This term is, however, likely to leave a present-day reader somewhat puzzled.[2] What exactly is this thing called 'self-love'? Very broadly speaking, the expression seems to invoke some kind of positive attitude towards our self – yet how exactly does this attitude manifest itself, when is it appropriate and when not? Is it really a form of love with the self as its object, as the expression suggests, or is it rather some form of self-approval, a good opinion about the self? Or does it simply refer to self-interested, egoistic desires for the agent's own advantage? Each of these answers, and others, were given at some point during the eighteenth century. Clearly, any more specific definition of the term will have an impact on discussions regarding the role of self-love in human psychology and society, and regarding its moral (and immoral) dimensions. Hence the crucial importance of dissecting the ambiguities surrounding the term 'self-love', which will be one of the chief tasks of this study.

The English term 'self-love' has a vivid history. In the seventeenth century it appeared very rarely in philosophical texts (Thomas Hobbes and John Locke, for example, almost never used it), though some-what more frequently in theological writings.[3] In the early eighteenth century, however, the term 'self-love' is quite suddenly omnipresent in Anglophone moral philosophy, especially in the 1720s and 1730s. At this time, it becomes part of the central vocabulary for discussing human behaviour from moral, psychological, theological, political and economic perspectives. If in seventeenth- and eighteenth-century Francophone philosophy and theology, a distinction between *amour-propre* and *amour de soi* was quite common, this was (generally) not the case in Anglophone philosophy – a fact that complicates the situation in interesting ways. Ultimately, even if the intense debates on self-love between thinkers in eighteenth-century Britain were influenced by other philosophical and theological traditions, especially French ones, it makes sense to concentrate on the British debates as a particularly intricate conversation.

The second term in the title of this book is *egoism*. Nowadays, we understand this term quite readily, since in the twentieth century it made its way into ordinary language with the now familiar opposition between egoism and altruism. 'Egoism' and 'egoistic' are, however, used in two somewhat different senses: first, in a more technical and morally neutral sense to contrast desires that are ultimately self-interested and aim at the agent's own benefit with desires that are altruistic or disinterested and aim at the benefit of someone else. Secondly, 'egoism' and its cognates are sometimes used in proximity to 'selfishness' to blame someone for having acted for her own benefit only, possibly to the detriment of others. In this book, and in accordance with much philosophical literature, I shall use the term 'egoism' in the first, morally neutral sense. This is also the sense underlying the more theoretical debates on the question of whether genuinely altruistic desires to promote the well-being of others for their own sake actually exist, or whether they are not some strangely disguised form of ultimately egoistic desire to promote one's own well-being. These debates concern the general (descriptive) theory of human psychology called 'psychological egoism', according to which all of our desires are ultimately egoistic.[4] I shall come back to this point shortly.

In early modern Anglophone philosophy, the term 'egoism' is more or less non-existent, yet the opposition between egoism and altruism is well known and often captured in contrasting pairs of expressions such as 'private interest' and 'public interest', 'self-interested' and 'disinterested', 'self-love' and 'benevolence'. A present-day reader might feel tempted to bring the terms 'self-love' and 'egoism' into direct conversation by translating 'self-love' as 'egoism'.[5] In several cases, this move is indeed appropriate. Consider the influential early eighteenth-century philosopher Francis Hutcheson. When he discusses the relation between what he terms 'self-love' and 'benevolence', or between the self-interested desire to promote one's private good and the disinterested desire to promote the public good, he has in mind something very close to our present-day opposition between egoism and altruism. However, as will become more evident shortly, this is far from true for all his contemporaries.[6] Too hasty a restriction of the semantic field of 'self-love' to our contemporary notion of egoism risks distorting our understanding of the period's debates, and rendering an appropriate analysis more difficult, as I will argue on several occasions throughout this book.

One of the main points I want to demonstrate is that in eighteenth-century British thought there were five distinct conceptions of self-love, namely 1) self-love as egoistic or self-interested desires, 2) self-love as love of praise, 3) self-love as self-esteem (or due pride), 4) self-love as *amour-propre* (or excessive pride) and 5) self-love as respect of self. I will say more on these conceptions in the next section, and refine them in their respective contexts. Clearly, an accurate analysis of the different conceptions of self-love, and of the debates surrounding them, will require some minimal understanding of the authors' theories of the emotions, since self-love is typically treated as a passion or affection, and quite often as one of the fundamental ingredients of human psychology.[7] As with other emotions or passions, the psychological dimension is conceived as inextricably connected to the moral one: self-love is indeed one of the passions that occupies a central place in eighteenth-century British moral debates.

The third expression in the title of this book is *selfish hypothesis*. This refers to a specific claim regarding self-love, which attracted a lot of attention especially in the early eighteenth century: the claim that *all* our motives and desires can be ultimately analysed in terms of self-love (in some sense).[8] The selfish hypothesis can often, but not always, be associated with the present-day theory of psychological egoism. In the early modern period, the selfish hypothesis was not considered a new theory of human psychology – it was famously connected with ancient Epicurean traditions and, in the seventeenth century, attributed to various authors such as Thomas Hobbes, John Locke, Samuel Pufendorf, French Augustinian moralists (of both Jansenist and Calvinist stripes) and others. In Anglophone philosophy, debates concerning the selfish hypothesis became particularly intense around the 1720s and 1730s. This can be partly explained as a reaction to some of the challenges posed by Bernard Mandeville – a fascinating and in various ways very influential thinker who will attract much of our attention.

The selfish hypothesis is primarily a *descriptive* theory of human psychology. However, it was (and still is) often associated with a pessimistic *moral* view of human nature as deeply corrupt and vicious.[9] It is significant that this connection between the descriptive dimension and the pessimistic moral dimension was made both by authors who rejected, as well as by authors who adopted the selfish hypothesis as a theory of human motivation. The making of this connection may have been reinforced by Hutcheson's influential approach to moral philosophy, but it was also supported by Calvinist and, more generally, Augustinian theological emphases on the Fall and original sin. Within such theological frameworks, asserting the descriptive psychological claim that all our desires are ultimately rooted in self-love meant *also* asserting the moral claim that therefore, in our present state, we do not have any genuinely virtuous desires – the dominance of self-love being one central aspect of postlapsarian corruption. Such pessimistic ideas sometimes still resonate in present-day debates on psychological egoism, albeit stripped of theological dimensions.

It is, however, crucial to highlight that a connection between the psychological and the moral dimensions was *not* univocally claimed to exist. Several eighteenth-century philosophers rejected the view that asserting the selfish hypothesis forces us into a view of human nature as morally corrupt. Archibald Campbell, John Gay and John Clarke of Hull, for example, defended the selfish hypothesis yet took great pains to make room for morality in human nature. Demonstrating awareness of the separateness of the descriptive and the moral dimensions, David Hume (who did not adopt the selfish hypothesis himself) suggested that we should distinguish between two versions of the selfish hypothesis, one connected with moral pessimism, the other rejecting such a connection.

In the eighteenth century the selfish hypothesis was often discussed in connection with an additional, epistemological thesis. In the search for the nature of our moral judgements, the claim that self-love is so strong as to influence or distort our moral judgements attracted quite a lot of attention. The claim that our self-love is ultimately the principle according to which we judge the moral value of motives, actions and characters often (but not always) comes close to what we nowadays call 'ethical egoism'. This is, roughly, the theory that our moral judgements are ultimately judgements about whether or not something is useful to further our private interest.[10] According to this theory, when I judge that something is morally good, I do not make a disinterested moral judgement, but I actually mean that something is good *for me*. This might be construed as a more general attack on the reality of objective moral values, which brings us to yet another question: if the claim is true that all our moral judgements are, in reality, judgements about whether something furthers our own interest, are we then not completely mistaken in our assumptions about what constitutes a moral practice, since we commonly think that morality is somehow connected to furthering the interests of others? Such were some of the worries about self-love connected to moral epistemology, and they were again often discussed in connection with Mandeville's provocative writings.

Both the question of whether the selfish hypothesis forces us into a pessimistic view of human nature and the question of self-love's potentially distorting influence on our moral judgements were part of a more general debate concerning the *moral status of human nature*. At the risk of oversimplification, one might state that British philosophy and theology in the seventeenth century often defended rather grim and pessimistic views of human nature (with interesting exceptions, of course – notably the Cambridge Platonists). The eighteenth century, by contrast, witnessed a broad range of efforts to put forward more positive views of human nature (again with interesting exceptions – notably Mandeville and various theologians). As suggested in Michael Gill's book *The British Moralists on Human Nature and the Birth of Secular Ethics* (Gill 2006), such positive views were often formulated against the Calvinist theological *topoi* of the irredeemable corruption of humankind after the Fall, our complete dependence on divine grace for salvation, and the impossibility of justification by works.

Such a contrast between the seventeenth and the eighteenth centuries is admittedly oversimplified, yet it points to profound changes in philosophical and theological reflections on human nature, where the debates on self-love and on the selfish hypothesis constituted a central battleground. Take, for example, those thinkers who wanted to morally rehabilitate human nature against the Calvinist *topos* of postlapsarian corruption: for some, this rehabilitation involved demonstrating the limits of corrupt self-love in human psychology. For others, however, it involved defending a more nuanced and positive account of self-love, which often required a distinction between 'true' self-love and other, passionate forms of self-love. And again, some of those who defended a more positive view of self-love rejected the selfish hypothesis (for example, Joseph Butler, David Hume and Adam Smith), while others adhered to it (for example, Archibald Campbell, John Gay and John Clarke).

From these reflections, three clusters of questions emerge that should be addressed for an appropriate understanding of the period's debates on self-love. First, the precise meaning of the term 'self-love' needs to be determined, and it needs to be investigated how different conceptions of self-love relate to our present-day notion of egoism. Secondly, we need to look at the central role of the selfish hypothesis for the period's moral philosophy, which will again invite comparisons with present-day debates on psychological egoism. A third cluster of questions concerns the place of the arguments concerning self-love and the selfish hypothesis in more general discussions of the moral status of postlapsarian human nature.

In analysing how these questions were addressed by various eighteenth-century British thinkers, this study follows two somewhat different yet complementary interests. First, it seeks to provide analyses of the individual authors' arguments. This is a stance quite common in the intellectual enterprise called 'history of philosophy' (which is often subsumed under the more general enterprise called 'philosophy'). Secondly, this study also wants to situate the philosophical conversations between the investigated authors in their broader intellectual context – philosophical, theological, political, and so on. This is commonly conceived as the central business of the enterprise called 'intellectual history'. The authors I analyse in this study were all contributors to the debates on self-love, but they have sometimes been treated more extensively in either philosophy and the history of philosophy (for example, Butler) or in intellectual history (for example, Mandeville and Campbell). This situation has produced sometimes very different bodies of secondary literature, which has in turn influenced my own study: depending on the figure under investigation, one or other of the two interests of argumentative analysis and of contextualisation may be somewhat in the foreground. In general, I hope to provide a more profound and accurate understanding of the debates on self-love by combining the two interests. The resulting attention accorded to non-canonical or 'minor' authors may strike some readers as unusual, but it is motivated by the goal of providing an accurate and comparative account of the debates on self-love.

The themes of self-love and egoism in general have been addressed in quite diverse studies dealing with eighteenth-century British philosophers. More on the side of intellectual history, and with a general focus on European debates, Arthur Lovejoy published in the early 1960s a series of lectures on theories of human nature and their implications for political and economic theories (Lovejoy 1961). Lovejoy introduced a series of distinctions that are particularly relevant for my discussion of the different conceptions of self-love, drawing attention to various dimensions of self-interest broadly conceived. Somewhat in the vein of Lovejoy's interest in political and economic theory, the intellectual historians Albert Hirschman (Hirschman 1977) and more recently Pierre Force (Force 2003) have been interested in the concept of self-interest and its role in theories of the passions. Their studies are primarily motivated by an interest in the history of economic ideas (broadly speaking) and in related topics, such as the social dimensions of the human passions. However, they also provide valuable insights for a history of moral philosophy of the (mainly) French and British seventeenth and eighteenth centuries. Force's analysis strongly relies on the tripartition between (neo-)Stoic, (neo-)Augustinian and (neo-)Epicurean currents of thought. I will comment on these categories on several occasions: to some extent, they are a useful tool for the reconstruction and contextualisation of the debates on self-love, but at the same time we need to keep in mind the risks of producing simplified narratives of reception and influence.[11]

With its more philosophical–argumentative approach, Michael Gill's study on what he terms the 'Human Nature Question' (Gill 2006) is very relevant for the present book. Gill analyses how various British philosophers responded to the Calvinist pessimistic view of the moral status of postlapsarian human nature as deeply corrupt. His study provides an important framework for my more focused interest in self-love. Gill regularly draws attention to the role of arguments concerning egoism in the struggle for more positive views of human nature, presenting rejections of psychological egoism as part of the development of such positive views. My interest in different conceptions of self-love and their contexts will, however, suggest some important additions and alterations to Gill's narrative.[12] In particular, I shall draw attention to authors who adopt the selfish hypothesis while *also* arguing for a positive view of human nature. And more generally, I will give attention to several non-canonical authors who are often neglected by present-day philosophers – most importantly Archibald Campbell and, to a somewhat lesser extent, Bernard Mandeville. Such figures are often under-represented in systematically oriented argumentative reconstructions, yet they are crucial to fully understand and contextualise the arguments in the debates on self-love. Furthermore, Colin Heydt's study (Heydt 2018) on the relations between the nowadays better known and canonical thinkers and the much less well-known Pufendorfian 'conventional moral philosophy' is very fruitful. Heydt occasionally relies on elements from Gill, for example when contrasting 'optimistic' and 'pessimistic' views of human nature. Crucially, however, Heydt builds his analysis on themes in Haakonssen (1996). Considering a broad range of thinkers, Heydt is interested in the light shed on nowadays canonical philosophers by the once conventional, early modern distinction between our moral relations to God, to the self and to others (Heydt 2018: 13–14).

1.2 FIVE CONCEPTIONS OF SELF-LOVE

Let me now turn to the key term of the present study, *self-love*. Again, this expression may be read as pointing in the direction of some kind of positive attitude towards one's self, or at least towards aspects of one's self. In principle, one can conceive of such an attitude as appropriate, within just bounds and connected to a legitimate and justified promotion of one's self-interest[13] – or, on the contrary, one can see it as inappropriate, excessive and unjustified, maybe even unjustifiable – 'selfishness', in other words. In this book, I want to show how eighteenth-century British moral philosophers use the term 'self-love' in five distinct ways, which we need to grasp in order to properly understand the various dimensions of the debates on self-love. I will elaborate more specific analyses of the conceptions of self-love in the subsequent chapters on individual authors, but here I introduce some preliminary distinctions for a systematic overview.[14]

The Conception of Self-love as Egoistic Desire, or Egoistic Self-love

One of the most widespread conceptions of self-love in the eighteenth century was self-love as egoistic desire, or egoistic self-love, which is also the default understanding of many present-day historians of philosophy. Self-love is here associated, broadly speaking, with self-interested desires for some benefit to the agent or, more specifically, with hedonistic self-interested desires for pleasure, but it is not blameworthy selfishness. Hutcheson, for example, defines self-love in terms of desires that 'pursue ultimately only the private Good of the Agent' (Hutcheson, *Essay*: 37; see Chapter 4.1), and he sometimes suggests that this good is ultimately the natural good of pleasure. Hutcheson's immediate contemporary Campbell follows him in proposing a hedonistic egoistic conception of self-love (Campbell, *Enquiry*: 5; see Chapter 6.1).[15] The term 'love' is here understood as 'desire', which was quite common in early modern theories of the emotions.

On a more conceptual level, distinguishing between egoistic or self-interested desires on the one hand, and altruistic or disinterested desires on the other, is essential to avoid falling into the tautological claim that desires are always self-interested, just because they are the desires of someone. Crucially, however, to distinguish between egoistic and altruistic desires is *not* to claim that they are necessarily in conflict: many authors insist that, thanks to providential design, the promotion of the private good and the promotion of the public good ultimately coincide.

Moreover, adopting an egoistic conception of self-love does not mean subscribing to the theory of psychological egoism, or to the claim that *all* our desires are egoistic.

Egoistic conceptions of self-love, then, are primarily concerned with qualities of desires and actions, but they do not imply the presence of a more complex attitude of the agent to her self, such as the emotion of love. The fact that an agent egoistically desires some advantage for herself does not require any positive self-evaluation. Mandeville points out that even an agent who hates herself can be motivated by egoistic desires (Mandeville, *Fable II*: 136; see Chapter 3.1). Also, one can be said to act 'against' one's self-love, for example by acting on an overriding altruistic motive or a motive of duty, or by giving way to less important and short-sighted egoistic desires and passions. In this latter case, one could also be said to act against one's self-interest duly considered. This last point will be particularly important in Campbell, who adopts the selfish hypothesis and wants to distinguish different ways of following self-love (see Chapter 6.2).

The Conception of Self-love as Love of Praise

In the eighteenth century, the term 'self-love' is often used for a person's desire for some form of approbation from others – a favourable opinion or a positive affective attitude. Self-love in this sense is also often called 'love of praise', 'desire of esteem' or 'love of honour'. Unlike the egoistic conception of self-love, self-love as love of praise presupposes a more complex cognitive structure in that the agent has to conceive of herself as part of a social context with certain normative standards. Yet again, self-love as love of praise does not require a positive view of oneself – Mandeville highlights that an agent suffering from low self-esteem may have an even greater desire for praise than one with a high self-esteem (see Chapter 3.1).

Philosophers as well as theologians have often discussed self-love as an important motivating factor in self-conscious human agents, who are naturally concerned about the opinions of others: love of praise can motivate us to socially useful or morally virtuous actions. However, the dangers of excessive or misplaced love of praise are also frequently highlighted, as shown for example in Hugh Blair's discussion in the *Sermon on the Love of Praise*, responding to John 12:43: 'For they loved the praise of men more than the praise of God' (Blair 1824: 1, 284). In principle, love of praise can be appropriate, but it can also degenerate into Augustinian vanity or into a Hobbesian competitive desire for glory.

The Conception of Self-love as Self-esteem or Due Pride

A third conception of self-love is connected to the notions of self-esteem, self-approbation and pride – insofar as pride is understood as a potentially appropriate, moderate and morally acceptable positive attitude towards one's self, and thus as distinct from its excessive cognate *amour-propre*. Self-love as self-esteem or due pride requires that the agent thinks of herself as, in principle, worthy of approbation, and it involves some positive self-evaluation. Unlike *amour-propre*, however, self-esteem does not imply that the agent thinks of herself as better than others, nor does it necessarily have *amour-propre*'s comparative and competitive tendencies.

Self-love as self-esteem cannot be understood simply in terms of specific egoistic desires. It requires the agent's awareness of being an agent who is the subject of evaluative criteria, moral or other, and who fares well on that respect – such an agent thus has some positive opinion, attitude or 'love' for herself. But an agent might also lose her self-esteem, and even fall into self-hatred. Since self-love as self-esteem may make the agent care more about herself, it is often treated as an important feature in moral education. Self-esteem may be supported by praise, but it may also lead to indifference with respect to the opinions of others about oneself (as in the Stoic sage, or Smith's perfectly virtuous agent; see Chapter 7.2). Self-esteem can also be inappropriate when it is based on wrong features, or on wrong estimates. Augustinian theology has a strong tendency to dispute that there are, in the deplorable reality of the postlapsarian state, any *legitimate* grounds for self-esteem – rather, it would be appropriate to feel utter humiliation in view of our corruption (Calvin 2008: 1, 248). Against this view, many eighteenth-century British moral thinkers are concerned precisely with arguing for the possibility of justified instances of self-love as self-esteem or due pride (see, for example, Chapters 5.2, 6.2, 7.1 and 7.2), thus opposing a crucial feature of Augustinianism.

Self-love as amour-propre or Excessive Pride

One of the most fascinating conceptions of self-love in the eighteenth century is self-love as *amour-propre*, excessive pride or narcissism. This is especially important for understanding Mandeville's claims and their Augustinian connections, as well as the numerous reactions to these in Britain and elsewhere in Europe, most famously in Rousseau. Self-love as *amour-propre* may be construed as an excessive form of self-love as self-esteem, essentially involving competitive behavioural tendencies and the agent's belief in or feeling of superiority over others. Since the term 'pride', on its own, is often used to refer to self-love as self-esteem in the sense of an appropriate and morally innocent pride, I will use the expressions '*amour-propre*' and '*excessive* pride' to mark the distinction between potentially appropriate or due pride on the one hand, and excessive pride on the other. Mandeville, in the second volume of *The Fable of the Bees*, famously coined the term 'self-liking' to contrast self-love as *amour-propre* with 'self-love', that is, hedonistic egoistic self-love (see Chapter 3.1).

Self-love as *amour-propre* (or excessive pride) differs from self-love as self-esteem (or due pride) in that the former not only is defined by an inappropriately positive self-evaluation, but also by a tendency to compare oneself with other agents, and by the belief in one's superiority. Furthermore, it crucially engenders both the tendency to compete with others in order to safeguard one's feeling of superiority, and a tendency to display or express this superiority while seeking confirmation from others. On this basis, self-love as *amour-propre* is frequently treated as a cause of self-love as love of praise – most explicitly by Mandeville (see Chapter 3.1). At this point, Hobbes's discussion of glory as a positional and thus limited good becomes particularly pertinent: desire for glory must result in enforced competition (see Chapter 1.3). Typically, self-love as *amour-propre* is not only treated as inappropriate (since based on a false belief in one's superiority over others), but also as morally problematic and potentially dangerous in its consequences. However, Mandeville also argues provocatively that in spite of the problematic dimensions of self-love as *amour-propre*, it is a passion that can be rendered most useful in the civilising process (see Chapter 3.2).

Self-love as Respect of Self

The fifth conception of self-love I term 'respect of self' – in allusion to Butler's somewhat vague expression of that principle in human nature which 'respects self' (see Chapter 5.2). Butler's conception of self-love is unique in the early eighteenth century, yet it proved to be influential in many ways: we find reflections of it, for example, in the writings of Henry Home, Adam Ferguson, Thomas Reid, Dugald Stewart and even Francis Hutcheson (see especially Chapters 5.4 and 7.4).

For Butler, the 'self' that is the object of self-love is the agent's 'true' nature, as it is designed by God. It is thus not the agent's actual or empirical self, as in self-love as self-esteem, but a normative self that the agent has to realise in self-cultivation. An agent can be said to 'love' herself if she is disposed to act in order to realise this true self, which she recognises as the proper goal of self-cultivation. In other words, the agent's love of herself in the sense of respect of self is characterised by a concern to form her own identity in view of what she recognises as her true self. In Butler, this forming of one's identity is described as a process that involves supporting and restricting various dispositions and desires in view of the realisation of one's true self. An action is in conflict with her self-love as respect of self if it prevents her from realising her true self. Thus, an agent who performs a viciously selfish deed can be said to act in conflict with her self-love as respect of self. If the agent is said to *really* love herself, this violation of what she should consider to be her true self needs to be reflected in a changing attitude towards her actual self, for example in terms of an experience of shame, or a decrease of her self-love as self-esteem.

1.3 CONTEXTS AND HISTORIOGRAPHIES – OLD AND NEW

One of the central goals of this book is to further our understanding of the debates on self-love in eighteenth-century British moral philosophy. On a more conceptual level, it is therefore essential to distinguish the five aforementioned conceptions of self-love, and to resist too hasty an assimilation of self-love with our present-day concept of egoism. Moreover, a complete understanding of the investigated arguments concerning self-love requires taking into account relevant contexts – especially philosophical, theological and political ones. Philosophical arguments often responded to theological points regarding the moral status of human nature after the Fall, the nature and extent of postlapsarian corruption, the role of grace in salvation, and the possibility or impossibility of justification by good works. Thus, theological reflections regarding the impact of the Fall on human nature and the role of the passion of self-love therein often set the tone for debates in moral philosophy. My analysis of the tensions between Archibald Campbell and the Committee for Purity of Doctrine, for example, will show how self-love played a crucial role at the overlap between philosophy and theology. Without consideration of theological context, an argumentative reconstruction ignores the famous elephant in the room.

Another aspect of context concerns the authors' own presentations of their ideas. As participants in eighteenth-century debates on self-love, they usually considered themselves as partakers in a debate with a longer history, and they often tried to situate themselves in one tradition or another. Of course, such narratives also serve the purpose of highlighting one's own contributions, and thus several 'histories' of the debates on self-love were presented, with different ways of conceiving competing traditions. Again, the most important English predecessors to the debates in the eighteenth century, Thomas Hobbes and John Locke, hardly ever used the term self-love, yet their positions regarding human motivation were commonly summarised in the terminology of self-love only a few decades later.

One particularly influential eighteenth-century 'history' of the debates on self-love is Francis Hutcheson's (and I shall argue in this book that it is a rather problematic 'history'). At the beginning of his *Illustrations Upon the Moral Sense* (1728), he opposes 'two Opinions' on matters of human motivation and moral approbation. The first is as follows:

> The one that of the old *Epicureans*, as it is beautifully explained in the first Book of *Cicero, De finibus*, which is revived by Mr. *Hobbes*, and followed by many better Writers: 'That all the Desires of the *human Mind*, nay of all *thinking Natures*, are reducible to *Self-Love*, or *Desire of private Happiness*: That from this Desire all Actions of any Agent do flow.' Our *Christian Moralists* introduce other sorts of Happiness to be desired, but still ''tis the *Prospect of private Happiness*, which, with some of them, is the sole *Motive of Election*.' (Hutcheson, *Essay*: 134–5)

In his brief presentation, which relies on a conception of self-love as hedonistic egoistic desires, Hutcheson explains that according to the mentioned thinkers, not only motivation in general and moral motivation in particular, but also the moral approval of one's own and others' actions is determined by their tendency to promote 'the Happiness of the *Approver*', that is, by a judgement of his own self-love. In Hutcheson's presentation, these thinkers claim that all our desires and motives and our moral judgements are equally self-interested.

To this account by the Epicureans, the Hobbesians and the Christian moralists, Hutcheson opposes a second, alternative view regarding motivation and moral approbation:

> That we have not only *Self-Love*, but *benevolent Affections* also toward others, in various Degrees, making us desire their Happiness as an *ultimate End*, without any view to private Happiness: That we have a *moral Sense* or Determination of our Mind, to *approve* every *kind Affection* either in our selves or others, and all publickly useful Actions which we imagined to flow from such Affection, without our having a view to our *private Happiness*, in our Approbation of these Actions. (Hutcheson, *Essay*: 136)

This second view, which defends the reality both of altruistic or benevolent motivational principles and of a disinterested moral sense, Hutcheson associates especially with the Stoics, Shaftesbury and some other thinkers – and he aligns himself with this tradition.[16]

Without assessing the accuracy of this presentation by Hutcheson, I want to draw attention to some noteworthy points. First, it is striking to see the crucial place Hutcheson accords to the selfish hypothesis – it really is one of the central lenses through which he looks at the history of moral philosophy. This also serves to highlight his own central contributions – his arguments for the reality of disinterested benevolence, and of a disinterested moral sense. Second, Hutcheson presents questions of motivation, moral motivation and moral approbation as intrinsically connected: even if the selfish hypothesis is primarily a descriptive claim about human motivation, to accept Hutcheson's view forces us to accept as well the claim that moral approbation is self-interested. However, we shall encounter several philosophers who rejected Hutcheson's association between motivation and moral approbation. Third, what resonates in these lines by Hutcheson (and is made more explicit elsewhere, for example in his *Inaugural Oration* from 1730) is the importance of questions of natural sociability – for Hutcheson, one cannot adopt the Epicurean account of human motivation without claiming that human nature is naturally unsociable. Others, most importantly Campbell, attacked this connection made by Hutcheson. Fourth, and most importantly, Hutcheson sees the assertion of the selfish hypothesis as connected to the adopting of a pessimistic view of the moral status of human nature – again a point strongly rejected by several of the thinkers studied in this book.

Without really elaborating this point, Hutcheson indicates nevertheless that there might be room to distinguish different versions of the selfish hypothesis: if the Epicureans and Hobbes claim that all our desires are self-interested and ultimately aim at private happiness, then the '*Christian Moralists* [. . .] introduce other sorts of *Happiness* to be desired'. Here might emerge a distinction between a selfish hypothesis based on self-love as a simple source of egoistic desires on the one hand, and a selfish hypothesis based on self-love as *amour-propre* on the other. The resulting versions look very different, and as we shall see, several authors suggest more fine-grained discussions of this point, most importantly David Hume (see Chapter 7.1).

I now want to focus on the quasi-historical dimension that Hutcheson invokes when opposing two traditions. On the one hand, he names ancient and modern Epicureans as well as 'Christian Moralists', all of whom support some version of the selfish hypothesis. On the other hand, he mentions those 'ancient' and modern thinkers who reject the selfish hypothesis. The application of such binary distinctions to the history of philosophy is quite frequent – Shaftesbury, for example, famously opposes the 'Socratic' tradition (which includes, first and foremost, the Stoics) to the 'Epicurean' tradition.[17] As mentioned above, Hutcheson opposes to the Epicureans a cluster of Stoic, Platonist and other philosophers – including the modern figures Richard Cumberland, Shaftesbury and himself. Again, this way of presenting a condensed history of philosophy might have appealed to Hutcheson since it highlights particularly well his own central contributions to moral philosophy.

In a somewhat similar spirit to Hutcheson's, more recent historians of ideas have suggested reading early modern sources through a tripartite lens that encompasses Stoics (and neo-Stoics), Epicureans (and neo-Epicureans) and Augustinians.[18] This has led to a number of inspiring discussions, since in contrast to de-contextualised argumentative reconstructions, the use of such 'school terms' helps to identify important similarities, overlaps and differences between various positions, and to situate them in their wider development. These terms and distinctions reveal a conversation between ancient and early modern approaches to philosophical questions, and they may be hints which point at paths of influence, which again often permit a more profound understanding of historical developments.[19]

However, school terms can be used in different ways. On the one hand, they can be used rigidly, for example by insisting on a narrow and fixed set of defining doctrines or tenets which form a coherent systematic unity – in our minds, often, rather than in the minds of the authors themselves. This might prevent us in turn from detecting interesting influences, and ways in which positions and schools develop over time. But on the other hand, school terms may be used too loosely, for example by interpreting the presence of some vague and isolated ideas in a thinker as a sign of his or her adherence to a specific tradition. This might result in oversimplified narratives of the development of positions and schools, which make us blind to the specific ways in which ideas are selectively adopted and adapted. If, for example, we call someone a 'Stoic' merely on account of a vague assertion that human nature is sociable, or that virtue can be cultivated and is not necessarily unpleasant, or if we call someone an 'Epicurean' simply by virtue of his or her adoption of the selfish hypothesis, we lose sight of crucial questions about the specific ways in which such ideas were adapted into new contexts, or how they were rejected and polemically attributed to someone else.

Early modern thinkers were often quite eclectic and strategic in their use of ideas from ancient thinkers, and we need to take this into account when studying the debates on self-love. Theological debates especially teach us how ideas could be used polemically, and how flexibly demarcation lines between orthodoxies, heterodoxies and heresies could be handled – a point that is no different in philosophy. Calling someone an Epicurean in the early modern period was typically an accusation of atheism, materialism or determinism, rather than an attempt to describe a similarity between a modern philosophical position and an ancient tradition. In other words, it is essential to look more precisely into how early modern philosophical claims or systems were associated with one school rather than another. With these reservations in mind, I want to cautiously use Hutcheson's very rough historiography as a basis for discussing some school terms and figures from the period, thereby also introducing some cornerstones for the debates on self-love.

The 'Epicureans' and Hobbes: Pleasure, Pain and Hedonism

The first group of thinkers mentioned by Hutcheson are the 'old Epicureans', with their early modern follower Thomas Hobbes, and he also counts John Locke and Samuel Pufendorf among them.[20] It was indeed quite common to attribute to the Epicureans, first, the view that all our motives can be analysed in terms of a self-interested pursuit of pleasure (that is, egoistic self-love or, in present-day terminology, the position of psychological egoism in its hedonistic variety), and secondly, the rejection of (some versions of) the claim that we are naturally sociable.[21] Further commonly mentioned features of Epicurean philosophy were materialism, determinism and atheism. As seen in Hutcheson, Hobbes was often portrayed as sympathetic to Epicurean ideas. It must be noted, however, that materialism, determinism and atheism were often *also* attributed to the Stoics, and that, especially in the seventeenth century, it was quite common to group together Hobbes and the Stoics.[22] This is fundamentally at odds with Hutcheson's presentation, and it is evidence of the struggle for interpretative authority: in a context dominated by theological debates on free will and the possibility of sin, the Stoic *fatum* and Hobbesian mechanistic determinism were seen as strikingly similar.[23] Hutcheson's strong focus on questions of sociability, by contrast, makes him put Hobbes in the 'Epicurean' camp, opposing the other 'Antients'.

Hobbes quickly became one of the key figures for eighteenth-century British debates on self-love, especially as a target for criticism in discussions regarding the selfish hypothesis, and in connected efforts to overcome a pessimistic view of the moral status of human nature. As mentioned above, Hobbes himself rarely ever used expressions such as 'self-love', 'love of self', *amor sui, amor proprii* and φιλαυτία (*philautia*). Yet his account of human psychology, with the fundamental pillar of self-preservation, offered itself very easily to presentations in the terminology of self-love – which was exactly what Hobbes's critics started to do at the turn of the century, as seen in Hutcheson. Today, it is relatively common (yet not undisputed) to present Hobbes's moral psychology as the seventeenth-century paradigm of psychological egoism, and his moral theory as a paradigm of ethical egoism.[24] Hobbes's political theory is often presented as an obvious consequence of this. The notorious saying *homo homini lupus*, 'man to man is an arrant wolf' (Hobbes 1991: 89), became the benchmark for Hobbes's view of human nature as aggressive, resulting in a conception of the state of nature as a state of war. All this is often supposed to dovetail with his assertion of the selfish hypothesis, usually backed by statements such as this: 'Of the voluntary acts of every man, the object is some *good to himself*' (Hobbes 1994b: I.xiv 82). Hobbes notoriously went so far as to analyse the passion of pity (which is often presented as the paradigmatically altruistic passion) in terms of an ultimately self-interested concern to avoid future calamities to ourselves.[25] This claim was frequently discussed in the context of eighteenth-century arguments concerning the selfish hypothesis. It is thus not surprising that Hobbes became important for the debates on self-love in a predominantly negative way. Almost all the philosophers and theologians who discussed his claims were explicitly hostile to Hobbes and used him as a negative point of reference.

However, it would be a mistake to think that the only way of attacking Hobbes would concern his endorsement of the selfish hypothesis – which Hutcheson's presentation seems to suggest. The vagueness of the concept of self-love made possible a broad range of presentations and criticisms of Hobbes's arguments. One other line of attack against Hobbes takes as its target his emphasis on aggressive competition. Campbell, for example, adopts the selfish hypothesis while attacking Hobbes on this point – which suggests, against Hutcheson, that asserting the selfish hypothesis does not mean sharing Hobbes's emphasis on competition and conflict (see Chapter 6.1).

In *De Cive*, which was discussed by several of our authors, Hobbes attacks Aristotle's claim that we are 'born fit for society' (Hobbes 1991: 110). Rather, for Hobbes, we are *made* fit for society by education. What we seek 'by nature' is honour and profit, rather than society itself – but we have come to understand that we can only satisfy the desire for honour when living in society. For Hobbes, the pleasures of the mind reside in glory – which is the same as 'to have a good opinion of one's self' (1991: 112). Crucially, glory and honour are presented as positional goods, that is, as goods which depend on the comparative distance of ourselves from others, and on our perceived superiority over them. In Hobbes's words: 'if all men have [glory] no man hath it' (1991: 113). As a result, our natural quest for the positional good of glory must engender constant competition and conflict, which undermines the foundations of society. For Hobbes, it follows that actually persisting societies are not grounded in mutual goodwill (*benevolentia*), but in mutual fear (*metus*) because of our natural equality and because of the will to hurt one another, in view of the limits of natural resources and glory. The point that glory, or the good opinion of ourselves, is a positional good is essential to a Hobbesian-style pessimistic view of human nature and society. Yet as we shall see, few emphasise the competitive element in self-love as strongly as Hobbes (in this reconstructed version of his philosophy). Mandeville notoriously does, and he is attacked by many for doing so – among others by Campbell, who himself defends a version of the selfish hypothesis.

'Christian Moralists' and Augustinians: Beloved Fallen Selves

The second group of thinkers that Hutcheson mentions he calls 'Christian Moralists'. Hutcheson is not very specific, but he might be thinking of philosophers and theologians such as French Jansensists and Calvinists, English Calvinists and Scottish Presbyterians. These are often collectively referred to as 'Augustinians' by intellectual historians, since their ideas are embedded in a theological framework centring on Augustine's doctrine of original sin and the Fall.[26] As noted by Hutcheson himself, some of their claims resemble those of the Epicureans. They characteristically adopt pessimistic views of human nature and society, and they typically emphasise the power of self-love as *amour-propre* in postlapsarian human nature.

Augustine himself put forward a famously negative view of postlapsarian human nature as deeply corrupt, and he connected this to a predominantly negative view of self-love. Augustine writes of self-love or *amor sui* as the first reason for man's Fall: 'Prima hominis perditio, fuit amor sui.'[27] Self-love it is the source of man's rebellion against God, and it is the dominant passion in corrupted human nature. It creates an insurmountable gap between heaven and earth: 'Fecerunt itaque ciuitates duas amores duo, terrenam scilicet amor sui usque ad contemptum Dei, caelestem uero amor Dei usque ad contemptum sui.'[28] Self-love is the source of all vices and the root of humankind's sins, and it is presented as closely associated with sins such as *avaritia* (avarice), *superbia* (pride) and the inappropriately strong love of one's own body and life.[29]

Such pessimistic conceptions of self-love as the primary source of vice, the claim that human beings are unavoidably subject to its power, and the claim that human nature is therefore morally corrupt and entirely dependent on divine grace for salvation, are typical of Reformed thinkers in the sixteenth century, and more generally of Augustinian moral philosophers and theologians in the seventeenth century. Augustinian views were particularly dominant in reformed moral theology throughout Europe, and they exerted a strong influence on moral philosophy. Calvin, for example, combines corruption and self-deception in the chapter on self-knowledge in his *Institution de la religion chrétienne*: 'Car comme ainsi soit que les hommes ayent une amour d'euxmesmes desordonnée et aveuglée, ilz se feront voluntiers à croire qu'il n'y a rien en eux digne d'estre desprisé' (Calvin 2008: 248–9). Augustinians in seventeenth-century France, whether of Catholic Jansenist stripe (for example, François de La Rochefoucauld, Jacques Esprit and Pierre Nicole) or of Protestant Calvinist stripe (for example, Jacques Abbadie), emphasised the fundamental motivational power of self-love as *amour-propre* in human nature. Abbadie writes, for example: 'Le coeur [. . .] pese l'utilité et non pas la lumière, et ce n'est pas la raison, mais l'amour de nous-mêmes qui nous détermine dans nos affections' (Abbadie 2003: 171). Self-love is conceived as a great vice, frequently associated with pride and vanity and not simply with the mere search for pleasure. Its dominance is related to the corruption and sinfulness of human nature after the Fall. To use Abbadie's words again:

> En un mot considérez bien tous les vices et toutes les passions de l'homme, vous trouverez au bout l'amour propre. C'est lui qui leur donne la naissance, puisque tous les motifs du vice sont pris de ce que nous recherchons ce qui nous flâte, et se rapporte à *ce moy*, qui tient le premier rang entre les objets de nos connoissances et de nos affections. (Abbadie 2003: 149)

Given the negative understanding of self-love, the analysis of social virtues in terms of *amour-propre* became one of the central themes of the French Augustinian moralists.[30] For them, what is commonly held to be virtuous behaviour in our societies is in fact ultimately motivated by self-love as *amour-propre*, and thus by a vicious principle of action. The social rules called 'virtues', 'honesty' or 'civility' are rooted in self-love and thus merely reflect the corruption of human nature. Thus, Augustinians often prided themselves on having unmasked our strategies to deceive ourselves about our real motives, and to conceal our selfish motives from others. La Rochefoucauld writes on friendship in one of his *Maximes morales*: 'Ce que les hommes ont nommé amitié n'est qu'une société, qu'un ménagement réciproque d'intérêts, et qu'un échange de bons offices; ce n'est enfin qu'un commerce où l'amour-propre se propose toujours quelque chose à gagner' (La Rochefoucauld 1976: 57, *maxime* no. 83).

However, another important theme of Augustinian thinkers is that in spite of its potential for conflict, self-love is providentially a useful (yet nevertheless morally corrupt) basis for a stable society of postlapsarian human beings, since individuals' selfish interests mutually restrain each other. This theme is most famously developed in Pierre Nicole's essay *De la charité et de l'amour-propre* from 1675. Such providential arguments about the potential utility of vicious principles had a most interesting impact on eighteenth-century moral and political philosophy (often via Mandeville, see Chapter 3.3), the most famous example being Smith's widely discussed metaphor of the 'invisible hand'.

Mandeville, on the basis of his emphasis on the power of self-love in human nature, his naturalistic approach to the civilising process, and his suspected atheism, has often been classified as an Epicurean. However, another viable interpretation takes into account the many dominant Augustinian elements in Mandeville's moral philosophy, which he himself presented first and foremost as anti-Shaftesburian. Augustinian ideas were also very prominent in an institutional religious context, most importantly in the Church of Scotland. The views of human nature and morality of authors such as Shaftesbury, Hutcheson, Butler and Smith were in clear opposition to these. Partly against a still very present Augustinian tradition with its emphasis on the narrative of original sin and the Fall, many eighteenth-century moral philosophers argued for more positive views of postlapsarian human nature, which often (but not always) included rejecting the selfish hypothesis. At the same time, much of the moral thinking of philosophers such as Hume and Smith can be interpreted as an interesting conversation with Augustinianism, in spite of their rejection of its central tenets.

Especially in Scotland, the Calvinist background nurtured interest in the debates on self-love. After the 1690s, the Westminster Confession of Faith from 1646–7 again emerged officially as one of the doctrinal pillars of the Church. In the *Larger Catechism*, Question 105, we find a list of sins forbidden in the First Commandment, 'Thou shalt have no other Gods before me' (Church of Scotland 1728: 241–5). After atheism, which is defined as 'denying, or not having a God', idolatry and neglecting our duties towards God, a cluster of sins consisting in the preference of ourselves over God is mentioned: 'Self-love, Self-seeking, and all other inordinate and immoderate Setting of our Mind, Will, or Affections upon other Things, and taking them off from Him in Whole or in Part'.[31] Such theological views of self-love as an obstacle to our love of God are part of the essential background to philosophical debates on self-love, and at different times they were taken up by more popular religious writers such as Thomas Boston, Alexander Forbes and Thomas O'Brien MacMahon in their treatises on the corruption of human nature and self-love.[32]

The 'Antients': Self-love, Sociability and Morality in the Stoics and 'Socratics'

The third tradition of thinkers Hutcheson simply terms the 'antients'.[33] He presumably had in mind the Stoics and, in line with Shaftesbury's broad category of the 'Socratics', figures from other philosophical traditions such as Platonism and Plotinism.[34] Hutcheson's interest in the Stoics is quite striking – it culminated in the anonymous publication of *The Meditations of the Emperor Marcus Aurelius Antoninus* in 1742, translated by Hutcheson himself and James Moor.

There is a tendency among recent historians of early modern thought to speak of 'Stoicism' in a vague sense. This sometimes runs the risk of oversimplifying the reception of Stoic ideas. The same holds for the category, of 'Christian Stoicism', which is regularly used to characterise the philosophical tonality of the Scottish Enlightenment.[35] (Countless early modern debates on heresy suggest that the very broad category of 'Christianity' is even more likely to render essential differences invisible than the category of 'Stoicism'.) It is crucial to keep in mind that the reception of Stoic (as well as Christian) doctrines was often very selective. Accordingly, we need to look at which available Stoic ideas were adopted and for which reasons, how they were adapted to fit into new philosophical contexts, and which Stoic ideas were rejected – explicitly or implicitly. This necessity becomes evident, for example, in our doubts about the accuracy of Hutcheson's own simplifying 'history' of philosophy, which focuses predominantly on questions of sociability, yet leaves out questions regarding free will and materialism.

Certain Stoic ideas were particularly well received by early modern philosophers – especially those dovetailing with the eighteenth-century emphasis on the themes of sociability and moral self-improvement. However, the latter theme especially was considered problematic in Calvinist-Christian contexts: approving of the Stoic idea that the cultivation of virtue is ἐφ' ἡμῖν (*eph' hêmin*) or 'in our power' was typically interpreted as contradicting the *topos* of our irredeemable corruption and complete dependence on divine grace.[36] Stoic views of the emotions, then, were often adapted, yet rarely adopted in their entirety: the Stoic division between violent passions and calm affections was crucial to eighteenth-century moral philosophy, yet Stoic claims concerning apathy, or the need to eradicate the passions, were generally rejected (with the exception of the more specific claim that some violent passions had to be overcome). Also, the strict Stoic opposition between the true good (that is, virtue) and indifferent things erroneously represented as good (health, life, riches and so on) was treated with care. Stoic objections to pity posed particularly tricky problems to stoically minded early modern thinkers, since pity had acquired the status of a paradigm for an other-directed passion, and was often invoked as a proof of the reality of disinterested benevolence. General Stoic claims about the difficulty of controlling the passions and of performing genuine moral self-improvement were sometimes modified and rendered less 'elitist', and the figure of the Stoic sage was sometimes criticised as making virtue a *private sublimely selfish Discipline*' (Hutcheson, *Essay*: 83).[37]

In spite of various criticisms, the Stoics seem to have been of particular interest to many philosophers who wanted to emphasise a view of human nature as naturally sociable. In this context, it is interesting to take a look at one of the central concepts of Stoic moral philosophy, that of οἰκείωσις (*oikeiôsis*).[38] The translation of this term has been a matter of debate: 'familiarisation', 'appropriation' and 'affinity' have been suggested.[39] The Stoic theory of οἰκείωσις describes the natural development of human beings. According to the Stoics, we are endowed not only with primitive natural instincts for self-concern, but also with primitive natural instincts for other-concern (Annas 1993: 265, 276). The process of 'familiarisation' thus involves the development of both natural self-directed and natural other-directed tendencies. For the Stoics, the sage has completed the developmental process of οἰκείωσις in both dimensions, and he has reached an impartial concern for humanity (rather than for particular persons) and a rational concern about his true good. The rough dichotomy between a private and a social dimension will reappear in various forms, for example in Shaftesbury's distinction between self-affections and natural affections, in Hutcheson's distinction between self-love and benevolence, and in Butler's distinction between private and public principles.

Several points are relevant for our investigation. First, there are good grounds to represent the Stoics as rejecting the selfish hypothesis. Even if the Stoic developmental account may allow for the interpretation that self-love (in the sense of an affection for the self and its preservation) is psychologically primary, the concern for others is best interpreted as an equally natural instinct, which develops according to nature and can be cultivated. Next, the 'elitist' figure of the Stoic sage notwithstanding, the Stoics can be presented as supporting a generally positive view of human nature, and as opposing the Augustinian doctrine of the total depravity of postlapsarian humanity. Virtue is said to be within the reach of human beings since they can cultivate their naturally virtuous dispositions and thus become more virtuous. Lastly, self-love is not considered morally problematic when in its natural degree, in contrast to the Augustinian view. Rather, it is treated as a natural and innocent concern for one's own well-being and self-preservation.

Other 'Schools' on Self-love: Aristotle and (Neo-)Platonist–Plotinist Traditions

I want to add some remarks on figures outside Hutcheson's tripartition. The questions of self-love have a long tradition in Western philosophy, and there have been other prominent positive views of it. The first substantial treatment can be found in Aristotle, who highlights both the negative and positive aspects of self-love. In his analysis of friendship in the ninth book of *Nicomachean Ethics*, Aristotle discusses in 1168a–1169b whether a man should love most himself or someone else. He distinguishes between two forms of φιλαυτία (*philautia*), a term that is generally translated as 'self-love'. The picture Aristotle draws of φιλαυτία is twofold, and this feature reappears during later debates on self-love: from the moral point of view, loving oneself can be either vicious or virtuous, depending on the part of the self that is the object of the agent's love. In Aristotle's view, one form of φιλαυτία is associated with 'those who assign themselves the larger share where money, or honours, or bodily pleasures are concerned' (Aristotle 2002: 235, 1168b15–1168b15). This way of loving oneself focuses on the wrong part of the self and has the consequence that one performs actions that harm others and ultimately oneself (2002: 235, 1169a10). It leads to a selfish focus on one's own interests, conceived in terms of pleasure, money and so on, which makes it a morally reproachable way of loving oneself.

The second form of φιλαυτία, more legitimately so called according to Aristotle, consists in a person's indulging 'the most authoritative element of himself, obeying it in everything' (Aristotle 2002: 235, 1168b25–30).[40] This way of loving oneself is compatible with being virtuous, for it is tied to the rational part of the self, which has moral authority over the other parts. Thus, to love oneself in the sense of φιλαυτία can be virtuous when it follows the dictates of the rational part of the soul, which does not exclude promoting the interests of others.

Aristotle concludes: 'Thus the good person should be a self-lover, since by doing what is fine he will both be better off himself and benefit others, but the bad one should not; for he will harm both himself and those round him through following worthless attractions' (Aristotle 2002: 235, 1169a10).

Aristotle's account of self-love has relatively few direct echoes in eighteenth-century British debates, yet as part of the general tendency to make room for more positive treatments of self-love against the Augustinian negative conception, references to Aristotle play a certain role. Campbell, who wants to put forward a very optimistic view of self-love, is well aware that this might pose problems in his Calvinist surroundings. He thus refers to the discussion in Aristotle just summarised with the declared purpose of preventing 'any Prejudices that may arise from introducing *Self-love* as a laudable Principle, in the Business of moral Virtue' (Campbell, *Enquiry*: 5). We shall see that the strategy of using the authority of Aristotle against potential criticisms did not work in Campbell's case (see Chapters 6.1 and 6.4).[41] More generally, and in a similar vein to Aristotle, several eighteenth-century thinkers put forward the idea of self-love as something not necessarily problematic, some even tending to morally rehabilitate self-love. This is most strikingly the case with Butler – in a theistic teleological framework, he relies on the idea of a hierarchy of authority between different parts of the agent's self (an idea that can be found both in Aristotle and the Stoics). Butler's point that self-love is a principle that aims at realising the agent's true self proved very influential for subsequent thinkers (see Chapters 5.2 and 5.4).

Another important background should be mentioned: the authors commonly referred to as the 'Cambridge Platonists', most importantly Benjamin Whichcote, Henry More and Ralph Cudworth. These authors were an important source of inspiration for Shaftesbury in particular, and they exerted significant influence on the Scottish universities in the second half of the seventeenth century via Henry More's *Enchiridion Ethicum* (1668) – an often-used, yet also much-attacked course book for ethics teaching.[42] The Cambridge Platonists put forward a generally positive view of postlapsarian human nature, and they presented the passions not as something to be overcome, but as fundamentally good and to be well used. In his *True Intellectual System of the Universe* (1678), Ralph Cudworth attacks the '*Villanizing* of *Humane Nature*' as one of the fundamentals of atheism, part of which is the claim that there is 'nothing of *Publick* and *Common Concern*, but all *Private* and *Selfish*' (Cudworth 1678: 890). And in his *Enchiridion Ethicum*, Henry More writes about the passions in general: 'we must maintain it against the *Stoicks*, that of their own Nature [the passions] are good' (More 1690: 34). The passions are part of divine providence, and they are useful and even necessary for moral self-cultivation. The intellectual part of the soul (which More famously calls the *boniform faculty*) is in a position to moderate the passions and direct them towards the 'best and greatest things' (More 1690: 41). For More, this positive view of the passions extends to self-love, and a citation from his *Divine Dialogues* in George Turnbull's *Principles of Moral and Political Philosophy* (1740) makes evident the importance of this point for the eighteenth century: 'Self-love is absolutely necessary: nay, it is no more than the desire of pleasure and happiness, without which a sensitive being cannot subsist' (Turnbull 2005: 320). The problem with self-love is when it becomes excessive and turns into a vice.

In a letter, presumably to Bishop Stillingfleet (first printed in 1708, and published in 1756 as a pamphlet by the Foulis Press in Glasgow),[43] More also explicitly addresses the selfish hypothesis in the form of the claim 'that self-love (or love of our selves) is the very principle of all love, whether to God, or any others' (More 1756: 2). Distinguishing between a selfish animal nature and a divine principle, he argues 'that self-love is not the very principle of all love whatsoever, to God or man' (1756: 24). He insists (in line with Fénelon) that there is a genuinely disinterested love, 'a love of God for his loveliness in himself' (1756: 5), which will make us love ourselves 'in reference to God' (1756: 11). It is not surprising that the Foulis Press, with its close ties to Hutcheson, published such a pamphlet. At the time of publication, the notion of disinterestedness was already part of the central vocabulary of Anglophone moral philosophy, and various attempts to present self-love as ultimately compatible with disinterestedness can be found.[44]

Let me take stock. Earlier in this chapter, I introduced several questions that are crucial for an appropriate understanding of the debates on self-love in eighteenth-century British moral philosophy: we need to comprehend the different conceptions of self-love, their relations to our contemporary notion of egoism, and their roles in context – most importantly in arguments for and against the selfish hypothesis, and in debates concerning the moral status of postlapsarian human nature. The moral rehabilitation of human nature often includes a moral rehabilitation of self-love, or so I shall argue. With these points in mind, I shall address the most important contributors to the debates on self-love in eighteenth-century British moral philosophy, and show how they were in conversation with each other. In comparison with other studies in the history of philosophy, I will pay more attention to less explored authors, such as Mandeville and Campbell. This will result in a broader understanding of what is at stake.

In Chapter 2, I look at Shaftesbury's treatment of the questions of self-love, which sets the tone for much of the subsequent debate. In the context of his arguments for natural sociability and virtue, Shaftesbury rejects the selfish hypothesis as an element of Hobbesian moral psychology. Yet in sum, the picture he paints of egoistic self-love is surprisingly positive – he declares self-love a necessary ingredient to the fully virtuous human agent. Mandeville, whom I discuss in Chapter 3, takes Shaftesbury as one of his main philosophical targets. Mandeville paints a very different picture of human nature and society as fundamentally driven by self-love as *amour-propre* and self-love as love of praise. Ultimately, self-love as *amour-propre* turns out to be really quite a beneficial vice – which does not mean, however, that it is morally rehabilitated: genuine moral virtue would require self-denial, not a Shaftesburian following of one's natural impulses.

Several subsequent authors claimed to defend Shaftesbury against Mandeville. The most influential was Hutcheson, whom I discuss in Chapter 4. Hutcheson argues extensively against the selfish hypothesis, and for the reality of disinterested benevolence. If benevolence is what makes us virtuous by nature, that does not, however, mean that self-love is a vicious principle: somewhat against Smith and present-day commentators, I shall argue that Hutcheson's overall view of egoistic self-love is less critical than commonly assumed. In Chapter 5, I analyse Butler's influential conception of self-love as respect of self. Based on their shared vocabulary, Butler's arguments often seem to be the same as Hutcheson's, but due to the fundamental differences in their conceptions of self-love, their arguments are sometimes very unalike indeed. Archibald Campbell, whom I discuss in Chapter 6, argues like Hutcheson for a very positive view of postlapsarian human nature – yet for once from within the framework of the selfish hypothesis. This undermines the validity of Hutcheson's widely accepted claim that if we adopt the selfish hypothesis, we accept at the same time a morally pessimistic view of human nature.

In the second half of the eighteenth century, arguing for or against the selfish hypothesis appears to have become less important – exploring this will be the main theme of Chapter 7. In Scotland, the selfish hypothesis was generally considered as refuted, and interest shifted to other issues, for example the exploration of sociability, and the moral rehabilitation of specific forms of self-love. I shall argue that Hume and Smith made room for more positive treatments of self-love, most importantly in the forms of self-love as due pride and self-love as love of praise, against both Mandeville *and* Hutcheson. In England, by contrast, the selfish hypothesis was widely accepted and continued to exert its influence in the psychologies of Associationists such as John Gay, David Hartley and Abraham Tucker.

NOTES

1. The two quotations are from Moncrieff (1735: 14–15) and Butler (*Sermons*: Preface, 40).
2. Blackburn (2014) is one of the very few contemporary philosophical books on self-love, with Frankfurt (2004).
3. We find, however, terms from the broader semantic family of self-love. Various Latin *Theses philosophicæ* from Scottish universities discuss some of Hobbes's central claims with the Greek term φιλαυτία, or its Latinised version *philautia*. Discussions by the French Augustinian moralists on *amour-propre* also came to be known. Locke, in his translation of three of Pierre Nicole's *Essais de morale*, uses the English term 'self-love' for the French term *amour-propre*.
4. Kavka (1986) offers a systematic and useful discussion of psychological egoism in Hobbes, as well as distinctions between psychological egoism, psychological hedonism, tautological egoism and ethical egoism applied to early modern authors. See furthermore Shaver (2014).
5. Many critical studies on Hobbes debate whether his positions can be presented as a version of egoism. This may also have led some commentators to frame eighteenth-century reactions to Hobbes as debates on egoism.
6. The word 'disinterested' is also quite commonly understood in the sense of altruistic – but I shall suggest in Chapter 5 that Butler is a most interesting exception.
7. In this study, I use the term 'emotions' in a generic sense to cover both affections (which in the early modern period are often, but not consistently, defined as *calm* emotions) and passions (which are often, but not consistently, defined as *violent* emotions). The term 'passions', too, is sometimes used in a generic sense to cover both calm and violent emotions, but more often in the specific sense of violent emotions. I shall regularly draw attention to this theme.
8. The expressions 'selfish hypothesis' and 'selfish system' were most famously used by David Hume (Hume, *Enquiry*: 297–8).
9. In accordance with commentators such as Gill (2006) and Heydt (2018: 158–79), I will use expressions such as 'optimistic' and 'pessimistic', or 'positive' and 'negative' to designate views of human nature as generally moral and sociable, or as generally immoral and unsociable. In the investigated period, the latter are most often connected to the Calvinist *topos* of postlapsarian corruption.

10. For further discussions on the concept of ethical egoism, as well as of the concept of egoism more generally, see Shaver (2014).

11. Furthermore, Herdt (2008) offers crucial insights for a study on self-love. Herdt takes serious the overlap between moral philosophy and theology in her discussion of pride, vanity and other notions commonly associated with self-love. Rivers (2000) provides a very impressive overview of seventeenth- and eighteenth-century moral discourse, and so does Robertson (2005) for the eighteenth century. Schrader (1984) is also often helpful in his presentation of the relations between the authors under discussion.

12. Similarly, I will occasionally comment on Irwin (2008) and Darwall (1995), two systematic studies on the history of ethics.

13. Commentators such as Hirschman (1977), Force (2003) and Heath (2013: 242–9) remind us that the relation between the agent's self-love and her self-interest is a matter of dispute. In some (but not all) understandings, the concept of self-interest is thought to include an element of calculation, whereas self-love is treated as a passion. On this understanding, it is possible that following one's self-love may counteract one's self-interest (or one's 'true self-love', as some authors prefer to put it). This looks different if the agent's self-interest is thought to be constituted by her self-love in the sense of the sum of her egoistic desires.

14. The following sections are partly indebted to reflections in Lovejoy (1961) and Solomon (1993), among others.

15. The Lockean contribution to the interest in hedonism in eighteenth-century moral philosophers is widely acknowledged – see, for example, Heydt (2018: 164). It is crucial to note, however, that not all 'hedonists' are 'egoists' in the sense that they support the selfish hypothesis. Hutcheson and Campbell are both hedonists in that they structure their psychologies around the notion of pleasure, but only Campbell is also an egoist.

16. This is most evident in Hutcheson's *Inaugural Lecture* (1730), which is marked by direct and indirect references to the Stoics and to Shaftesbury. See Hutcheson (*Inaugural Lecture*, 204–8), and furthermore Brooke (2012: 159–64).

17. On this point, Jaffro (2008) and Sellars (2016a) offer insightful discussions. See also Maurer and Jaffro (2013) on Shaftesbury's manuscript *Pathologia*.

18. This tripartition has been particularly important in studies of intellectual historians for example Force (2003), Robertson (2005) and, more recently, Brooke (2012). It partly goes back to Lafond (1996).

19. For the advantages of reconstructing past philosophical debates as broader conversations with their continuities and changes, which include non-canonical 'minor' figures, see Hutton (2015: 2–3; 2014).

20. The Epicurean tradition, which is here of particular interest for its moral psychology and its account of sociability, has been studied in particular in Leddy and Livschitz (2009) and Wilson (2008).

21. In this context, Book V of Lucretius' *De rerum natura*, with its narrative about the formation of society, saw a vivid reception in early modern philosophy – see, for example, Wilson (2016).

22. See, for example, Brooke (2012: 101–5) on Bramhall's presentation of Hobbes as a Stoic. Similar points were made in numerous *Theses philosophicæ* in late seventeenth-century Scotland – see, for example, Maurer (2016d: 202–5).

23. Similarly, Stoic theology was regularly subject to criticism. Campbell, for example, wrote: 'The *Stoicks* in particular, notwithstanding their great Zeal in the Cause of Moral Virtue, give out the supreme Being to be only *anima mundi*, the Mind of the World; and they deny the *Eternity* or Immortality of the Soul' (*Enquiry*: xxvii).

24. For a detailed discussion of the classification of Hobbes as an 'egoist', see Kavka (1986).

25. In *Human Nature*, Hobbes proposes his notorious definition of pity as '*imagination* or *fiction* of *future* calamity to *ourselves*, proceeding from the sense of *another* man's calamity' (1994a: 53). See also Maurer (2013b: 76–9).

26. For more detailed accounts of the French Augustinians' philosophico-theological treatments of various theological *topoi*, see especially Moriarty (2006; 2011), Stiker-Métral (2007) and Herdt (2008: 235–67). Force (2003) treats them in connection with eighteenth-century debates.

27. Augustinus, *Sermo* XCVI.2: 'The primal destruction of man was self-love.' See the translation and discussion in O'Donovan (1980: 96).

28. Augustinus, *De Civitate Dei*, Lib. XIV, Cap. XXVIII: 'Two loves made two cities. Self-love to despite of God made the earthly city, love of God to despite of self the heavenly.' See the translation and discussion in O'Donovan (1980: 93).

29. It is noteworthy that Augustine also develops a more positive view of self-love. When discussing the command that 'you shall love your neighbour as yourself', Augustine invokes a concept of self-love as the recognition of one's true nature and dignity, which relates to loving oneself in God, or to the seeking of one's true welfare in the love of God. If the self is improperly understood, then loving oneself is evil, but if the creature sees herself in her relation to God as her creator, her love of self will coincide with her love of God (O'Donovan 1980: 112, 147). In comparison, many early modern Augustinian moralists have an even stronger tendency to emphasise the corrupt form of *amor sui*.

30. Jacques Esprit, for example, wrote an entire treatise with the title *La fausseté des vertus humaines*, which was first published in 1678 (Esprit 1996). On the French Augustinian critique of the virtues, see also Force (2003: 57–63), Moriarty (2006; 2011) and Stiker-Métral (2007).

31. One of the Scripture references is to Paul's pastoral letter 2 Tim. 3:2. 'For men shall be lovers of their own selves' (φίλαυτοι/*philautoi*).

32. See Boston (1787), Forbes (1734) and MacMahon (1774).

33. Christopher Brooke (2012) has recently discussed the multifaceted and complex history of reception of the Stoic tradition in early modern political and moral philosophy. Brooke focuses on political and moral philosophy, and describes how various Stoic thinkers and doctrines were embraced and rejected in very different ways. For the debates on self-love, it is particularly interesting to see how the Stoics became, through the interpretations of Shaftesbury and Hutcheson especially, proponents of sociability – against the Epicureans and Hobbes. Sellars (2016b) offers a broad overview of the history of the reception of Stoicism.

34. Gill (2010) offers important insights not just on the proximities, but also on the differences between Hutcheson and Shaftesbury in their relation to the Cambridge Platonists. Drawing on Carey (2006), Gill highlights how Hutcheson shares the Cambridge Platonists' more 'democratic' view of human nature's moral capacities.

35. See the influential Sher (1985), on which I have commented in Maurer (2016c: 254–7). The expression 'Christian Stoicism' has been taken up by numerous commentators.

36. To my mind, one of the most illuminating texts in this respect is Pascal's *Entretien avec M. de Saci* (1655), which illustrates the Augustinian rejection of basic Stoic tenets. See also Brooke (2012: 83–6). An eighteenth-century testimony of the critical orthodox attitude towards Stoicism is Witherspoon (1763).

37. On the theme of Stoic 'elitism', see Gill (2010). In Maurer (2010), I describe the combination of attraction to and criticism of Stoic ideas in Hutcheson. See furthermore Brooke (2012: 162–4) and Maurer (2016c).

38. The most important classical sources for the Stoic concept of οἰκείωσις are Chrysippus, as summarised in the 7th book of Diogenes Laertius' *Lives of the Philosophers*, as well as Cicero's analysis in the 3rd book of *De finibus*.

39. See, for example, Annas (1993: 262) and Sellars (2006: 107). The present section is much indebted to Annas's discussion of οἰκείωσις.

40. Annas (1993: 257) makes the interesting suggestion that commendable φιλαυτία is not distinguished from reproachable φιλαυτία in that the latter is competitive and the former is not. Rather, Annas distinguishes two different objects of competition. For many, self-love consists in competing for bodily and external goods, which are limited and thus involve competition at others' expense. The 'real' self-lover, however, competes with others to be virtuous, which is not competition for a limited good.

41. It is furthermore noteworthy that about a century later, in 1829, Dugald Stewart refers to the very same passage in Aristotle in his *Philosophy of the Active and Moral Powers of Man* (Stewart 1829: 101–2), see also Chapter 7. 4.

42. I have addressed some aspects of the reception of More's *Enchiridion Ethicum* in Scotland in Maurer (2016d: 206–8).
43. On the fascinating role of the Foulis Press in the dissemination of unorthodox ideas, see Rivers (2000: 184–7).
44. On the French background of the notion of disinterestedness, see Force (2003: 183–200) and, more generally, Le Brun (2002).

2. *Shaftesbury on the Self-affections and the Selfish Hypothesis*

In Shaftesbury's *Sensus Communis, an Essay on the Freedom of Wit and Humour* (1709), we find the somewhat puzzling phrase: 'It is the height of wisdom, no doubt, to be rightly selfish' (Shaftesbury, *Sensus Communis*: 56). Is this an incitement to be selfish? Already in the eighteenth century there were different interpretations of the phrase 'rightly selfish' in Shaftesbury, as we shall see, and this is partly connected to the presence of different conceptions of self-love.

Anthony Ashley Cooper, the third Earl of Shaftesbury (1671–1713), was indisputably a crucial figure for eighteenth-century philosophy in Europe, in particular for aesthetics and moral philosophy. The author of *Characteristicks of Men, Manners, Opinions, Times*, a collection of treatises published in 1711, he was famous for his reflections on the moral sense, which influenced Hutcheson's subsequent more systematic elaboration of a moral sense theory.[1] Commentators correctly highlight Shaftesbury's strong affinities with Stoic ideas, as well as his interest in Platonism and neo-Plotinism, fostered by personal relationships with the Cambridge Platonists. Shaftesbury, who had close ties to John Toland, was tutored by John Locke, whose philosophical principles he later attacked alongside those of Hobbes – a move that is connected to the theme of self-love. Shaftesbury can be considered the thinker who set the stage for the debates on self-love in eighteenth-century British moral philosophy. In various ways, he strongly contributed to a revival of interest in Stoic philosophy, and developed an influential anti-Hobbesian account of sociability.

In his study *The Development of Ethics*, Terence Irwin points out that Shaftesbury's 'critics and interpreters agree that he criticizes Hobbesian egoism' (Irwin 2008: 354). This is not an incorrect description of Shaftesbury's position, yet in order to understand his influence on the subsequent debates we need to look more precisely into his ideas, analyse how he criticises the position that Irwin calls 'Hobbesian egoism', and study how he conceives of both egoistic and non-egoistic features of human nature. I shall argue that there is a particularly important combination of theses in Shaftesbury, as far as the debates on self-love are concerned: Shaftesbury rejects the selfish hypothesis, that is, the claim that we are only motivated by self-love (of some sort), by means of an influential account of natural sociability, which he sees as supported by Stoic ideas. However, he does not complement this rejection with a negative view of self-love. Rather, in his theory of the affections, he proposes an ultimately positive and again influential view of what he terms the 'self-affections', that is, self-love as egoistic desire.

2.1 'HOBBESIAN EGOISM' AND THE RIGHT LOVE FOR ONESELF

Let me start this analysis of Shaftesbury's contribution to the debates on self-love with another passage from *Sensus Communis*. At one point, Shaftesbury focuses on the 'common saying that "interest governs the world"' (Shaftesbury, *Sensus Communis*: 53). For Shaftesbury, this view is false, since as a matter of fact we often act 'counter to self-interest' (*Sensus Communis*: 54), for example when we are moved by violent passions and partisan zeal. Note that if this is an attack on the selfish hypothesis, it is only targeting one specific version, namely the claim that we always act upon a rational assessment of how best to promote our interest. This claim is invalidated, for Shaftesbury, by the reality of passionate, irrational actions – think of angry revenge, which may be extremely costly for us, but which we passionately engage in even if it is ultimately 'against our interest'. The reality of such actions does not falsify all versions of the selfish hypothesis, however: if the notion of interest is conceived in terms of the most strongly felt desire (which is one possible interpretation of Hobbes's motivational theory), Shaftesbury's point does not hold.

Shaftesbury continues to criticise those ancient and modern philosophers who analyse human behaviour exclusively in terms of self-interest, excluding everything 'on the side of the better and more enlarged affections' (*Sensus Communis*: 54) – for example kindness, generosity and friendship. For Shaftesbury, this account of human psychology is not only false, but as a theory it also distorts our ethical reflections. 'Modern projectors', Shaftesbury claims, are even worse than the ancients, since they 'would new-frame the human heart and have a mighty fancy to reduce all its motions, balances and weights to that one principle and foundation of a cool and deliberate selfishness' (*Sensus Communis*: 54).[2] In other words, modern philosophers in the vein of Hobbes are obsessed with analysing all 'enlarged' (that is, benevolent, disinterested or altruistic) affections in terms of self-interested or egoistic ones, presenting human beings as rational, egoistic calculators.

Elaborating on his comparison between the ancients and the moderns, Shaftesbury points out that Epicurus, interestingly, asked his followers not to marry and to retire from public life in order to be assured that they were 'conquering nature in themselves' (*Sensus Communis*: 54). The ancient Epicureans knew very well that in contact with other humans, strong affections of a non-egoistic sort towards family and friends, society and humankind, would naturally arise and make the crucial task of conquering one's passionate nature more difficult. Shaftesbury here insinuates that after all, the ancient Epicureans would not fully subscribe to the selfish hypothesis, and that they allowed for the reality of altruistic desires while remaining critical about their psychological consequences.

The modern followers of Epicurus, however, went even further in misrepresenting human nature as entirely selfish. They

> thought to alter the thing by shifting a name. They would so explain all the social passions and natural affections as to denominate them of the selfish kind. Thus civility, hospitality, humanity towards strangers or people in distress is only a more deliberate selfishness. An honest heart is only a more cunning one, and honesty and good nature, a more deliberate or better-regulated self-love. (*Sensus Communis*: 55)

According to these thinkers, among whom Shaftesbury mentions Hobbes most prominently, familial and parental affections, affection for one's country and humankind, as well as virtues such as magnanimity and courage are nothing but 'modifications of this universal self-love!' (*Sensus Communis*: 55). Again, Shaftesbury disapproves of presenting human agents as rational, egoistic calculators prone to deceive others – a theme to which he here attaches the English expression 'self-love'.

In *Sensus Communis*, Shaftesbury attacks Hobbes explicitly. In his correspondence, however, we also find him mentioning Locke, his former tutor, in a similar criticism:

> It was Mr. Locke that struck the home blow: for Mr. Hobbes's character and base slavish principles in government took off the poison of his philosophy. 'Twas Mr. Locke that struck at all fundamentals, threw all *order* and *virtue* out of the world, and made the very ideas of these (which are the same as those of God) *unnatural*, and without foundation in our minds. (Shaftesbury 1900: 403)[3]

If Hobbes was a recognisably corrupt philosopher, then Locke was far more dangerous, since he presented his pernicious ideas about human nature and virtue in a more seditious and apparently innocent manner. However, moral virtue is real, for Shaftesbury, and as we shall see in the subsequent sections, it has indeed a 'foundation' in our minds – virtue is not a mere invention of selfish creatures.

In *Sensus Communis*, Shaftesbury continues to write the following on modern authors besides Hobbes, culminating in the expression quoted at the beginning of this chapter:

> Other authors there have been of a yet inferior kind, a sort of distributors and petty retailers of this wit, who have run changes and divisions without end upon this article of self-love. You have the very same thought spun out a hundred ways and drawn into mottoes and devices to set forth this riddle, that 'act as disinterestedly or generously as you please, *self* still is at the bottom, and nothing else'. Now if these gentlemen who delight so much in the play of words, but are cautious how they grapple closely with definitions, would tell us only what self-interest was and determine happiness and good, there would be an end of this enigmatical wit. For in this we should all agree – that happiness was to be pursued and in fact was always sought after. But, whether found in following nature and giving way to common affection or in suppressing it and turning every passion towards private advantage, a narrow self-end or the preservation of mere life, this would be the matter in debate between us. The question would not be 'who loved himself or who not?' but 'who loved and served himself in the rightest and after the truest manner?'
>
> It is the height of wisdom, no doubt, to be rightly selfish. (Shaftesbury, *Sensus Communis*: 56)

A note in the French translation, referred to approvingly by Shaftesbury in the 1711 and 1714 editions, suggests that Shaftesbury may have had in mind French moralists such as La Rochefoucauld, and thus the debates on *amour-propre* with the central theme of humankind's moral corruption. Shaftesbury complains that such 'inferior' authors, in order to protect their false claims about human nature, do not provide us with a more specific explanation of what a properly self-interested pursuit of happiness might look like.[4] Even if we agreed that happiness is *de facto* the ultimate goal of all our actions, these authors hide behind a crucial ambiguity, which is connected to the vocabulary of self-love.

In his answer to them, Shaftesbury does not really argue in favour of the existence of disinterested or altruistic social affections. Simply presupposing their reality, he highlights how different accounts of happiness in different moral psychologies recommend either gratifying or suppressing these social affections. In the closing sentence to this passage, which will be taken up by several later authors, Shaftesbury suggests that being 'rightly selfish' or loving oneself in the right manner (that is, promoting one's genuine long-term interest, and thus one's happiness) means living a life in which the social affections, which are part of our nature, are *not* suppressed[5] – a point directed against both the ancient and modern Epicureans. Strictly speaking, Shaftesbury does not here attack an analysis of the social affections in terms of self-affections. Rather, he suggests that given the nature that we have, promoting our own happiness requires gratifying the social affections instead of suppressing them. In other words, he points towards an egoistic reason for realising our nature by cultivating natural sociability.[6] As we shall see below, several other authors (some rejecting the selfish hypothesis, for example Hutcheson and Butler, others accepting it, for example Campbell) would produce similar arguments against suppressing the social affections.

From a purely terminological point of view, the quoted passages are actually rather unusual for Shaftesbury, since in his other writings the term 'self-love' occurs very rarely. Especially in the *Inquiry*, Shaftesbury prefers expressions such as 'self-affections', 'private affections' and 'selfishness' to speak of what I have termed 'egoistic self-love'. This terminology sets him slightly apart from subsequent British eighteenth-century thinkers, for whom the term 'self-love' was much more common. I shall now look more closely into Shaftesbury's *Inquiry* in order to discuss his arguments against the selfish hypothesis, as well as his psychological and moral analysis of self-love as one of several essential ingredients of human nature. This will allow me to suggest, in the end, a more refined discussion of Shaftesbury's account of what it is to love oneself 'in the rightest and after the truest manner'.

2.2 SHAFTESBURY ON THE SELF-AFFECTIONS IN THE *INQUIRY*

Human Nature, Natural Goodness and Moral Virtue

Shaftesbury's main contributions to the debates on self-love, in particular his psychological analysis of self-love, his rejection of the selfish hypothesis and his quite positive moral assessment of self-love, are best understood through the lens of his treatment of human nature and morality in *An Inquiry Concerning Virtue or Merit* (1699/1711), which is also his most systematic text in moral philosophy (though not necessarily his most influential).[7] Analysing the treatment of self-love in the *Inquiry* requires first looking into Shaftesbury's general account of human nature, goodness and virtue.

Shaftesbury declares that one of his main goals in the *Inquiry* is to provide an answer to the question of *'what honesty or virtue is considered by itself'* (Shaftesbury, *Inquiry*: 163), and to investigate the relation between virtue and religion. In Shaftesbury, 'honesty' stands for the Stoic *honestum*, which is the moral good, and which is to be distinguished from the *utile*, that is, the natural good produced by an action.[8] Furthermore, Shaftesbury famously argues with Bayle that it is possible to be a virtuous agent and to have a correct sense of right and wrong without having religious beliefs, even if religion is of great utility for the cultivation of virtue.[9] Crucially, then, Shaftesbury argues for a close link between moral virtue and human nature when rooting virtue in the right balance of several kinds of affections – a point on which Smith would insist half a century later.

Arguments from divine design are crucial in Shaftesbury. He conceives of the universe as a providentially designed and harmonious system. In Shaftesbury, this idea is better understood as reflective of his interest in Stoicism and other ancient schools rather than as an adherence to Christianity.[10] Every human creature is part of the human species, which is again part of the system of animals, which is 'together with that of vegetables and all other things in this inferior world [. . .] properly comprehended in one system of a globe or earth' (Shaftesbury, *Inquiry*: 169). Ultimately, everything is part of 'a system of all things and a universal nature' (*Inquiry*: 169). Every creature has a role attributed by design, and 'a certain end to which everything in his constitution must naturally refer' (*Inquiry*: 167). This designed end is, first, the promotion of the good of the species and, ultimately, the promotion of the good of the whole.

Of course, one species can affect the well-being of other species, and be a natural good or ill for them. A species of predators, for example, is an ill for its prey. Considering the whole, however, 'there is no such thing as real ill in the universe, nothing ill with respect to the whole' (*Inquiry*: 165). The existence of a real evil would imply that the designing principle, God, is 'itself corrupt' or 'cannot be the cause of all things' (*Inquiry*: 165) – which is, for Shaftesbury, absurd.[11] In our universe, the relations between different species are ultimately well ordered and promote the good of the universe.

This generally optimistic outlook with respect to the universe is reflected in Shaftesbury's treatment of human nature.[12] Even if his terminology is sometimes ambiguous, Shaftesbury distinguishes quite systematically between *natural* goodness (that is, the Stoic *utile*) and *moral* goodness or virtue (that is, the Stoic *honestum*). Both the natural goodness of non-rational and rational creatures and the moral virtue of rational creatures are again determined by reference to providential design. Every sensible creature – be it non-rational or rational – has 'a private good and interest of his own, which nature has compelled him to seek' (*Inquiry*: 167). The affections of the creature have the function of guiding it in the promotion of its private good, and in the promotion of the good of its species. Thanks to providential design, the creature naturally contributes to the preservation of the species, and the species naturally contributes to the creature's good (*Inquiry*: 167).

The *natural goodness* or illness of an individual creature ultimately depends on its overall tendency to promote or hinder the good of its species:

> When in general all the affections or passions are suited to the public good or good of the species, as above-mentioned, then is the natural temper entirely good. If, on the contrary, any requisite passion be wanting or if there be any one supernumerary or weak or anyway disserviceable or contrary to that main end, then is the natural temper, and consequently the creature himself, in some measure corrupt and ill. (*Inquiry*: 172)

In other words, the individual creature's natural goodness or illness is determined by its affections and their effects for the species' good. A creature has a naturally good character if its affections in general tend to promote the good of the species. At this point, it is essential to note that Shaftesbury claims that a creature is naturally good if and only if it has both affections tending to promote the good of its species ('natural affections'), *as well as* affections tending to promote its private good ('self-affections') in their natural, that is, designed and appropriate degree.[13] This announces a positive outlook on the self-affections, as opposed to treating them as corrupt.

Moral virtue, then, is a feature that only rational creatures can possess: 'And in this case alone it is we call any creature worthy or virtuous, when it can have the notion of a public interest and can attain the speculation or science of what is morally good or ill, admirable or blameable, right or wrong' (*Inquiry*: 173). Non-rational creatures 'are only capable of being moved by sensible objects' (*Inquiry*: 175). Their behaviour is guided by 'perceptions, sensations, and presensations' (Shaftesbury, *Moralists*: 282) – they are moved by mere impulses and by affections that involve representations, which they are, however, unable to critically evaluate or to rationally control. Rational creatures, on the other hand, are 'capable of framing rational objects of moral good' (Shaftesbury, *Inquiry*: 175), and they can critically assess their representations: in a Stoic vein, Shaftesbury asserts that they have the liberty to assent to the impressions from their senses, which constitute the cognitive basis for their affections. Their affections thus become the object of other affections:

> In a creature capable of forming general notions of things, not only the outward beings which offer themselves to the sense are the objects of the affection, but the very actions themselves and the affections of pity, kindness, gratitude and their contraries, being brought into the mind by reflection, become objects. So that, by means of this reflected sense, there arises another kind of affection towards those very affections themselves, which have been already felt and have now become the subject of a new liking or dislike. (*Inquiry*: 172)

This passage is best interpreted through a distinction between first-order and second-order affections.[14] Second-order affections, which are rational dispositions towards first-order affections, make rational agents conscious of their first-order affections, and allow them to take an evaluative stance towards them. Second-order affections are generated immediately and 'naturally': 'the heart cannot possibly remain neutral [. . . and . . .] in all disinterested cases, must approve in some measure of what is natural and honest and disapprove what is dishonest and corrupt' (*Inquiry*: 173). The origin of these second-order affections is the moral sense – 'a sense of right or wrong, a sentiment or judgment of what is done through just, equal and good affection or the contrary' (*Inquiry*: 173). It is ultimately by virtue of their moral sense that rational creatures can be said to be *morally* good or evil, virtuous or vicious.[15]

In sum, the conditions for a rational creature to be *morally* good or virtuous are that, first, the creature is naturally good (meaning that it has first-order affections which in their combination ultimately promote the good of its species) and, secondly, that it has the appropriate second-order affections, which are rooted in the moral sense, and which endorse or oppose first-order affections in accordance with divine design. In an important sense, we can see Shaftesbury arguing for a more generally positive view of postlapsarian human nature: as rational creatures, we are designed to have natural tendencies towards virtue.[16] Without any mention of the Fall, Shaftesbury's opposition to the Calvinist *topos* of postlapsarian corruption is evident. But what is the role of self-love in Shaftesbury's account of naturally virtuous human nature? In the following sections, I shall answer this question, first by focusing on his classification of the affections, and then on his moral assessment of them.

The Inquiry's Classification of the Affections

In the *Inquiry*, Shaftesbury suggests a classification of first-order affections into natural affections, self-affections and unnatural affections:[17]

> The affections or passions which must influence and govern the animal are either:
> 1. the *natural affections*, which lead to the good of the public; or
> 2. the *self affections*, which lead only to the good of the private; or
> 3. such as are neither of these nor tending either to any good of the public or private, but contrariwise, and which may therefore be justly styled *unnatural affections*.
>
> So that according as these affections stand, a creature must be virtuous or vicious, good or ill.
> The latter of these affections, it is evident, are wholly vicious. The two former may be vicious or virtuous according to their degree. (Shaftesbury, *Inquiry*: 196)

Two main topics emerge here: first, the classification of the affections, and second, their evaluation in terms of natural goodness and moral virtue. With regard to the classification of the affections, some points can be noted straight away. First, what Shaftesbury terms 'unnatural' affections (for example, malice and delight in viewing distress) are *not* presented as self-affections in an unnaturally strong or weak degree. Rather, they form a separate kind of affection, characterised by the fact that they do not aim at *any* good, not even a mistaken conception of the good. The value of natural affections and self-affections depends on their degree of strength, but unnatural affections are always ill, whatever their degree. Secondly, the distinction between 'private' and 'public' applies to non-rational instincts as well as to those affections that are guided by 'general notions of things' (*Inquiry*: 172). Both non-rational and rational creatures can be moved by non-rational instincts for self-preservation and for the preservation of their species. Rational creatures, however, also act on affections that depend on a general notion of private or public interest.[18]

Let us now look at the three kinds of affections in some more detail:

1. *Natural affections*: According to Shaftesbury, rational and non-rational creatures have, by nature, strong disinterested tendencies to associate with other members of their species and to promote their species' good.[19] He also terms the 'natural' affections 'social' or 'public affections'. Examples of such natural affections are 'pity, kindness, gratitude', 'pity, love, kindness or social affection', 'gratitude, kindness,

and pity' and 'affection of love, gratitude, bounty, generosity, pity, succour or whatever else is of a social or friendly sort' (Shaftesbury, *Inquiry*: 172, 178, 182, 201). In *Miscellaneous Reflections* IV.2, Shaftesbury explains that

> as the design or end of nature in each animal system is exhibited chiefly in the support and propagation of the particular species, it happens, of consequence, that those affections of earliest alliance and mutual kindness between the parent and the offspring are known more particularly by the name of *natural affection*. (Shaftesbury, *Miscellanies*: 432)

In a footnote to this passage, Shaftesbury uses the Stoic term στοργή (*storgê*) to explain what the natural affections are – he evidently interprets the Stoics as supporters of his claim that there are natural affections for the well-being of others.[20] Both non-rational and rational creatures act instinctively for the sake of their species. Rational creatures, however, also form a notion of the public good, and act with the intention of promoting it (Shaftesbury, *Inquiry*: 173). In this case, the natural affections are governed by reason. Natural affections are 'natural' in a negative sense in that they do not depend on education, habits or punishments and rewards. They are 'natural' in a positive sense in that they are said to exert their motivational power as part of the design or teleological constitution of every creature in the harmonious universe.

The passages discussed from *Sensus Communis* suggest that natural affections, for Shaftesbury, are irreducible to self-affections. Claiming the reality of natural affections means by the same token rejecting the selfish hypothesis, according to which there are ultimately only self-affections. Here, Shaftesbury may be seen to rely on a Stoic idea, namely that both self-concern *and* other-concern are part of the natural constitution of human beings. The fact that Shaftesbury calls altruistic affections 'natural affections' highlights the importance he attributes to them in his opposition to Hobbes, Locke and the Augustinian moralists. Against these, Shaftesbury claims that the natural affections are not just a natural, but even a *powerful* motivational force in human nature:

> Thus it may appear how much natural affection is predominant, how it is inwardly joined to us and implanted in our natures, how interwoven with our other passions and how essential to that regular motion and course of our affections on which our happiness and self-enjoyment so immediately depend. (Shaftesbury, *Inquiry*: 216)

For Shaftesbury, the fact that self-affections and natural affections form two distinct kinds clearly does not imply that they oppose each other.

Rather, given the providential design of the universe, the promotion of the private and the public good are interconnected and ultimately coincide.

In the context of his anti-Hobbesian assertion that society is not 'a kind of invention and creature of art', but is naturally based on a 'herding principle and associating inclination' (Shaftesbury, *Sensus Communis*: 52), Shaftesbury also highlights potential problems with the natural affections. Natural affections can have very different scopes: 'Universal good, or the interest of the world in general, is a kind of remote philosophical object' (*Sensus Communis*: 52). Thus, the natural affections are sometimes confined to smaller communities, where men can 'better taste society and enjoy the common good and interest of a more contracted public' (*Sensus Communis*: 52). In vast societies, this 'cantonising' is quite common, but it may lead to a problematically narrow 'spirit of faction', which 'seems to be no other than the abuse or irregularity of that social love and common affection which is natural to mankind'. In such a spirit, 'separate societies' can be 'formed in opposition to the general one of mankind and to the real interest of the State' (*Sensus Communis*: 53). Excessive natural affections can thus turn out to be problematic, and we can 'readily affirm it was even from the violence of this passion that so much disorder arose in the general society of mankind' (*Sensus Communis*: 52). Thus, if Shaftesbury rejects the selfish hypothesis and argues for the reality of natural sociability, he does so with critical awareness – but his treatment of the problematic sides of natural affections which are restricted in scope also gives him an additional point against Hobbes, since he does not need to invoke selfishness as an explanation of 'cantonising'.

2. *Self-affections*: The second kind of affections are those Shaftesbury terms in the *Inquiry* 'self-affections', 'private affections' or 'affections towards private good' (Shaftesbury, *Inquiry*: 197). Examples of self-affections, or of

> those home-affections which relate to the private interest or separate economy of the creature [. . . are . . .] love of life, resentment of injury, pleasure or appetite towards nourishment and the means of generation, interest or desire of those conveniences by which we are well provided for and maintained, emulation or love of praise and honour, indolence or love of ease and rest. (*Inquiry*: 216–17)

The self-affections come in different degrees of strength, and they can have very different objects, such as self-preservation, pleasure or praise. Since they ultimately aim at some kind of benefit for the agent, the

self-affections are best understood in the broad sense of self-love as egoistic desire. Non-rational as well as rational creatures are instinctively
moved by self-affections, yet rational creatures can form a notion of
what is in their true interest and act upon a reflective intention of promoting their own well-being.

In a similar vein to *Sensus Communis*, Shaftesbury critically notes
in the *Inquiry* that the self-affections become problematic from a moral
and rational point of view when they rise 'beyond a moderate degree':
'These affections, as self-interesting as they are, can often, we see,
become contrary to our real interest' (*Inquiry*: 225). However, Shaftesbury does not criticise the self-affections *per se*, which is a substantial
contrast to the Augustinian narrative of self-love as *amour-propre*. For
Shaftesbury, the moral value of the self-affections depends on their
degree of strength considered in relation to the other affections in the
creature. By themselves, however, they are neither a sign of depravity, nor are they, in general, found to be overly strong. If they are in
their natural (that is, providentially designed) degree, they have positive
effects for both the agent *and* the species (a feature subsequent authors
such as Hutcheson and Butler also explicitly emphasise). Thus, the
promotion of the private and the public good are not in conflict, but
connected thanks to the harmonious design of the universe. As we shall
see below, Shaftesbury treats having self-affections in their natural
degree as necessary for the goodness of a creature – they are required
not only in view of self-preservation, but also in view of the promotion
of the good of the species.

3.*Unnatural affections*: The third kind of affections neither tends to
the private nor to the public good. Examples of unnatural affections are
'unnatural and inhuman delight in beholding torments and in viewing
distress, calamity, blood, massacre and destruction with a peculiar joy
and pleasure' (*Inquiry*: 226). Shaftesbury furthermore mentions malice,
malignity, ill will, envy, hatred of humankind and society, and unnatural lusts in foreign kinds or species (*Inquiry*: 226). Again, he avoids
presenting these as forms of self-affections by distinguishing excessive
self-affections or 'extended self-passions' (*Inquiry*: 226), which presuppose an erroneous notion of private interest, from unnatural affections,
which involve no notion of good at all. This allows again for a more
positive presentation of the self-affections against the Augustinian and
Hobbesian stance. Shaftesbury is straightforward about the value of
unnatural affections: they are always ill or vicious, independently of
their degree (*Inquiry*: 196). And as far as happiness is concerned, to
have unnatural affections is 'wholly and absolutely unnatural as it is
horrid and miserable' (*Inquiry*: 226). It is not possible to derive any

real pleasure or original joy from the gratification of unnatural affections, since they are 'original misery and torment, producing no other pleasure or satisfaction than as the unnatural desire is for the instant satisfied by something which appeases it' (*Inquiry*: 228). The unnatural affection 'has been the reigning passion of many tyrants and barbarous nations' (*Inquiry*: 226).[21]

Evaluating the Affections

Natural and private affections can be evaluated in terms of natural goodness (as far as all creatures are concerned) and in terms of moral virtue (as far as rational creatures are concerned). In the *Inquiry*, Shaftesbury argues that the natural goodness or illness of natural affections and self-affections depends on their respective degree of strength. When natural affections and self-affections are in their natural, providentially designed degree, they are naturally good. But if they become too strong or too weak, they are naturally ill. Shaftesbury focuses on two main ways in which things typically go wrong: first, there is the combination of too weak self-affections with too strong natural affections (what he calls the 'unusual' part of illness and vice), and second, there is the combination of too strong self-affections with too weak natural affections (what he calls the 'more essential' part of illness and vice).

1. *Self-affections too weak and natural affections too strong*: Having introduced the distinction between the three kinds of affections, Shaftesbury discusses first the 'unusual' part of illness and vice:

> It may seem strange, perhaps, to speak of natural affections as too strong or of self affections as too weak. But to clear this difficulty we must call to mind what has been already explained, that natural affection may, in particular cases, be excessive and in an unnatural degree, as when pity is so overcoming as to destroy its own end and prevent the succour and relief required or as when love to the offspring proves such a fondness as destroys the parent and consequently the offspring itself.
>
> [. . .] Now, as in particular cases, public affection, on the one hand, may be too high, so private affection may, on the other hand, be too weak. For if a creature be self-neglectful and insensible of danger or if he want such a degree of passion in any kind as is useful to preserve, sustain or defend himself, this must certainly be esteemed vicious in regard of the design and end of nature. (Shaftesbury, *Inquiry*: 196–7)

Note again that the expression 'unnatural degree' refers explicitly to the *degree*, not to the *kind* of affection (a point that is different in *Pathologia*). Shaftesbury focuses on the directly pernicious effects for the creature, and on the indirectly pernicious effects for the species. If natural affections are too strong, their excessive degree is likely to make the realisation of their end impossible (as in the case of excessive pity, which prevents the agent by its violence from effectively relieving the sufferer's distress). This may even lead to the destruction of the creature by pushing it into dangerous situations (*Inquiry*: 172, 196). On the flip-side of the coin, if the self-affections are too weak, then neglect is likely to engender self-destruction (*Inquiry*: 197). Yet since the well-being of the species depends on the well-being of its creatures, what harms the creature also indirectly harms the species. Shaftesbury points out that all this may seem unusual. Yet he insists on the fact that 'to have any natural affection too high or any self-affection too low, though it be often approved as virtue, is yet, strictly speaking, a vice and imperfection' (*Inquiry*: 200).

Most significant for our study, Shaftesbury explicitly claims that 'the affections towards private good become necessary and essential to goodness' (*Inquiry*: 197). When the self-affections are too low, the creature has a tendency to destroy itself and thus to harm the species, which is unnatural and, in the case of rational creatures, becomes a vice. Again, compared to the Augustinian treatment of self-love as a sign of moral corruption, this inclusion of egoistic self-love in natural goodness and even moral virtue amounts to a moral rehabilitation of self-love. As I shall show in subsequent chapters, quite diverse authors join Shaftesbury in his positive view of self-love. Hutcheson and Butler do so while rejecting the selfish hypothesis, and Campbell does so while adopting it. Smith is fully aware of Shaftesbury's positive view of the self-affections and lists him in Part VII of *The Theory of Moral Sentiments* among those who claim that 'virtue consists in propriety; or in the suitableness of the affection from which we act', specifying that Shaftesbury 'places [virtue] in maintaining a proper balance of the affections, and in allowing no passion to go beyond its proper sphere' (Smith, *TMS*, VII.ii.1.48, 2002: 346).[22]

2. *Natural affections too weak and self-affections too strong*: According to Shaftesbury, this is the 'plainer and more essential part of vice' (Shaftesbury, *Inquiry*: 200). First, if the natural affections are too weak, then the creature's tendency to promote the good of its species is too weak, and the creature's natural affections are likely to be over-ridden by self-affections. This makes the creature naturally ill or morally vicious. Yet Shaftesbury insists that even if natural affections are more commonly found too weak than too strong, this does not justify the false claim that they do not exist at all. So here again Shaftesbury rejects the selfish hypothesis.

Secondly, if the self-affections are too strong and go beyond their natural and necessary degree, they become problematic. Shaftesbury writes that in rational creatures,

> these affections, if they are moderate and within certain bounds, are neither injurious to social life nor a hindrance to virtue, but, being in an extreme degree, they become cowardice, revengefulness, luxury, avarice, vanity and ambition, sloth, and, as such, are owned vicious and ill with respect to human society. (*Inquiry*: 217)

The self-affections can be in conflict with the natural affections and keep the creature from promoting the good of the species. This is not, however, to claim that there is a necessary oppostion between self-affections and natural affections, in the sense that they mutually exclude each other's gratification. Rather, Shaftesbury argues that 'to be well affected towards the public interest and one's own is not only consistent but inseparable' (*Inquiry*: 193), and he claims that if the self-affections are in a reasonable degree, then 'the public as well as the private system is advanced by the industry which this affection excites' (*Inquiry*: 223). A natural degree of the self-affections is thus in both the agent's *and* the species' interest.

On a more terminological note, 'selfishness' for Shaftesbury describes the state in which the self-affections are passionate to a degree that cannot be rationally controlled any more, which is unnatural and, in a rational creature, vicious:

> But if the affection [towards self-good] be then only injurious to the society when it is immoderate and not so when it is moderate, duly tempered and allayed, then is the immoderate degree of the affection truly vicious, but not the moderate. And, thus, if there be found in any creature a more than ordinary self-concernment or regard to private good, which is inconsistent with the interest of the species or public, this must in every respect be esteemed an ill and vicious affection. And this is what we commonly call selfishness and disapprove so much in whatever creature we happen to discover it. (*Inquiry*: 170)

In such a state, the agent's self-affections are in conflict with the natural affections, and thus with the good of the species. They may even cause the loss of the creature's natural affections (*Inquiry*: 225). Shaftesbury claims furthermore that a selfish character dominated by excessive self-affections is in conflict with the agent's 'real interest':

> Thus have we considered the self-passions and what the consequence is of their rising beyond a moderate degree. These affections, as

self-interesting as they are, can often, we see, become contrary to our real interest [. . .] They are original to that which we call selfishness and give rise to that sordid disposition of which we have already spoken. (*Inquiry*: 225)

Self-affections in an excessive or passionate degree put at risk not only the good of the species, but also the pursuit of the agent's own long-term self-interest. But Shaftesbury also carefully distinguishes cases of selfishness from the case of animal parents that are incapable of resisting their enemies and thus flee for the sake of self-preservation, thereby abandoning their offspring. If they stayed, both parents *and* offspring would be killed. Shaftesbury considers this fleeing behaviour 'no way unnatural or vicious' (*Inquiry*: 198) and does not treat it as a case of selfishness, in spite of the fact that there might be a conflict between self-affections and natural affections.[23]

Table 2.1 Shaftesbury on the natural and moral values of the affections

	Degree of affection		
Type of affection	*Too weak*	*'Natural' (i.e. providentially designed)*	*Too strong*
Self-affections (also called 'self-love' or 'private affections' by Shaftesbury)	naturally ill/ morally vicious (the 'unusual' part of vice)	naturally/ morally good, preserving the individual and thus promoting the public good	naturally ill/ morally vicious (the 'plain' part of vice; sometimes called 'selfishness' or 'self-passions')
Natural affections	naturally ill/ morally vicious (the 'plain' part of vice)	naturally/ morally good, promoting the public good	naturally ill/ morally vicious (the 'unusual' part of vice)
Unnatural affections	always naturally ill/morally vicious		

To sum up this reading of the *Inquiry* on self-love and the self-affections: a creature is *naturally good* if motivated by a combination of natural affections *and* self-affections in their natural degree, and if it has no unnatural affections. Besides having the right second-order affections originating in the moral sense, a *morally virtuous* rational creature also has this balanced state of affections. A creature with a naturally good character *'is such a one as by the natural temper or bent of his affections is carried primarily and immediately, and not secondarily and accidentally, to good and against ill'* (Shaftesbury, *Inquiry*: 171). When the creature has its affections in their natural degree, it promotes the good of its species *and* its own good, which is again best for the species. Shaftesbury may more frequently emphasise the requirement of having the natural affections in the right degree, yet his claim that 'the affections towards private good become necessary and essential to goodness' (*Inquiry*: 197) emphasises that both natural affections *and* self-affections are required for goodness and moral virtue. Only their combination guarantees the well-being of the species.

Given the dependence of virtue on the degree and combination of affections, 'vice and virtue are found variously mixed and alternately prevalent in the several characters of mankind' (*Inquiry*: 176). According to Shaftesbury, however, there are no wholly vicious creatures: 'Nothing is more just than a known saying that "it is as hard to find a man wholly ill as wholly good" because, wherever there is any good affection left, there is certainly some goodness or virtue still in being' (*Inquiry*: 177). Since there are no morally insensible rational creatures who entirely lack any notion of a public interest (*Inquiry*: 177), there are also no rational creatures without any trace of virtue left that could be cultivated. Human nature is capable of both 'the highest improvements of temper' and the 'greatest corruptions and degeneracies' (*Inquiry*: 199), but it is never *entirely* corrupt and deprived of goodness and virtue. The contrast to the Calvinist *topos* of postlapsarian corruption is quite striking. Yet again, especially when it comes to the cultivation of virtue, Shaftesbury shows his more 'elitist' Stoic side, as becomes evident in other texts: very few people will be able to cultivate virtue to the highest degree. Even if he claims in the *Inquiry* that no one is entirely vicious, his account of how we can reach virtue is definitely more 'elitist' than, say, Hutcheson's account of self-cultivation.

2.3 A SIDE-NOTE ON PRIDE IN *PATHOLOGIA* AND *MISCELLANEOUS REFLECTIONS*

In the foregoing sections, I have focused on Shaftesbury's treatment of self-love in his remarks in the *Inquiry* on the self-affections, that is, on egoistic self-love. The *Inquiry* is his most systematic treatise in moral philosophy, but it is not fully representative of all his writings. I thus want to briefly compare this text to some of his other, more 'Stoical' writings. In his Latin manuscript *Pathologia* (*A Theory of the Passions*, written in 1706), Shaftesbury presents and defends the Stoic theory of the emotions, in dialogue with Cicero's *Tusculan Disputations* and Diogenes Laertius' *Lives of the Philosophers*.[24] Shaftesbury begins with an essential Stoic distinction in moral ontology: first, there are things truly good and ill, which are internal or ἐφ' ἡμῖν, that is, 'in our power'.

These are virtue and vice, and nothing else. Secondly, there are things 'fancied', or erroneously represented by us as good or ill, which are in reality indifferent and external, thus not ἐφ' ἡμῖν. These are typically health, riches, honour and offices (Shaftesbury, *Pathologia*: 222, 231–2). For the Stoics, these two kinds of things produce different emotions when we represent them to ourselves: truly good or ill things (virtue and vice) produce calm or constant emotions (εὐπαθείαι or *constantiæ*), which are often called 'affections' in English. 'Fancied' good or ill things produce violent or perturbed emotions (πάθη or *perturbationes*), which are often called 'passions' in English. As Shaftesbury shows with a very detailed table in the continuation of his manuscript, all these emotions are further subdivided by the Stoics (*Pathologia*: 223–4, 233–4).

Self-cultivation, according to the model in *Pathologia*, consists primarily in the rectification of our representations of things: the virtuous agent avoids the erroneous representation of genuinely indifferent things as goods or ills. This account is very different from that of the *Inquiry*, where the focus lies on controlling the degree and balance of two different *kinds* of affections, namely natural affections and self-affections. According to *Pathologia*, then, one of the most problematic passions is admiration, which is 'the greatest cause of all vices, and that which increases and strengthens them' (*Pathologia*: 224–5, 235; Maurer and Jaffro 2013: 218). The problem with admiration is that it represents external things, which are in reality indifferent, as 'the highest beauties' and as worthy of possession (Shaftesbury, *Pathologia*: 225, 235). The psychological consequence of this misrepresentation is that he who possesses such falsely admired goods 'attributes no lesser beauty to himself and admires himself' (*Pathologia*: 225, 235). The specific form of self-admiration (*admiratio sui ipsius*) produced is pride (*superbia*), which includes the joy of being superior to others in view of the possession of these external things, which are in reality indifferent (*Pathologia*: 225, 236). In some remarks on the subject, *superbia* is explained as a morally problematic passion that is based on the erroneous attribution to oneself of beauty or goodness because of one's possession of external things, which one erroneously 'fancies' true goods. It involves an unjustified highly positive opinion of oneself, paired with the comparative tendency to consider oneself superior to others.

In Shaftesbury's *Miscellaneous Reflections on the Preceding Treatises and Other Critical Subjects*, IV (1711), *Pathologia*'s presentation of admiration and pride shines clearly through. Shaftesbury does not simply present the Stoic theory of the emotions – to quite some extent he adopts it himself. He discusses the following example of passionate desires for external things which are erroneously fancied as truly good or excellent in themselves, and tells us how we have to avoid these passions:

> Again, I consider with myself that I have the imagination of something beautiful, great and becoming in things. This imagination I apply perhaps to such subjects as plate, jewels, apartments, coronets, patents of honour, titles or precedencies. I must therefore naturally seek these not as mere conveniences, means or helps in life (for as such my *passion* could not be so excessive towards them) but as excellent in themselves, necessarily attractive of my admiration and directly and immediately causing my happiness and giving me satisfaction. Now if the passion raised on this opinion (call it avarice, pride, vanity or ambition) be indeed incapable of any real satisfaction, even under the most successful course of fortune, and then too, attended with perpetual fears of disappointment and loss, how can the mind be other than miserable when possessed by it? But if, instead of forming thus the opinion of good, if instead of placing worth or excellence in these outward subjects, we place it where it is truest, in the affections or sentiments, in the governing part and inward character, we have then the full enjoyment of it within our power: the imagination or opinion remains steady and irreversible, and the love, desire and appetite is answered without apprehension of loss or disappointment. (Shaftesbury, *Miscellanies*: 422)

The passage explains how our admiration for external things, which are not within our power, causes violent emotions, that is, perturbed passions such as pride, vanity and ambition – as seen in *Pathologia*. All these passions necessarily make us unhappy, since their object is not within our power, and because they are 'incapable of any real satisfaction'. Since these passions or *perturbationes* are likely to remain ungratified, they cause the further passion of fear that the original passion is not satisfied. All this results in a very perturbed state of mind.

In contrast, the correct representation of the virtuous dispositions of the soul as the only true good, and as something that is fully within the agent's power, results in a 'steady and irreversible' opinion and is the foundation of calm affections or *constantiæ*. 'Placing worth or excellence' in the internal goods of the soul allows the rational person to have 'the full enjoyment' of what is within her power. In other words, if we value our virtuous dispositions, we develop affections that can be gratified 'without disappointment', whereas the valuing of external things necessarily leads to misery. Thus, Shaftesbury insists in the subsequent passages on self-cultivation that we have to 'rectify opinions' – the account of self-cultivation developed focuses on Stoic moral ontology. The questions that were central to the *Inquiry*, concerning the degree of strength and the distinction between private and public, are merely subordinated to the distinction between 'true' and 'fancied' goods and ills.

2.4 CONCLUSION

With the remarks on the *Inquiry*'s treatment of the affections, we are in a better position to understand the passage quoted initially from *Sensus Communis*, where Shaftesbury attacks the views of human nature and self-love of Hobbes and others. Remember how Shaftesbury's critical commentary ended in the slightly obscure statement: 'It is the height of wisdom, no doubt, to be rightly selfish' (Shaftesbury, *Sensus Communis*: 56). We have now seen the crucial place that Shaftesbury attributes in the *Inquiry* to the distinction between self-affections and natural affections or, in present-day terminology, between egoistic and altruistic desires. In both *Sensus Communis* and *Inquiry*, he argues against the selfish hypothesis or, in his proper language, against attempts to reduce all natural affections to affections of the 'selfish kind': human behaviour cannot be explained in terms of self-affections only, and we must furthermore assume with the Ancients (particularly the Stoics) that we share a sense of the common good, or what he terms *sensus communis* (*Sensus Communis*: 48). Shaftesbury furthermore rejects claims about a necessary opposition between private and public interest: thanks to providential design, these coincide, at least as far as our true self-interest is concerned (*Sensus Communis*: 55).

To come back to the statement in question: Only if we properly distinguish between self-affections and natural affections, and only if we acknowledge the fact that our nature is equipped with affections for the public good, can we reasonably treat the question of whether we best promote our happiness *either* by satisfying both natural affections and self-affections (which is in accordance with nature, since both are part of human nature), *or* by frustrating the natural affections in favour of the self-affections (which would be against our nature). Shaftesbury argues for the first solution, and the *Inquiry* spells out how: happiness is found in 'following nature', that is, in realising our selves by keeping both natural affections *and* self-affections in their natural, that is, providentially designed degree. This keeping the right balance constitutes what it is to love oneself 'in the rightest manner'; it is the best way of taking care of the realisation of the self.[25]

The expression 'loving oneself in the rightest manner' remains somewhat peculiar. Loving oneself should not be mistaken here for a first-order self-affection, or for egoistic self-love. Rather, it seems to point to self-cultivation connected to the reflected promotion of one's true happiness, where this is gained by living according to one's true nature, and thus by keeping public *and* private affections in their natural degrees.[26] Loving oneself is concerned with gaining happiness by means of realising the agent's true nature, which includes the cultivation of virtue by means of cultivating one's affections, both self-affections and public affections. Such an understanding of 'self-love' is only suggested in this passage, but it is not really elaborated – the fullest and most influential account of self-love as respect of self to be found in eighteenth-century British moral philosophy would be presented by Butler in his *Sermons* some years later.

Thus, how does Shaftesbury criticise 'Hobbesian egoism', as Irwin puts it (Irwin 2008: 354)? Again, it seems most apposite to interpret Shaftesbury's 'self-affections' in terms of egoistic self-love. In our providentially designed universe, this leads to the promotion of the private good, and indirectly to the promotion of the good of the species – under the condition that the self-affections are in their natural degree, and are neither excessive nor too weak. With his conception of the natural affections, Shaftesbury defends the reality of social affections which naturally lead to the promotion of the public good, and which are irreducible to the self-affections. Thereby he also attempts to refute the selfish hypothesis. We have seen that he explicitly attacks two types of egoistic psychologies: first, the claim that we are motivated only by self-affections, be they reflected or not (that is, psychological egoism), and second, the more specific claim that we act only upon calculation of our self-interest (that is, prudential egoism). Both theories are false and dangerous in that they may impede our cultivation of virtue, for example by bringing us to counteract or frustrate our social affections, against our own nature.

There are good reasons why Shaftesbury is known as a philosopher who attacked the selfish hypothesis by emphasising natural sociability – his anti-egoist stance is important and influential. Nevertheless, we should not forget that in his rejection of the selfish hypothesis, Shaftesbury also puts forward a very positive account of self-love, especially in comparison with the Augustinian point of view. If the self-affections are in their natural degree, they are not only no hindrance to virtue (since due to divine design they are not in conflict with the natural affections). Shaftesbury insists that they are required for goodness and, in rational agents, for virtue: 'the affections towards private good become necessary and essential to goodness' (Shaftesbury, *Inquiry*: 197). Indeed, Shaftesbury claims that the self-affections can be too weak – a fully virtuous agent requires them.[27] Again, it is true that Shaftesbury depicts the cultivation of virtue as a most challenging enterprise, which cannot be successfully accomplished by just anyone – this is quite different in Hutcheson. In comparison to Augustinian and Hobbesian views, however, Shaftesbury is still very positive about natural sociability, about postlapsarian human nature's capacity for virtuous action and character, and about the role of the self-affections. It is this general optimism of Shaftesbury that attracts the attention of Bernard Mandeville, who is the second cornerstone for our debates in the early eighteenth century.

Before focusing our attention on Mandeville, one last point should be addressed. One specific interpretation of Shaftesbury was quite widely adopted in the eighteenth century, and it is connected to the previously discussed question of how to be 'rightly selfish'. Shaftesbury was quite often portrayed as claiming 'that there can be but one ultimate end of the agent's cool and deliberate pursuit, viz. his own highest interest or personal happiness' (Leechman 1755: xlv).[28] In other words, Shaftesbury would admit only an egoistic reason (namely the agent's own happiness) for being virtuous. Indeed, Shaftesbury strongly highlights the beneficial effects of being virtuous in the *Inquiry*. However, Michael Gill points out that there is also a 'teleological' reason to be virtuous in Shaftesbury, grounded in the idea that we are providentially designed for virtue, and that we should realise our nature in self-cultivation (Gill 2006: 118–21). From this point of view, gaining happiness is not considered the reason for being virtuous, but a mere consequence of what it is to realise or fulfil our nature – which may be again a Stoic point. Interestingly, Hutcheson can be seen to make a very similar point when introducing the idea that there is a hierarchy of the pleasures (see Chapters 4.2 and 4.3), and Butler and many others defend the virtuous way of life, all things considered, as pleasurable (see Chapter 5.2). Thus, their presentation of Shaftesbury as reducing the reason for virtue merely to that of pleasure may have been a strategic distancing of themselves from potential objections against their own moral philosophies, which also emphasised the pleasurable aspects of virtue, as opposed to self-denial.

NOTES

1. *Characteristicks* is a collection of several texts, some of which were published previously. It includes *A Letter Concerning Enthusiasm* (1708/1711), *Sensus Communis, an Essay on the Freedom of Wit and Humour* (1709/1711), *Soliloquy, or Advice to an Author* (1710/1711), *An Inquiry Concerning Virtue or Merit* (1699/1711), *The Moralists, a Philosophical Rhapsody* (1709/1711) and *Miscellaneous Reflections* (1711). Shaftesbury also left a large body of manuscripts, for example

Askêmata and *Pathologia*. For more information on Shaftesbury, see in particular Grean (1967), Klein (1994; 2004) and Darwall (1995). In the present chapter, I concentrate on Shaftesbury's contributions to the debates on self-love.

2. This passage is quoted in, among others, Forbes (1734: 324) – see Chapter 4.4.

3. This famous passage is discussed by numerous commentators, for example Darwall (1995: 177), Gill (2006: 81), Carey (2006: 98) and Brooke (2012: 114).

4. In Maurer (2015), I analyse how specific themes of the French moralists were discussed by early eighteenth-century British moralists.

5. See also Grean (1964: 41).

6. Against certain interpretations of Shaftesbury, contemporary and present-day, we should emphasise that here Shaftesbury does *not* make the claim that the egoistic reason indicated (happiness) is the *only* possible reason for living virtuously in his sense. See Gill (2006: 118–23) on a similar issue.

7. According to Shaftesbury himself, the 1699 publication by the Deist John Toland of the *Inquiry* was against his wishes – see also Klein (2004). Shaftesbury's *Moralists*, written in the form of a dialogue, was possibly his most influential text.

8. See Jaffro (2013) on the importance of the distinction between *honestum* and *utile* in Shaftesbury and Hutcheson.

9. See Shaftesbury (*Inquiry*: 163–4) and Harris (2003) for further discussion. The difference between Bayle's conception of civic virtue and Shaftesbury's conception of moral virtue is an additional important point.

10. See Force (2003: 81), yet note the reservations in Grean (1967) against too unqualified a classification of Shaftesbury as a (neo-)Stoic. See also Brooke (2012: 118–19) and Maurer and Jaffro (2013) regarding *Pathologia* and *Miscellaneous Reflections*.

11. Hume subjects this opinion to sharp criticism in several of his writings, most importantly in his *Dialogues concerning Natural Religion* (1779).

12. See, however, Gill (2010: 20–1; 2006: 83–8) and Brooke (2012: 120) on the limits of Shaftesbury's optimism in some of his other texts, and on his 'elitist' or 'aristocratic' approach to questions of moral culture, which contrasts with those of Hutcheson and the Cambridge Platonists.

13. Darwall clarifies that Shaftesbury uses the adjective 'natural' often as 'a synonym for "good". Standing behind this identification is a teleological picture of the natural order as an integrated system in which sub-systems function together to realize a well-functioning whole' (1995: 183–4). This does not hold for the adjective 'natural' in the expression 'natural affections', however. Here, 'natural' means 'social', 'public' or, in our present-day vocabulary, 'altruistic'.

14. See Jaffro (2000: 68) for this suggestion.

15. Several commentators have emphasised that Shaftesbury does not have a sentimentalist conception of the moral sense as a passive recipient of moral sentiments, but a rationalist conception that highlights the importance of active reflection on the notion of the public good. See, for example, Darwall (1995: 187) and Jaffro (2000: 65–6).

16. The overall picture of Shaftesbury's account looks more nuanced and less simplistically optimistic. Elsewhere, Shaftesbury highlights the great difficulties of cultivating virtue to its highest possible degree, which may be a reminiscence of the figure of the Stoic sage. See again Gill (2006: 83, 111).

17. This classification of the emotions is strikingly different from the approach in *Pathologia* and, to quite some extent, in *Miscellaneous Reflections*. Based on Stoic moral ontology, emotions are there fundamentally distinguished into calm εὐπαθείαι (*eupatheiai*) or *constantiæ* on the one hand, which are directed towards the one true good (virtue), and violent πάθη (*pathê*) or *perturbationes* on the other hand, which are directed towards external things erroneously represented as good. The distinction between public and private affections, which is essential for the *Inquiry*, plays almost no role, however, in *Pathologia* and *Miscellaneous Reflections*. See Chapter 2.3 and Shaftesbury (*Pathologia*: 221–3); Maurer and Jaffro (2013: 211–16).

    On a more terminological issue, the *Inquiry* has a strong tendency to use the term 'affections' (and sometimes the term 'passions', too) in a generic sense to refer to all the emotions. There is no strict distinction between calm affections and violent passions, even if sometimes the term 'passions' is used in the narrower sense of emotions that are too strong or violent, as opposed to 'affections' in the narrower sense of emotions that are in their natural degree. Other terms, such as 'appetites' or 'desires', are often used indiscriminately.

18. Some philosophical commentators have noted that a distinction based not on the objects of affections, but on their normal causal tendencies (an interpretation which may be suggested by Shaftesbury's words 'lead' and 'tend' in the quoted passage), may blur the distinction between natural affections and self-affections (McNaughton 1996: 206–7). However, if we consider Shaftesbury's conception of the universe as a harmonious designed system, in which, for example, the direct causal tendencies of private affections, which are initially positive for the individual creature, also lead to positive indirect causal tendencies for the public good, then the point seems less important, at least insofar as non-rational creatures are concerned. See also Darwall (1995: 184).

19. Shaftesbury claims in *Sensus Communis*: 'For my own part, methinks, this herding principle and associating inclination is seen so natural and strong in most men' (*Sensus Communis*: 52). This is in clear contradiction

to Hobbes, according to whom there is no such natural principle of association. Mandeville ridicules Shaftesbury on this point with a rather fishy tale of 'Fresh Herrings' – see Mandeville (*Search*: 337).

20. There are numerous points that demonstrate Shaftesbury's affinities with Stoicism. Grounded on Shaftesbury's affirmation of the reality of the natural affections, Force claims that Shaftesbury takes part in a neo-Stoic refutation of the selfish hypothesis (2003: 80–2). However, some aspects in Shaftesbury are more difficult to combine with Stoicism, for example his positive treatment of the passion of pity. Carey prefers to speak of a 'Stoic pedigree' in Shaftesbury (Carey 2006: 112). See furthermore Grean (1967), Carey (2006: 110–16), Brooke (2012: 111–24) and Maurer and Jaffro (2013: 214–16).

21. This point is similar to Hutcheson's discussion of disinterested hatred – see Hutcheson (*Inquiry*: 105). Hutcheson calls such emotions 'disinterested' because they do not aim at any private advantage for the agent herself, but only at the misery of the other person. Hutcheson agrees with Shaftesbury that these cases are neither occurrences of excessive self-affections (or of 'passionate self-love' in Hutcheson's terminology), nor caused by an erroneous representation of the private good.

22. Turnbull (2005: 1, 221) highlights the same point, clearly in the vein of Shaftesbury: in some 'constitutions self-love is really too weak, and some generous affection is too strong'.

23. Shaftesbury is more ambiguous regarding the term 'self-love', which in the *Inquiry* he often uses in a generic sense to refer to self-affections in their natural degree, that is, to 'the affections which relate to the private system and constitute whatever we call interestedness or self-love' (*Inquiry*: 217). Unlike 'selfishness', 'self-love' is not associated with vice, unless it is in an immoderate degree. The passages quoted from *Sensus Communis* at the beginning of this chapter suggest a different view, however – one that is closer to self-love as *amour-propre*.

24. With Laurent Jaffro (Université Paris-1 Panthéon-Sorbonne) and Alain Petit (Université Clermont Auvergne), we have edited, translated and critically commented on this manuscript by Shaftesbury – see Shaftesbury, *Pathologia*, and Maurer and Jaffro (2013).

25. In *Miscellaneous Reflections* IV, Shaftesbury writes on the *Inquiry*: 'This is the main problem which our author in more philosophical terms demonstrates in this treatise: that, for a creature whose natural end is society, to operate as is by nature appointed to him towards the good of such his society or whole is in reality to pursue his own natural and proper good; and that to operate contrariwise, or by such affections as sever from that common good or public interest, is in reality to work towards his own natural and proper ill' (*Miscellanies*: 432), The public and the private good are connected, by providential design, and so are self-love and benevolence, to use Hutcheson's more common terminology.

26. In this context, Shaftesbury's deep engagement with Stoicism is particularly important, but differences need to be kept in mind. See again Grean (1967: 7), Brooke (2012: 118) and Maurer and Jaffro (2013: 214–16).
27. This point must caution us against presenting Shaftesbury's ethics as an ethics of benevolence – a point Smith saw very clearly in his comparison of Hutcheson and Shaftesbury. I will discuss this point in greater detail in Chapter 7.2.
28. Similar claims can be found in Hutcheson himself, in Blair's review of Leechman's edition of Hutcheson's *System*, and in Butler's preface to the *Sermons*. This point has also attracted the attention of present-day commentators, for example Ahnert (2014: 52) and Grote (2006; 2010). For further discussions, see Chapter 4.5.

3. Mandeville: Self-love, Self-liking and Augustinian Themes

Bernard Mandeville's essay *A Search into the Nature of Society* was included in the second edition from 1723 of *The Fable of the Bees*. Its beginning states that the noble author Shaftesbury

> Fancies, that as Man is made for Society, so he ought to be born with a kind Affection to the whole, of which he is a part, and a Propensity to seek the Welfare of it. [. . .] The attentive Reader [. . .] will soon perceive that two Systems cannot be more opposite than his Lordship's and mine. His Notions I confess are generous and refined: They are a high Compliment to Human-kind, and capable by the help of a little Enthusiasm of Inspiring us with the most Noble Sentiments concerning the Dignity of our exalted Nature: What Pity it is that they are not true. (Mandeville, *Search*: 323–4)

Many central ideas of the moral philosophy of Bernard Mandeville (1670–1733), a Dutch immigrant and medical doctor to the London poor, can indeed be fruitfully understood through their provocative contrasts to the English Lord Shaftesbury's perspective of the '*Beau Monde*' (Mandeville, *Fable II*: 11). Mandeville likes to present his disagreements with Shaftesbury as centring on the question of the dignity or moral status of human nature, in which the debates on self-love play a crucial role.[1] In their opposition, Shaftesbury and Mandeville influenced much of the subsequent discussion in Britain and elsewhere.

Mandeville may not be one of the most systematic, but he is certainly one of the most fascinating moral philosophers of the period. He has received a considerable amount of attention from intellectual historians, yet he is still quite neglected in much present-day Anglophone history of philosophy. Even in major studies in the field, Mandeville has received only marginal attention, and he is often only discussed indirectly through the reactions of other philosophers who are considered more serious.[2] Admittedly, Mandeville was not only a philosopher, he was also a literary writer and a medical doctor, and this may make Mandeville the philosopher's claims more difficult to reconstruct and assess: one of his preferred registers is clearly that of provocation, much more so than analytic exposition of theses and arguments. In addition, his preferred form is the dialogue rather than the philosophical treatise. The form of the dialogue was not at all unusual for the period, but nowadays we have become less comfortable with this once very common and reputable ways of presenting philosophical reflections. I shall not attempt here to solve the many issues of interpretation concerning Mandeville, yet I want to see what light his contributions to the debates on self-love shed on his moral philosophy.

Mandeville, who may have been taught by Pierre Bayle in Rotterdam, studied medicine in Leyden and emigrated to London in 1693. There he worked as a medical doctor and soon embarked upon a literary career. Some of his central philosophical texts are the various pieces contained in *The Fable of the Bees* (first edition 1714, second enlarged edition 1723), *Free Thoughts on Religion, the Church, and National Happiness* (1720), *The Fable of the Bees, Part II* (1729) and *An Enquiry into the Origin of Honour, and the Usefulness of Christianity in War* (1732). Mandeville's other writings are indeed noteworthy, but I shall here concentrate on those that are most relevant for understanding his conceptions of self-love.[3]

Concerning the debates on self-love, Mandeville's original and influential voice is frequently summarised under the general label of 'egoism'. In some sense, this classification is not incorrect, since Mandeville indisputably adopts a version of the selfish hypothesis.[4] However, I think that labelling Mandeville an egoist is insufficient and blinds us to the most interesting facets of his position – facets that his contemporaries perceived only too well. Crucially, it is the interplay between the conceptions of self-love as *amour-propre* and self-love as love of praise that most profoundly marks his thinking about human nature and morality. Behind his generally pessimistic view of postlapsarian human nature we find a playful use of ideas found in the French Augustinian moralists and Bayle, and I think that Mandeville can be fruitfully interpreted as adapting many of these for an early eighteenth-century English context, with Shaftesbury as a most inviting target.[5]

In his moral philosophy, Mandeville famously claims that rather than looking with Shaftesbury at the beautifully presented surfaces of human nature and society, he wants to concentrate on their anatomies – which means taking into account the ugly parts as well.[6] One of the results of this method is that we must acknowledge that human nature is dominated by passions rather than by reason. And those passions are utterly selfish:

> But be we Savages or Politicians, it is impossible that Man, mere fallen Man, should act with any other View but to please himself while he has the Use of his Organs, and the greatest Extravagancy either of Love or Despair can have no other Centre. (Mandeville, *Search*: 348)

Again, based on isolated quotations like this one, we may quickly wish to locate Mandeville as a psychological egoist of the hedonistic variety. Yet matters are far more interesting: Mandeville's developmental narrative about sociability and the civilising process, his treatment of the social virtues of politeness and honour, and his discussion of moral virtue and religion deserve deeper discussion. In this chapter, I shall only be able to present a selective look at Mandeville's rich *oeuvre*, with the goal of contributing to a more fine-grained view of his contributions to the debates on self-love. As far as the treatment of Mandeville in philosophy is concerned, many commentators have too narrowly concentrated on some selected passages from essays from *Part I* of the *Fable*. I will focus instead on the less studied *Part II* of the *Fable* (1729), and on the *Enquiry into the Origin of Honour* (1732). These are styled as dialogues between Horatio, a supporter of Shaftesbury, and Cleomenes, a supporter of Mandeville who explains the principles of *Part I* of the *Fable* to Horatio.[7] In the following, I shall first discuss the core features of Mandeville's passion of 'self-liking', that is, self-love as *amour-propre*, and then look at its role in connection with the distinction between the social virtues and moral virtue.

3.1 MANDEVILLE ON THE PASSION OF SELF-LIKING

In the context of an attack in the *Enquiry* on Shaftesbury's claim that virtue is congenial to human nature, and thus requires no self-denial but our 'living according to nature', Cleomenes distinguishes between two kinds of self-love – one he terms 'self-love', the other 'self-liking'. The two are 'plainly distinct' (Mandeville, *Honour*: 3).[8] In the state of nature, the passion Mandeville terms 'self-love' 'would first make [a creature] scrape together every thing it wanted for Sustenance, provide against the Injuries of the Air, and do every thing to make itself and young Ones secure' (Mandeville, *Fable II*: 133). 'Self-love', Cleomenes claims, 'was given to all Animals, at least, the most perfect, for Self-Preservation' (*Fable II*: 129).

Mandeville does not offer a very detailed account, yet as far as *Fable II* is concerned, we may best interpret 'self-love' as a conception of self-love as hedonistic egoism. This kind of self-love is a fundamental motivational power that makes the creature seek pleasure and avoid pain, and that under *normal* circumstances leads to its preservation (*Fable II*: 139).[9] However, in Mandeville's version of the selfish hypothesis, what he terms 'self-liking' is much more central.

The passion of self-liking, which turns out to be a conception of self-love as *amour-propre* or excessive pride, makes the creature 'seek for Opportunities, by Gestures, Looks, and Sounds, to display the Value it has for itself, superiour to what it has for others' (*Fable II*: 133). Self-liking is said to be 'that great Value, which all Individuals set upon their own Persons; that high Esteem, which I take all Men to be born with for themselves' (Mandeville, *Honour*: 3). Self-liking is not self-love as self-esteem, which is based on a potentially appropriate self-evaluation, and it involves much more than just some psychological primacy of self-concern over other-concern. To begin with, self-liking makes the individual value itself more than all other creatures – it is connected to a belief or sentiment of one's superiority over others, it is the creature's 'real liking to its own Being, superior to what they have to any other' (Mandeville, *Fable II*: 129). Self-liking thus involves a very specific comparative stance.

Furthermore, Mandeville claims that human beings not only have a high regard for themselves, but that they objectively *over*estimate their own value. Self-liking is an instinct, given from nature, 'by which every Individual values itself above its real Worth' (*Fable II*: 130).[10] Mandeville does not explain in greater detail what the 'real' worth of an individual consists in, but opposing his view to Shaftesbury's, Mandeville suggests on several occasions that we contrast our subjective self-approbation with the objective reality of postlapsarian humankind. The self-approbation involved in the passion of self-liking, or self-love as *amour-propre*, is not justified, since after the Fall human beings are hardly capable of genuine moral virtue. From the moral point of view, no human agent is really justified in approving of herself, given our psychological make-up. Mandeville's detailed description of the consequences of self-liking, and his discussion of the origins of politeness in society, show how self-liking engenders expressive and competitive behavioural tendencies that are problematic for society – unless the passion is modified during the civilising process. As we shall see, unmodified self-liking is likely to give offence to the self-liking of others, and thus to cause conflicts. All these features show the proximity of Mandeville's 'self-liking' to the French Augustinians' passion of *amour-propre*.[11]

Mandeville points out an interesting problem with our belief in our superiority: human beings are intelligent enough to have at least a suspicion that this belief in their own superiority cannot be justified. This valuing oneself over one's real worth and over the worth of others

> in us, I mean, in Man, seems to be accompany'd with a Diffidence, arising from a Consciousness, or at least an Apprehension, that we do over-value ourselves: It is this that makes us so fond of the Approbation, Liking and Assent of others; because they strengthen and confirm us in the good Opinion we have of ourselves. (*Fable II*: 130)

Self-liking and the belief in my superiority are undermined by the apprehension that my attribution of superior value to myself may not be justified. Doubts are raised by my apprehension of others who express their respective beliefs in their own superior value, but not because of my insight that my belief in my own superiority is incorrect. Such doubts endanger the gratification of the passion of self-liking.

The far-reaching consequence of this situation is that we become excessively eager to be praised. In other words, self-love as love of praise is boosted due to the fragilities inherent to self-liking. Praise gives the agent an external confirmation of her imagined value and temporarily stabilises her belief in her superiority over others. Mandeville regularly highlights the power of love of praise in human motivation and explains that this selfish desire for approbation from other agents is the hidden motive for many apparently benevolent actions (Mandeville, *Fable II*: 130; *Honour*: 4–6; *Enquiry*: 55). According to Mandeville, human creatures are so excessively desirous of praise that they even derive pleasure from being praised when they know that it is inappropriate, rests on false assumptions, or is insincere and nothing but flattery – *any* praise is welcome and will provide them joy (Mandeville, *Honour*: 7). In Adam Smith's terms, since Mandevillian humans have no conception of praise*worthiness*, they do not distinguish between appropriate and inappropriate praise. Smith's distinction between 'love of true glory' and 'love of vanity', which we shall discuss in greater detail in Chapter 7.2, has no room in Mandeville. In a more political context, praise is presented as nothing but an 'imaginary' reward grounded in our eagerness to be flattered, and providing us with 'superlative Felicity' (Mandeville, *Enquiry*: 42, 55; *Fable II*: 95). Yet besides producing the pleasure of being praised (for false reasons), praise does not involve any benefits.

This reinforcement of self-love as love of praise is not the only psychological consequence of the insecurity of the gratification of self-liking, that is, self-love as *amour-propre*. In the state of nature, where manners are not yet cultivated, humans tend to display their assumed superiority, which will offend others (Mandeville, *Fable II*: 133). This expression of an agent's self-liking offends the self-liking of other agents, which renders human beings unbearable, 'insufferable' and 'hateful' to each other and threatens the cohesion of society (*Fable II*: 138).[12] Due to the instability of their self-liking, human beings in the state of nature tend to be competitive and aggressive (*Fable II*: 138). Self-deception is another way of securing the gratification of the passion of self-liking, and Mandeville often emphasises the tendency to conceal one's real motives from others and also from oneself (*Fable II*: 139; *Remarks*: 135, 230; *Charity*: 281–2). Compared to the French Augustinians' treatment of *amour-propre*, Mandeville may insist more strongly on the developmental aspects of self-liking and less on its connection to theological *topoi*, but the structural features of self-liking are closely modelled on *amour-propre*. These points must be kept in mind when we broadly qualify Mandeville as an 'egoist'.

Mandeville calls self-liking a passion (Mandeville, *Honour*: 2; *Fable II*: 138). Without taking into account a subdivision of emotions into calm, controllable affections and violent, uncontrollable passions, Mandeville states that we cannot govern our passions, and especially that we cannot counteract them with reason – only passions can overrule passions (Mandeville, *Remarks*: 201).[13] However, self-liking has different degrees of strength: it can be 'excessive', 'moderate and well regulated' (Mandeville, *Honour*: 6–7), or weak and even absent – which is unnatural. Mandeville highlights that there is a social policy with respect to the naming of the passion of self-liking, depending on its degree of strength: '[w]hen it is kept out of Sight, or is so well disguis'd as not to appear in its own Colours, it has no Name, tho' Men act from that and no other Principle' (*Honour*: 3). Mandeville continues:

> [Self-liking], when it is moderate and well regulated, excites in us the Love of Praise, and a Desire to be applauded and thought well of by others, and stirs us up to good Actions: but that the same Passion, when it is excessive, or ill turn'd, whatever it excites in our Selves, gives Offence to others, renders us odious, and is call'd Pride. (*Honour*: 6–7)

Self-liking, that is, self-love as *amour-propre*,[14] in both its moderate and its excessive degree engenders self-love as love of praise. In a civilised society, moderate self-liking, even if it is based on an unjustifiably positive opinion of oneself, is not offensive to others since its expressive tendencies are well concealed. This is the aim of the social practice of politeness, as we shall see in the next section. Concealed self-liking is still self-liking, and it still involves the belief in one's superiority – but

in society, it is not given any name. If self-liking has an excessive degree
of strength, it is not concealed and offends other agents, since they see
their own self-liking and the belief in their superiority undermined by
the other's displayed belief in their superiority. In this case, self-liking is
given the names of 'pride' or 'vanity'.[15]

Mandeville's analysis of suicide clarifies the interplay between the
two passions he terms 'self-love' and 'self-liking'.[16] Self-liking (self-love
as *amour-propre* or excessive pride) orients self-love (egoistic self-love
of the hedonistic variety) towards the preservation of one's beloved self.
Mandeville claims that without self-liking, the creature 'can taste no
Pleasure' (Mandeville, *Fable II*: 136). The ability to have pleasurable
experiences, or to gratify the passion Mandeville terms 'self-love', seems
to presuppose that the creature has the passion of self-liking in some
minimal degree. If self-liking is entirely absent, hedonistic self-love will
cause the agent to kill herself:

> no Man can resolve upon Suicide, whilst Self-liking lasts: but as soon
> as that is over, all our Hopes are extinct, and we can form no Wishes
> but for the Dissolution of our Frame: till at last our Being becomes so
> intollerable to us, that Self-love prompts us to make an end of it, and
> seek Refuge in Death. (*Fable II*: 136)

Thus, the presence of self-liking, the passion that is grounded in the belief
in one's superior value over others, is a condition for hedonistic self-love
to take its natural direction of self-preservation. If the creature has lost its
self-liking, it will have a tendency to avoid the pain of being intolerable
to itself by committing suicide. All these reflections show the importance
of going beyond the superficial classification of Mandeville as an 'egoist'.

3.2 SELF-LIKING AND THE CIVILISING PROCESS: POLITENESS AND HONOUR

It is obvious why, for Mandeville, the passion of self-liking has potentially very problematic dimensions, especially in the state of nature.
Our tendency to display the excessively high and objectively unjustifiable value we put on ourselves offends the self-liking of others, which
may lead to competition and aggression. Encountering others who are
also experiencing the passion of self-liking may cause hate and anger. In
Hobbes's *Leviathan*, egoistic fear of a violent death was presented as the
prime reason for the instrumentally rational decision to leave the state
of nature, and egoistic fear of death by punishment as the reason for
remaining in society. Mandeville produces a different argument, based
on a developmental story of the civilising process, centred on the passion

of self-liking or self-love as *amour-propre*, and its two facets of honour and shame.[17]

Mandeville's account of the civilising process in *Fable II* starts with a description of the necessity of protecting oneself against attacks from wild animals. There is, however, an even more challenging danger, arising from 'that stanch Principle of Pride [i.e. self-liking] and Ambition, that all Men are born with' (Mandeville, *Fable II*: 266). To stabilise a society of creatures dominated by self-liking, conflicts provoked by this passion must be avoided. Here, fear becomes crucial. Mandeville claims, in accordance with Hobbes, that fear is the 'only useful Passion then that Man is posses'd of toward the Peace and Quiet of a Society' (Mandeville, *Remarks*: 206). Fear has as its object either real dangers, such as death, or others such as shame, where 'the Evil to be fear'd from it is altogether imaginary, and has no Existence but in our own Reflection on the Opinion of others' (Mandeville, *Fable II*: 95). Both fear of death and fear of shame can be used to curb anger, which is raised when the satisfaction of our desires is in danger (for example, if our self-liking is endangered by others' expression of this passion).[18]

Since society also needs to defend itself against threats, an appropriate balance between fear and courage must be established. In a civilised society, artificial rather than natural courage should be used – natural courage is based on anger, artificial courage on pride and fear of shame, which makes the latter much more controllable, since shame 'may be fix'd on different Objects, according to the Lessons we have receiv'd, and the Precepts we are imbued with' (*Fable II*: 95; see also *Remarks*: 207–11). The process of civilisation requires the manipulation of various self-interested passions – against Shaftesbury, society is not said to be based on our mutual natural affections or στοργή. Mandeville sometimes presents the process as managed by 'skilful politicians' or 'moralists' (more so in *Fable I*), and sometimes as a more natural development based on providential design (more so in *Fable II*). Whichever his preferred version, it is of primary importance that the problematic passion of self-liking, that is, self-love as *amour-propre*, be modified in ways that turn it into a benefit for society. According to Mandeville, there are two essential ingredients to this modification: the rules of politeness and the rules of honour, which offer solutions to the potential of self-liking to cause conflicts.

Politeness and the Notion of Self-denial

Politeness is the answer to the need for concealment of the problematic expressive tendencies of self-liking. The rules of politeness only concern the expressive dimension of self-liking, but not the passion itself.

Remember that our belief in our own superiority is undermined by the expression of the self-liking of others, which puts the gratification of the passion in danger and causes anger. Concealing self-liking's expressive tendencies avoids these consequences, and this is basically 'what we call good Manners and Politeness' (Mandeville, *Fable II*: 138).

In the voice of Cleomenes, Mandeville elaborates on a claim made in the first part of the *Fable*, namely that 'all good Manners consist in flattering the Pride of others, and concealing our own' (*Fable II*: 108). Politeness and good manners have two principal aspects. First, they involve praising and flattering others, and thus supporting their self-liking by satisfying their love of praise. Since the agent who praises another still naturally believes in her own superiority, her praise cannot be sincere. Even if the praised person is aware of this, the flattery is causally efficient due to her great eagerness to be praised. Secondly, politeness involves concealing one's own self-liking by suppressing its expressive tendencies, and thereby refraining from offending other agents' self-liking. However, the concealment of a passion's expressive tendencies is not to be mistaken for suppressing or frustrating the passion itself. The practices of politeness remain rooted in self-liking (*Fable II*: 133). Note how this conception of politeness contradicts ideas about politeness, civility and good breeding as a genuine moral quality of a refined heart, as found for example in Shaftesbury.[19]

At this point, a clarifying note on the crucial notion of *self-denial* is required – a notion often found in theological documents.[20] Mainly in his later writings, Mandeville uses the term 'self-denial' exclusively in the strong sense of a voluntary frustration or suppression of self-liking, rather than in the weak sense of a mere modification of the passion's behavioural tendencies. The strong sense will be crucial for Mandeville's distinction between moral virtue (singular) and the social virtues (plural) (see Chapter 3.3). The mere modification of one's natural passions and the concealment of their expressive tendencies (which would be self-denial in the weak sense) do not count as the strong kind of self-denial that is required for moral virtue.[21] Crucially, the modification of the passions during the civilising process, with the goal of behaving according to the rules of politeness, involves the reward of praise, and is thus compatible with the satisfaction of self-liking. According to Mandeville, this is the fundamental difference between politeness, a mere social virtue, and genuine moral virtue.

For Mandeville, the rules of politeness or good manners vary strongly across societies. Nevertheless, the underlying psychological mechanisms remain the same: behaviour in accordance with good manners ultimately aims at getting praise and avoiding shame, and thus at satisfying the passion of self-liking in a specific social context. Mandeville claims that the seeds of politeness 'are lodg'd in this Self-love and Self-liking' (*Fable II*: 133). In society, human agents have an interest in concealing their passion of self-liking (that is, in performing self-denial in the weak sense, not in the strong sense). Once the rules of politeness have been fixed through education, psychological modification and, possibly, manipulation, human agents will have a strong egoistic interest in obeying these rules, since violating them by not concealing one's passions will deprive the agent of the applause she needs in order to gratify her self-love as love of praise, and her self-liking, and will cause trouble with other members of society.[22]

Mandeville claims that in a well-functioning civilised society, men are also taught the superior art of being 'proud of hiding their Pride' (*Fable II*: 128). Since the concealment of one's self-liking is socially approved, we are psychologically manipulated into gratifying the passion of self-liking by concealing its expressive tendencies. Concealing counts as good manners and as praiseworthy, and will thus be seen in turn to be a sign of superiority over those who are unable to keep to these social rules. In another passage, Mandeville goes even further and claims that self-liking 'is not to be gratify'd without being conceal'd, and never enjoy'd with greater Ecstasy than when we are most fully persuaded, that it is well hid' (*Fable II*: 100). Yet again, even if the members of a civilised society successfully *conceal* the expressive sides of their self-liking, it remains their fundamental passion. The contrast with Shaftesbury is striking: much of the behaviour Shaftesbury explains as originating from kind affections of the heart, Mandeville explains as based on the passion of self-liking, or self-love as *amour-propre*. The anatomist looks behind the beautiful skin.

Honour

The rules of politeness have the principal function of restricting the *expressive* tendencies of self-liking. Honour, then, principally serves as a source of reward for the modification of one's passions according to the given rules of a society – a most effective and simultaneously inexpensive invention. The introduction of the concepts of honour and shame, Mandeville claims, are the most important steps during the civilising process. 'Honour owes its Birth' to the passion of self-liking (Mandeville, *Honour*: 7). According to one of his descriptions of the civilising process, politicians have discovered the strong passion of self-liking, and the connected strong love of praise, which makes us susceptible to flattery. Acting according to the rules of honour, which are established as part of the 'dextrous Management' of human behaviour (Mandeville, *Search*: 369), meets with praise or flattery, thus helping to satisfy the desire for praise and ultimately supporting self-liking. Acting against the rules of honour meets with shame and puts the gratification of self-liking in danger. By virtue of this psychological mechanism, the natural passion of self-liking provides the agent with powerful self-interested motives to act according to the specified rules of honour. This holds even if honour and shame are 'Chimera without Truth of Being' and are 'not related to Religion' (Mandeville, *Remarks*: 198). The pleasure we derive from being praised for acting in accordance with the rules of honour is real, even if it is caused by a belief in a good, namely honour, that has no reality independent of the agent's mind (Mandeville, *Honour*: 6).

Mandeville invokes two different kinds of praise. The first concerns the qualities of humans *qua* species, without attention to individual merit. The invention of honour, he writes 'was an Improvement in the Art of Flattery, by which the Excellency of our Species is raised to such a Height, that it becomes the Object of our own Adoration, and Man is taught in good Earnest to worship himself' (Mandeville, *Honour*: 42). This is one reminder of the Augustinian point that in the postlapsarian state, *amor sui* replaces the love of God. The second kind of praise is connected to the notions of individual honour and shame, or 'Dishonour' (*Honour*: 9–10). Praise is given for individual behaviour that accords to a fixed set of rules of honour. This kind of praise directly gratifies the individual's passion of self-liking. The notions of honour and shame, and associated rules of behaviour, have to be taught during the civilising process.

Honour in the sense of a taught set of rules, in tandem with fear of shame or dishonour, are invented and

> may be fix'd on different Objects, according to the different Lessons we have receiv'd, and the Precepts we are imbued with; [. . .] tho' Shame is a real Passion, the Evil to be fear'd from it is altogether imaginary, and has no Existence but in our own Reflection on the Opinion of others. (Mandeville, *Fable II*: 95)

In this way, politicians can direct the individual's passions and behaviour with a set of rules that is determined in view of the desired behaviour. Individuals are likely to act according to these rules because it allows them to gratify their passion of self-liking. Ultimately, fear of dishonour or shame, that is, fear of an imaginary object, can be so strong as to overcome fear of death, which is a natural fear of a real evil (*Fable II*: 96).

Following the suppression of the natural passion of anger, however, honour and shame are used to create artificial courage, and to increase fear of shame in order to engage the members of society to participate in wars (Mandeville, *Remarks*: 211). A corollary effect (or, rather, a collateral damage) of artificial courage is the tenacious persistence of the practice of duelling, which is a consequence of the constellation of the passions of a civilised (male) human being.[23]

As in the case of politeness, Mandeville insists that honour is merely a *social* virtue, yet not a *moral* virtue. The word 'Honour'

> is a Technic Word in the Art of Civility, and signifies a Means which Men by Conversing together have found out to please and gratify one another on Account of a palpable Passion in our Nature, that has no Name, and which therefore I call Self-liking. [. . .] Honour signifies likewise a Principle of Courage, Virtue, and Fidelity, which some Men are said to act from, and to be aw'd by, as others by Religion. (Mandeville, *Honour*: 14)

Honour is often *erroneously* counted as a virtue, but it is not a *real* virtue, since it does not require self-denial in the strong sense of frustrating our passions, and since it often encourages actions that are in conflict with the precepts of religion (*Honour*: 43–5). But when comparing honour with religion, Mandeville admits that the former, for psychological reasons, is 'more skilfully adapted to our inward Make' (*Honour*: 42). In the present state, the passion of self-liking is so strong that frustrating it seems quite impossible. By supporting self-liking, honour rewards the agent, and it is thus a more successful means of influencing the subject's behaviour.

To summarise: self-liking, or self-love as *amour-propre*, is both a most dangerous and a most useful passion. It dominates human nature and has the potential to cause conflict – yet during the civilising process, it constitutes the glue that keeps stubborn, selfish individuals in society. For the persistence of society, it is not necessary that individuals have 'a kind Affection to the whole, of which he is a part, and a Propensity to seek the Welfare of it' (Mandeville, *Search*: 323–4), as claimed by Shaftesbury. Rather, the rules of politeness and honour, which are the two fundamental social virtues, allow for the modification of the passion of self-liking in ways that make it most useful for society – without, however, extinguishing it.

In Mandeville's description of self-liking, and in his discussion of the psychological mechanisms behind the norms of politeness and honour, we find a series of references to the French Augustinians, whose ideas are turned into attacks on the Shaftesburian idea that politeness is a morally admirable quality of the cultivated heart. The 'anatomist' Mandeville combines a very specific version of the selfish hypothesis (namely one in which self-love as *amour-propre* plays the central role, rather than self-love as egoistic desire) with a pessimistic view of post-lapsarian human nature, often within a fine-grained 'scientific' discussion of the passions. In other words, it is not just 'egoism' broadly speaking that marks Mandeville's psychology, but a very specific kind of egoism. The contrast with Campbell, who adopts a version of the selfish hypothesis based upon self-love as egoistic desire (rather than self-love as *amour-propre*), and who nevertheless argues for an utterly optimistic view of human nature as naturally virtuous, will further clarify the importance of this point (see Chapter 6).

3.3 MANDEVILLE ON THE SOCIAL VIRTUES (PLURAL) AND ON MORAL VIRTUE (SINGULAR)

I have stated above that Mandeville the writer sometimes makes Mandeville the philosopher tricky to interpret. This is especially true when it comes to his provocative and ambiguous claims regarding virtue and morality. Mandeville's most notorious catchphrases, picked up over and over again by his critics, are 'Private Vices, Publick Benefits' (the subtitle of the *Fable*), and 'the Moral Virtues are the Political Offspring which Flattery begot upon Pride' (Mandeville, *Enquiry*: 51). Even more confusingly, such statements come alongside the praise of the social utility of 'invented' rules of behaviour, institutions and social practices based on self-liking (that is, on self-love as *amour-propre*), and they come in combination with what Kaye and others have called an 'ascetic' and 'rigorist' conception of morality (that is, a conception based on self-denial in the strong sense of the frustration of our passions). Furthermore, it seems that Mandeville's conception of moral virtue is compatible with the view that, in reality, there are no morally virtuous actions at all, due to our psychological make-up. Some commentators thus ask whether Mandeville could have sincerely held such views. Another problematic domain concerns Mandeville's view of religion: neither English Anglicans nor Dutch Calvinists would have counted him among their 'orthodox' members – but was he therefore irreligious, as many of his contemporaries objected? In the present section, I want to describe how different interpretations of Mandeville result in different pictures of his claims regarding morality and religion, and I have the limited goal of suggesting that a reading of Mandeville as sincere in contrasting genuine moral virtue to mere social virtues can be coherent, and should not be dismissed too rapidly.

Many of Mandeville's contemporaries were quick to present him as recommending vice and attacking morality in his notorious statement 'Private Vices, Publick Benefits', which in more present-day terminology they may have read as an endorsement of a form of ethical egoism or moral anti-realism.[24] However, this is one of Mandeville's vaguest phrasings – as Hutcheson noted very well by readily distinguishing five possible meanings (Hutcheson, *Remarks*: 41–2). A more refined version of the statement is found in the conclusion of Mandeville's *Search*, where he writes that 'Private Vices by the dextrous Management of a skilful Politician may be turned into Publick Benefits' (*Search*: 369). This is preceded by this paragraph:

> I flatter my self to have demonstrated that, neither the Friendly Qualities and kind Affections that are natural to Man, nor the real Virtues he is capable of acquiring by Reason and Self-Denial, are the Foundation of Society; but that what we call Evil in this World, Moral as well as Natural, is the grand Principle that makes us sociable Creatures, the solid Basis, the Life and Support of all Trades and Employments without Exception: That there we must look for the true Origin of all Arts and Sciences, and that the Moment Evil ceases, the Society must be spoiled, if not totally dissolved. (Mandeville, *Search*: 369)[25]

Again, in opposition to Shaftesbury, the Stoics and Aristotle, Mandeville claims that society is not based on natural, kind affections but on natural and moral evil. If there was no such evil, a society of postlapsarian human beings could not possibly persist. Once the civilising process has started, the opportunities created for the gratification of the passion of self-liking will keep a society of human creatures together. This points to both a specific version of the selfish hypothesis and a view of human nature as dominated by the morally problematic passion of self-liking.

Did Mandeville therefore *encourage* vice, and did he undermine the distinction between moral good and evil, as some of his contemporaries alleged? Must his claims be understood as attempts to present so-called moral virtue as a facet of self-love? Was Mandeville a moral sceptic, an ethical egoist, or a moral anti-realist who undermined a proper distinction between moral good and evil? Undeniably, Mandeville argued that much of what is commonly considered vicious (luxury, avarice, vanity, excessive drinking, prostitution, even robbery)[26] had, under specific circumstances, useful consequences for society. Furthermore, he argued that a lot of what commonly counts as virtuous (such as building charity schools, being compassionate and acting from pity)[27] had potentially harmful consequences for society. And he asserted that many actions commonly treated as virtuous were actually not truly virtuous because they were based on concealed selfish motives, or simply consisted in the gratification of a natural passion rather than in a conscious effort to be virtuous. In line with many seventeenth-century French Augustinian moralists, Mandeville often presented himself as an unmasker of hidden vicious motives, arguing that many so-called 'virtuous' practices, and many rules of behaviour that commonly, but mistakenly, count as moral norms, had their origin in nothing else but the passion of self-liking. Even if the resulting actions have beneficial consequences, self-liking remains a morally problematic motive – and like most other moral philosophers of his time, Mandeville explicitly denies that utility trumps morality.[28] On such a reading, he cannot simply be said to encourage vice, nor to undermine the distinction between virtue and vice.

During his own times, and later, Mandeville received many labels – some more, some less convincing, and many obviously stemming from attempts to counter his polemical attacks. Present-day commentators are equally split in their interpretations of him. I shall not attempt here to distil Mandeville's deepest and most sincere convictions regarding morality and religion from his writings, which often strike us with their confusing rhetorical strategies and ambiguities.[29] I want to describe, however, how Mandeville's contributions to the debates on self-love (especially in *Part II* of the *Fable* and in the *Enquiry into the Origin of Honour*) suggest at least that we should not dismiss an interpretation of Mandeville as a thinker who often gets his inspiration from the French Augustinian moralists, and who adapts their ideas for an English context.[30] This is not to deny that Mandeville may have had doubts of his own about such a narrative, but it is to give this interpretation additional weight by taking seriously the philosophical and rhetorical context of his attacks on Shaftesbury.

Consider the following passage from *Part II* of the *Fable*, where Cleomenes defends the principles of the first volume against Horatio's objections and comments on what we should think of the author's intention:

It is his [i.e. Mandeville's] Opinion, that there is no solid Principle to go by but the Christian Religion, and that few embrace it with Sincerity: Always look upon him in this View, and you'll never find him inconsistent with himself. Whenever at first sight he seems to be so, look again, and upon nearer Enquiry you'll find; that he is only pointing at or labouring, to detect the Inconsistency of others with the Principles they pretend to. (Mandeville, *Fable II*: 102)

Even if we take this advice seriously, we will not therefore blind ourselves to Mandeville's frequent use of sarcastic and polemical registers. However, it will remind us that his target is not religion and morality *per se*, but rather Shaftesbury's then influential approach to them. And this should shed doubts on a, say, broadly consequentialist reading of Mandeville that takes him to be positively insincere in his rigorism, or even to be performing an ironical *reductio ad absurdum* of the suggested conception of moral virtue.[31] This seems to me an anachronistic reading that neglects both the strong presence of Augustinian and Calvinist themes, and Mandeville's predilection for attacks on Shaftesbury.

It is not a bad strategy to begin by taking seriously Mandeville's distinction between real moral virtue (singular) on the one hand, which he regularly equates with religion and 'Christianity', and the mere social virtues (plural) on the other, which he opposes to religion and claims to be rooted in self-liking. Whether or not Mandeville wholeheartedly embraces these elements with all of their consequences, especially the engendered pessimistic account of postlapsarian human nature, such a reading takes into account his rhetorical and philosophical strategies, especially when considering the background of his contributions to the debates on self-love.[32] We can then take at face value Mandeville's comments in *Part II* of the *Fable*, and his regular assertions to be a sincere Christian (of sorts). There may be compelling reasons not to rest with such an interpretation, but these reasons must be more than reflections of our twenty-first-century outlook on moral philosophy.

Social Virtues, Moral Virtue and the Vices

To further examine Mandeville's theses and to assess the objections to them, we need to look at his accounts of virtue and vice. In a nutshell, according to Mandeville it is extremely difficult, maybe even impossible, to be morally virtuous, and extremely easy to be vicious. Mandeville's conceptions of self-love play a crucial role on this point. Throughout his writings, Mandeville speaks of 'virtue' in two fundamentally different senses. First, he speaks of the social virtues (in the plural), among which we find the 'invented', artificial and arbitrary norms of politeness, good manners and honour, which characterise civilised society (Mandeville, *Search*: 354). Social virtues must not, however, be confused with moral virtue (in the singular). This claim is one of the pillars of Mandeville's anti-Shaftesburian attacks. Good manners, politeness and the like have

nothing to do with Virtue or Religion, tho' it seldom clashes with either [. . .] All the Precepts of good Manners throughout the World have the same Tendency, and are no more than the various Methods of making ourselves acceptable to others, with as little Prejudice to ourselves as is possible: by which Artifice we assist one another in the Enjoyments of Life, and refining upon Pleasure; and every individual Person is rendred more happy by it, in the Fruition of all the good Things he can purchase, than he could have been without such Behaviour. (Mandeville, *Fable II*: 146–7)

Social virtues are designed to effectively guide the behaviour of the members of a society and to allow for a peaceful and well-functioning society of individuals, in spite of their being determined by self-liking. Most importantly, the social virtues fulfil this aim by imposing restrictions on the natural expressive tendencies of the passion of self-liking (that is, by requiring self-denial in the weak sense). They aim at social utility or public benefit by means of the uncostly reward of praise, and thus by gratifying the self-liking of individuals who comply. Yet acting in accordance with the social virtues does not require self-denial in the strong sense of frustrating or suppressing one's self-liking. 'Good Manners have nothing to do with Virtue or Religion; instead of extinguishing, they rather inflame the Passions' (Mandeville, *Remarks*: 79). Again, these points can be seen as connected to an Augustinian critique of the social virtues. Also, criticising the social virtues as being grounded in self-liking is not the same as recommending vice.

Secondly, Mandeville uses the terms 'virtue' and 'vice' in a proper *moral* sense, and he often opposes genuine moral virtue to the social virtues, especially in his discussions of politeness and honour (*Remarks*: 222). In contrast to the social virtues, moral virtue tends to 'extinguish' the passions – it requires self-denial, that is, the voluntary frustration of the passions in general, and of self-liking in particular. Moral virtue is independent of the accepted social virtues of a given society, and acting in accordance with the social virtues does not make one morally virtuous. Social virtues can even be in conflict with moral virtue – more often in the case of honour than in the case of politeness. The norms of honour incite to the morally vicious practice of duelling, which directly contradicts the precepts of the Christian religion.[33] Mandeville often identifies these precepts with genuine moral virtue. Note that his claim that the social virtues are not part of moral virtue is not a denial of the reality of moral virtue, nor an attack on the distinction between moral virtue and vice. The rhetorical gesture, however, is that of unmasking the non-moral foundations of the social virtues.

Moral virtue requires self-denial in the strong sense of the frustration of one's passions, whether they be selfish or not. Being motivated by a mere natural kind affection, such as Shaftesburian natural affections,

Hutchesonian benevolence or the passion of pity, does not make one virtuous – rather, there needs to be a 'Rational Ambition of being good' (Mandeville, *Enquiry*: 49). In Mandeville (as in Shaftesbury), whether an action counts as morally virtuous depends on the agent's intentions, and *not* on the consequences of the action – even if these latter are paid a great deal of attention in the context of Mandeville's discussion of the social virtues, and in his narrative of the civilising process. Actions that turn out to be beneficial to others, yet are performed with the ultimate aim of gratifying the passion of self-liking (for example, by means of being praised), are not morally virtuous. This is the case with all actions that merely presuppose a modification of one's natural passions, but still involve the gratification of one's passion of self-liking within the social framework of a civilised society (for example, the suppression of anger in exchange for praise). Hedonistic self-love, self-love as love of praise and self-love as *amour-propre* may all motivate actions that are in accordance with the social virtues, but they cannot give rise to morally virtuous actions.

There is an important consequence of Mandeville's account of moral virtue, given the dominance of self-love and self-liking in his psychological theory of human nature: there are, in reality, very few virtuous actions – if any at all. Mandeville presents this as a rejection of Shaftesbury's claim regarding our naturally virtuous tendencies. If Mandeville is indeed a 'psychological egoist' of sorts, as many commentators have claimed, then this may exclude the reality of virtuous actions, and lead to an even more strikingly pessimistic view of human nature. Again, this is in line with Mandeville's declared anatomist goal of unmasking the hidden selfish motives behind apparently virtuous actions, and with the importance he attributes to flattery and self-deception in his psychology and social philosophy. Furthermore, it seems that, for Mandeville, the obligation to moral virtue persists even if the dominance of our selfish passions does not allow for genuinely virtuous actions.

Yet another consequence of Mandeville's account of virtue concerns the reasons to be virtuous. Here, the distinction between the social virtues and moral virtue is again essential. Given what Mandeville claims about the social virtues and their role in the civilising process, it is evident that it is in our self-interest to act in accordance with them, since they allow us to gratify our self-liking. By contrast, since *moral* virtue requires self-denial in the strong sense of the frustration of self-liking, and since we are determined by or at least strongly subject to selfish passions, there is an important sense in which being virtuous is 'against' our (corrupt) human nature.

Again, Mandeville emphasises the intricate relation between moral virtue and the 'Christian religion', sometimes to the point of identifying them (Mandeville, *Remarks*: 222; *Honour*: 42–5). Especially in the *Enquiry into the Origin of Honour*, this allows him to criticise the principles of honour by contrasting them with the principles of Christianity, and by arguing that 'there are many Allowances, gross Indulgences to Human Nature in the Principle of Honour, especially of modern Honour, that are always exclaim'd against by the Voice of Virtue, and diametrically opposite to the Doctrine of Christ' (Mandeville, *Honour*: 45). However, when comparing virtue and honour, Mandeville admits that from the *psychological* point of view, honour is 'more skilfully adapted to our inward Make' (*Honour*: 42). Honour involves rewards in the form of gratifications of self-liking, and it does not require the difficult (or even impossible) task of self-denial in the strong sense. Ultimately, then, honour is a more efficient principle for the manipulation of creatures with our (corrupt) psychological make-up. Hence, the 'Invention of Honour has been far more beneficial to the Civil Society than that of Virtue, and much better answer'd the End for which they were invented' (*Honour*: 43). However, if as a matter of fact in our corrupt state, moral virtue is less *useful* than self-liking-based social virtues such as honour or politeness, this does not mean that the obligation to be morally virtuous ceases to exist, or that the advantages produced by our vices turn them into moral virtues.

As far as Mandeville's account of vice is concerned, we find a narrow account of vice introduced in the *Enquiry* in *Fable I*, which focuses on the absence of an agent's regard for the public good, and the action's potentially negative consequences for the public good (Mandeville, *Enquiry*: 48). There is, however, also a broad sense of vice, which comes forth throughout Mandeville's writings. From an Augustinian point of view, the selfishness inherent in human nature is a moral vice that is fundamental to the moral corruption of post-lapsarian humankind, whether or not it has negative consequences for society. The Augustinian pessimistic view of human nature is based on some version of 'egoistic' psychological theory, which emphasises the dominance of the passions of egoistic self-love, self-love as love of praise, and especially self-love as *amour-propre*. Thus, even if self-love, pride, vanity and self-liking may have positive consequences in a providentially ordered world if they are well managed, they are still considered vicious in this broader sense since they put the self before God. The perfectly polite person who suppresses the expressive tendencies of her self-liking and flatters the vanity of others is still vicious insofar as, at the bottom of her heart, she is motivated by self-liking and not by a concern for others.

Mandeville's Provocative Statements Reconsidered

Given these remarks on virtue and vice, I want to focus on three of Mandeville's provocative statements. First, what are we to make of his famous (and notorious) subtitle for the *Fable*, 'Private Vices, Publick Benefits'? In principle, several non-comparative readings are possible: some (or all) private vices are (or engender) *some* public benefits (always or under certain circumstances). Several comparative readings are possible, too: some (or all) private vices are sometimes (or always) *more beneficial* to society than some (or all) private virtues. On various occasions throughout his writings, different readings are encouraged by Mandeville.[34] However, he ultimately favours specific interpretations.

In the *Search*, Mandeville spells out that there is an important condition for vice to be advantageous: 'Private Vices by the dextrous Management of a skilful Politician may be turned into Publick Benefits' (Mandeville, *Search*: 369). And in the *Moral* to the *Grumbling Hive*, he writes: '*So Vice is beneficial found, / When it's by Justice lopt and bound*' (Mandeville, *Fable I*: 37). Mandeville often points to specific requirements for vices to have useful consequences, namely a legal and civic framework, guidance by politicians, and thus at least some external control over the vicious passions. Mandeville also does not simply claim that *all* vices *always* lead to public benefit. In addition, he seems to contradict his own thesis in the *Preface* to the *Enquiry Into the Origin of Honour*:

> I am likewise fully persuaded, that to govern our selves according to the Dictates of Reason, is far better than to indulge the Passions without Stop or Controul, and consequently that Virtue is more beneficial than Vice, not only for the Peace and real Happiness of Society in general, but likewise for the Temporal Felicity of every individual Member of it, abstract from the Consideration of a future State. (Mandeville, *Honour*: ii)

It can be especially disputed that Mandeville *recommends* or encourages vice – typically, in the manner of a proto-sociologist, he points at the connections between vicious actions and their potentially useful consequences, thus provoking his contemporaries.[35]

What are Mandeville's examples of such vicious actions? In *Remark G*, Mandeville argues for the paradox that the deeds of thieves, house-breakers, pickpockets, highwaymen and those who form '*the worst of all the Multitude*' have (some) beneficial effects for a commercial society (Mandeville, *Remarks*: 86). Yet what about the *ratio* between private loss and public benefit? Mandeville's paradigm cases are rather vices in the broad sense – self-liking, pride and vanity. It holds for those especially that if they are well hidden, they are extremely beneficial for society, even if they remain vices: 'Pride and Vanity have built more Hospitals than all the Virtues together' (Mandeville, *Charity*: 261). According to Mandeville, such vices are essential for society: 'the good and amiable Qualities of Man are not those that make him beyond other Animals a sociable Creature' (Mandeville, *Search*: 325). Given postlapsarian humanity's corrupt nature, society depends on its members' self-liking – a very useful passion indeed, as we have seen in our reconstruction of Mandeville's story of the civilising process.

Can Mandeville be said to encourage the *performance* of all or some vicious actions? Alternatively, does he encourage *toleration* of some vicious actions, or does he merely *state* a correlation between certain types of behaviour and public benefit within his social theory? Given Mandeville's different rhetorical strategies and registers in his various works, we may not want to give a single answer. He certainly attracts his readers' attention to the link between vicious behaviour (in both the narrow and the broad sense) and its potential beneficial outcome in a commercial society. Furthermore, the passion of self-liking, a fundamental human passion that is vicious in a broad sense, is depicted as the paradigmatic example of a private vice that produces public benefits. In a well-governed social structure, the pursuit of private interests leads to the flourishing of the whole. However, there seems to be no ground to suggest that Mandeville would seriously *recommend* the performance of vices – which is precisely what many attacked him for. By contrast, he repeatedly insists on the contrary. For example, he comments on his recommendation of the institution of public brothels in order to preserve the chastity of women as follows:

I am far from encouraging Vice, and think it would be an unspeakable Felicity to a State, if the Sin of Uncleanness could be utterly Banish'd from it; but I am afraid it is impossible: The Passions of some People are too violent to be curb'd by any Law or Precept; and it is Wisdom in all Governments to bear with lesser Inconveniences to prevent greater. (Mandeville, *Remarks*: 95)

This is an example of Mandeville's pragmatic approach to vice: if it is impossible to get rid of it, try to restrict the damage and make the best out of it. Nevertheless, it remains a vice – there might be an 'ought' even without a 'can'.

Secondly, what should we think of the anti-Shaftesburian claim that society is based on moral and natural evil, and neither on the natural and amiable qualities in human beings, nor on moral virtue? Mandeville states in the *Search*: 'I flatter my self to have demonstrated that, neither the Friendly Qualities and kind Affections that are natural to Man, nor the real Virtues he is capable of acquiring by Reason and Self-Denial, are the Foundation of Society' (Mandeville, *Search*: 369). It seems unlikely that this claim refers exclusively to vices in the narrow sense, which involve direct harm to the public. What Mandeville emphasises in his story of the civilising process, which is closely structured around the passion of self-liking, is the importance of pride and vanity for the creation, persistence and cohesion of society.[36] He can indeed also be taken to argue that *some* examples of vices in the narrow sense, that is, vices with harmful consequences for some parts of society, *also* have beneficial consequences. From this, we cannot conclude that he would claim that *all* vices in the narrow sense *always* have beneficial consequences for society, to the degree that society could be claimed to be based on them. And again, we cannot conclude that Mandeville recommends vice from the moral point of view. Rather, he opposes to Shaftesbury's optimistic view of human nature and society a picture of human agents as dominated by self-liking. A society made up of such selfish human beings can function in perfect harmony under the condition that the vicious sides of human nature are managed well enough.

Thirdly, what are we to make of the provocative statement that 'Moral Virtues are the Political Offspring which Flattery begot upon Pride' (Mandeville, *Enquiry*: 51)? This notorious formulation from 1714 (one of the rare occasions where the expression 'moral virtues' is in the plural) is likely to confuse. Besides having led astray present-day commentators, it motivated an entire series of contemporary attacks against Mandeville, often culminating in the accusation that he reduces morality to pride or self-love. However, this accusation is on shaky ground in light of the essential distinction between social virtues (plural) on the one hand, and moral virtue (singular) on the other, which is defended in all his other writings. There, not moral virtue but the social virtues are said to be the invention of politicians who want to govern the members of a society by flattering their self-liking. The social virtues are psychologically built upon, and may thus be said to have their origin in self-liking, pride and flattery. Once again, they do not require self-denial, but only the modification of one's natural passions, and they allow for the gratification of self-liking or pride by praise. On this reading, Mandeville does not claim that there are no real *moral* virtues, or that there is no distinction between moral good and evil. Rather, he attacks the *social* virtues, which he sees praised by Shaftesbury, and unmasks their origin in self-liking, arguing that the rules of honour and politeness especially are mistakenly presented as *moral* virtues.

On this reading, Mandeville has not 'reduced' moral virtue to self-love or self-liking, or undermined the distinction between virtue and vice. He may be counted as a sceptic and relativist with respect to the social virtues, and he may be a pessimist with respect to the reality of morally virtuous actions in the world. According to Mandeville, the ultimate motive for actions that are in accordance with social norms is self-liking, not some kind affection, and the social virtues are to a certain extent arbitrary, since invented to benefit some given society. But then again, the social virtues have to be sharply distinguished from moral virtue, and any action motivated by self-liking, by definition, cannot be a moral action. Even if, in reality, there is no action that fulfils the conditions for being a *moral* action, this would still not allow for the conclusion that Mandeville undermines the distinction between virtue and vice, or that he reduces moral virtue to self-love.

3.4 CONCLUSION

An impressive number of contemporary authors reacted critically to Mandeville's claims.[37] Given the indirect influence of his contributions to eighteenth-century British debates on self-love, he is clearly under-represented in many studies of the history of philosophy (much more so than in studies of intellectual history). His position is often vaguely summarised as a version of 'egoism', which his contemporaries would then have opposed. In some sense, Mandeville is indeed an egoist, but this qualification is not precise enough to understand either his own claims or many of the more interesting criticisms they provoked. The shortcomings of our present-day use of the notion of egoism appear most clearly in the case of Campbell's criticisms of Mandeville – these are formulated from within the framework of an egoistic psychology, which is, however, fundamentally different from Mandeville's.

Crucially, the central position in Mandeville's moral and political philosophy is not occupied by egoistic self-love, but by self-love as *amour-propre* or excessive pride (Mandeville's 'self-liking'), and by self-love as love of praise. For Mandeville, our excessive and undue pride, and our desire to seek confirmation from others of our superiority over them, are both the main problem for society and the glue that keeps it together. By emphasising such features in human psychology, and by adopting and adapting a series of Augustinian themes for an early eighteenth-century English context, Mandeville provocatively opposes Shaftesbury's conception of human nature as naturally sociable and naturally virtuous. In Chapter 2, I showed that Shaftesbury is even quite positive about the moral value of the self-affections, that is, egoistic self-love – the self-affections are presented as a necessary ingredient for a fully virtuous rational creature. Mandeville attacks Shaftesbury's 'social system' and his ideas about naturally virtuous tendencies as ideas of the 'beau monde': moral virtue and the social virtues are to be strictly distinguished. The social virtues have nothing to do with genuine moral virtue or religion, since instead of requiring self-denial, they are built on the vicious passion of self-liking.

Mandeville's detailed explorations of the socially useful sides of the morally problematic passion of self-liking should not, however, be mistaken for a moral rehabilitation of self-love as *amour-propre*. Mandeville's version of the selfish hypothesis connects with the Augustinian emphasis on the morally corrupt aspects of human nature – which does not involve a denial that our providentially ordered world functions in orderly ways, even in a state of moral corruption. None of this is adequately nuanced in the vague qualification of Mandeville as an 'egoist', since this does not take into account the most interesting and provocative aspects of his philosophy – which are also those that attracted most attention from his contemporaries.

Mandeville has often been fruitfully read as an economic theorist, and as a contributor to debates on luxury.[38] Yet he must also be acknowledged as a moralist and social theorist, especially in his dealing with Shaftesbury. The proximity of Mandeville's arguments to those of the French Augustinians is most obvious in his contributions to the debates on self-love, which concern issues of moral, social and political philosophy. The following chapters present a selection of reactions to Mandeville, which are sometimes also introduced as defences of Shaftesbury against the attacks by the author of *The Fable of the Bees*. Yet in some cases, Mandeville may also simply have served as a useful straw man to put forward claims that were in turn considered problematic from other points of view, such as the orthodox Calvinist one. I shall argue this especially in the case of Campbell in Chapter 6.

NOTES

1. Hont (2006) has furthermore highlighted the importance of Fénelon for the early Mandeville's political thought. Shaftesbury occupies a more central place as Mandeville's counter-figure especially from the second edition of *Fable I* onwards.
2. Otherwise excellent systematic in-depth studies in the history of philosophy such as Darwall (1995), Gill (2006) and Irwin (2008) unfortunately do not take Mandeville seriously enough. This is not the case with French scholars, most notably Carrive (1980), who has a profound understanding of the French Augustinian background to

Mandeville. Historians of ideas and historians of philosophy more interested in context have taken Mandeville more seriously, for example Monro (1975), Goldsmith (1985), Hundert (1994), Force (2003), Peltonen (2003: 263–302), Robertson (2005: 261–80), Hont (2006), Herdt (2008: 268–80), Brooke (2012: 153–9) and Tolonen (2013). Their interpretations often diverge, which emphasises the interesting facets of Mandeville's thought.

3. Mandeville's other writings include, for example, his medical treatise *A Treatise of the Hypochondriack and Hysterick Passions* (1711), *A Modest Defence of Publick Stews* (1724) – a treatise on prostitution attributed to him – and *A Letter to Dion* (1732). For more on Mandeville's writings, see, for example, Carrive (1980) and Hundert (1994).

4. For the classification of Mandeville as an 'egoist', see, for example, the discussions in Gill (2006: 141–50) and Irwin (2008: 404–7). Tolonen (2013: 29, 73–86) rejects this classification based on Mandeville's remarks on the natural affections in *Fable II*. It seems to me, however, that Tolonen overemphasises the possibly non-egoistic dimension of the natural affections, an interpretation I see undermined by Mandeville himself, for example in *Fable II* (177–83). More generally, I think that the 'intellectual change' between *Fable I* and *Fable II* is smaller than suggested by Tolonen. In my reading of Mandeville, what Tolonen defines as 'Hobbism' (Tolonen 2013: 42) is already less important in *Fable I*, mainly because the fundamental features of what Mandeville terms 'self-liking' in *Fable II* are already present in *Fable I*, most importantly in the *Remarks*. However, these features are discussed in the vocabulary of 'pride' and 'self-love' rather than in the terminology of 'self-liking'.

5. To some extent, my interpretation of Mandeville as a moralist who adapts Augustinian themes into a new context contradicts Hundert, who insists on a contrast between the French *moralistes* and Mandeville. For Hundert, Mandeville 'abandoned the Augustinian premises' by placing them on 'scientific foundations' rather than on theological ones (Hundert 1994: 36–7). I think, however, that the 'anatomist' gesture can be combined with an Augustinian-themed moralist project.

6. See the discussion of the metaphor, and its link with Hume, in Herdt (2008: 221), Tolonen (2013: 153–7) and Harris (2015: 121–39).

7. *Fable II* contains furthermore direct reactions to Hutcheson and Alexander Innes, who plagiarised Archibald Campbell's *Enquiry* and printed it under his own name in 1728. On the fascinating publication history of *Fable II*, see Tolonen (2013: 103–46).

8. This may remind us of the distinction in French between *amour de soi* (Mandeville's 'self-love') and *amour-propre* (Mandeville's 'self-liking'), which is most famously present in Rousseau, and somewhat less famously so in some seventeenth-century French Augustinians such as Pierre Nicole. However, there are important differences between Mandeville and Rousseau, especially in that Mandeville assumes that

self-liking is as natural as *self-love* for human beings after the Fall, whereas for Rousseau, the morally corrupt passion of *amour-propre* is a product of the civilising process. On this point, see also Carrive (1980: 44–8).

9. The exceptional circumstance is that of suicide. I will discuss Mandeville's account of suicide towards the end of Chapter 3.1.

10. Mandeville highlights the same point about the passion he names 'pride' in *Fable I* (Mandeville, *Remarks*: 124): 'every Mortal that has any Understanding over-values, and imagines better Things of himself than any impartial Judge, thoroughly acquainted with all his Qualities and Circumstances, could allow him'.

11. See famously Nicole (1999: 381ff.) on the subsequent features.

12. This point is famously highlighted in very similar terms by the French Augustinians and Hobbes, among others, and it is acknowledged as 'a trite observation in philosophy' in Hume's *Treatise* 3.3.3(596) – see Chapter 7.1.

13. Hirschman's contextualising reflections on these themes are still inspiring (1977: 14–42).

14. Note that in Chapter 1.2, I also termed self-love as *amour-propre* 'excessive pride'. This is to more clearly oppose it to possible *due* forms of pride, as suggested by Hume and Smith. Self-liking, Mandeville suggests, cannot be justified, whatever its degree of strength.

15. Mandeville does not clearly distinguish between pride and vanity, and neither does he draw a distinction between justified and unjustified comparative self-esteem, nor between comparative and non-comparative self-esteem. It seems that in his view all forms of self-esteem are essentially comparative and competitive and, given our corruption, unjustified. In Chapter 7.2 I discuss Smith's reactions to this point.

16. See also the contextualisation of Mandeville on suicide in Force (2003: 55).

17. Heath (1998) analyses Mandeville's account of how social norms emerge, without contract, in a society of creatures dominated by the passion of self-liking. For analyses of Mandeville's developmental narrative and descriptions of the broader connections with the French moralists, see, for example, Carrive (1980), Peltonen (2003: 268–85) and Tolonen (2013: 65–102).

18. A third crucial passion is pity, which may stop anger, crucially the anger of parents towards their children. Mandeville's discussion of pity highlights that it is the 'most gentle and the least mischievous of all our Passions' (Mandeville, *Remarks*: 56). However, as a passion it does not give rise to morally virtuous actions, which require self-denial. Also, Mandeville analyses actions motivated by pity as attempts to remove the unease of seeing someone suffering. This contrasts with Shaftesbury's and Hutcheson's treatment of pity as a paradigmatically sociable passion.

19. See also Klein (1994) and Tolonen (2008: 23). In similar ways, the French Augustinians attacked the notions of *honnêteté* and *civilité*.

20. The English expression 'self-denial' would play an interesting role in the Committee for Purity of Doctrine's attack on Archibald Campbell. Campbell, with many others, claimed that Mandeville exaggerated the duty of self-denial, and Campbell himself was attacked for this claim by orthodox Calvinists (see Chapter 6.4). Hutcheson and Smith both rejected the selfish hypothesis, and also highlighted that Mandeville went too far – see Hutcheson (*Remarks*: 81) and Smith (*TMS*, VII. ii.4.11, 2002: 368).

21. In *Fable I*, Mandeville has a tendency to speak of self-denial in the weaker sense of a mere modification of one's natural passions, which may include the concealment of their expressive tendencies during the civilising process (*Enquiry*: 42; *Remarks*: 222). In such cases, passions are redirected towards new objects (fear of death becomes fear of shame, for example), some of their facets are concealed, or they are opposed by other, stronger passions (anger is opposed by fear of death, for example). However, self-denial in this weak sense is fully compatible with the continuous satisfaction of the underlying passion. An interesting complementary discussion concerns the social virtue of modesty. See Mandeville (*Remarks*: 68–9).

22. Here we can see reflections of French Augustinian ideas, as well as elements of Bayle's arguments for the possibility of a society of atheists in *Pensées diverses sur la comète* (1680) – see, for example, Bayle (2007: *Pensées* 172–9).

23. For further reflections on duelling in Mandeville, see Peltonen (2003: 285–302) and Branchi (2014).

24. In Maurer (2014: 4), I draw attention to six very common points of attack against Mandeville: 1) Mandeville's motivational egoism (broadly speaking); 2) his claim in *An Enquiry Into the Origin of Moral Virtue* (*Enquiry*: 51) about the origin of the 'moral virtues' in flattery and pride (here, exceptionally, the adjective 'moral' is followed by the noun 'virtues' in the plural, an expression we find very rarely, and which should be taken to refer to what he elsewhere calls the 'social virtues' in the plural, opposing it to 'moral virtue' in the singular); 3) his claims about the link between vice and social utility; 4) his claim that moral virtue requires self-denial; 5) his treatment of the social virtues of honour and politeness as based on the corrupt principle of self-liking or self-love as *amour-propre*; and 6) his view of human nature as fundamentally asocial and tricked into society by politicians.

25. There are numerous occasions on which Mandeville explains and defends his subtitle, among others in *A Letter to Dion* (Mandeville 1732b: 36–7) in response to George Berkeley's attacks in *Alciphron*.

26. See, for example, Mandeville (*Remarks*: 86–93, 100–2, 107; *Search*: 350–3; *Defence*).

27. See especially Mandeville (*Enquiry*: 56; *Charity*: 272).

28. Jaffro (2013) sets out the importance of the distinction between the moral and the natural good for Shaftesbury and Hutcheson. In my opinion, the same point holds for Mandeville.

29. In a similar vein, Heydt (2018: 162) states with caution: 'It can be hard to disentangle the relative influence of Augustinian and Epicurean thought in Mandeville's writing.'

30. On this point, I hope to raise at least some doubts regarding Herdt's view, which rests mainly on Part I of the *Fable*. For her, 'Mandeville's tone of detached amusement' puts him at quite some distance from the Augustinians, Herdt (2008: 269). Considering both the crucial Augustinian goal of humiliating our vanity and Mandeville's anti-Shaftesburian rhetoric in his later moral writings, I think there are good grounds to treat them as closer than Herdt suggests.

31. Cf. Kaye on this point in his introduction to Mandeville, *Fable I* (lv). According to Kaye, Mandeville's rigorism is ultimately arbitrary.

32. See also Carrive (1980: 192) and Scott-Taggart (1966: 222).

33. See, for example, Mandeville (*Honour*: 43–5). Mandeville describes the conflict between honour and Christianity in the following words: 'What I would demonstrate, is, that there are many Allowances, gross Indulgences to Human Nature in the Principle of Honour, especially of modern Honour, that are always exclaim'd against by the Voice of Virtue, and diametrically opposite to the Doctrine of *Christ*.' On politeness, he writes in *Fable II* (146) that 'the Art of good Manners has nothing to do with Virtue or Religion, tho' it seldom clashes with either'.

34. See also Hutcheson (*Remarks*: 41–2).

35. In this context, Scott-Taggart highlights that 'although Mandeville did not plead the cause of vicious actions, he did make a plea for the toleration of many of these actions. It is still easy today, and was even more easy in the eighteenth century, to make the slide from the charge that someone is encouraging toleration through the charge that he is not discouraging vice to the conclusion that he is encouraging vice' (Scott-Taggart 1966: 221).

36. In a similar vein, Nicole famously emphasises that a society that is driven by *amour-propre* can work perfectly well: 'Quelque corrompue que cette société fût au-dedans et aux yeux de Dieu, il n'y aurait rien au-dehors de mieux réglé, de plus civil, de plus juste, de plus pacifique, de plus honnête, de plus généreux; et ce qui serait de plus admirable, c'est que n'étant animée et remuée que par l'amour-propre, l'amour-propre n'y paraîtrait point, et qu'étant entièrement vide de charité, on ne verrait partout que la forme et les caractères de la charité' (Nicole 1999: 408).

37. MacMahon (1774) is one of the rare exceptions of a positive reaction, announcing on the title page of his *Essay on the Depravity and Corruption of Human Nature* that he follows the opinions of Mandeville and others on the subject.

38. See especially Hont (2006: 387–95) and Sagar (2013).

4. Hutcheson on Self-love, Benevolence and Self-cultivation

The subtitle of the first edition of the *Inquiry into the Original of our Ideas of Beauty and Virtue* (1725) by the Scottish-Irish philosopher Francis Hutcheson (1694–1746) famously runs as follows:

> In which the principles of the late Earl of Shaftesbury are Explain'd and Defended, against the Author of the *Fable of the Bees*: and the Ideas of Moral Good and Evil are establish'd, according to the Sentiments of the Antient Moralists. With an Attempt to introduce a Mathematical Calculation in Subjects of Morality. (Hutcheson, *Inquiry*: 199)[1]

This announcement by Hutcheson of his intention to defend Shaftesbury against Mandeville seems slightly at odds with a claim that he made at the beginning of his *Remarks upon the Fable of the Bees* (1725). This is the text in which Hutcheson presented his most explicit and detailed criticisms of Mandeville, and there he writes: 'I do not intend any answer to that book [i.e. *Part I* of *The Fable of the Bees*]; but rather hereafter to shew it to be unanswerable, notwithstanding the zealous attempts of some of the clergy' (Hutcheson, *Remarks*: 41). To what extent and on which points did Hutcheson consider Mandeville thus answerable in terms of philosophical arguments? What role do the 'Antient Moralists' play in this? And what are Hutcheson's positions in the debates on self-love?

At the end of Hutcheson's *Remarks*, much of which focuses on Mandeville's conception of self-love as *amour-propre*, on his attacks on 'kind affections' and natural sociability, and on his ambiguous and provocative statements on moral virtue and vice, Hutcheson writes that Mandeville 'has probably been struck with some old fanatic sermon upon self-denial in his youth', which forced him into a scheme of thought in which it is 'absolutely impossible [. . .] that God himself can make a being naturally disposed to virtue' (Hutcheson, *Remarks*: 81). Throughout his writings, Hutcheson argues for the opposite view, namely that God has indeed equipped us with natural virtuous tendencies, namely benevolence, and that instead of 'denying' our nature by frustrating our passions, we can 'follow' and cultivate our nature, thus becoming more virtuous. Hutcheson's comments on Mandeville and self-denial also constitute an implicit attack on some central Calvinist *topoi*: moral virtue is not a matter of grace, but it is in our hands to cultivate it – a point on which the 'Antients' and especially the Stoics have a lot to say. In orthodox terms, however, Hutcheson here opens the gate for justification by works.

Hutcheson was born the son of a Presbyterian Scottish minister in Ireland. He studied at the University of Glasgow under Gershom Carmichael (1672–1729), who introduced natural law into the Scottish curriculum, and under John Simson (1667–1740), the controversial theologian who was condemned for heresy in 1717 and 1727, and who was also the teacher of Archibald Campbell. Hutcheson returned to Ireland in 1718 to become the head of a dissenting academy. He had close contact with Lord Robert Molesworth and his circle, where Shaftesbury's philosophy was discussed. Hutcheson succeeded Carmichael in the chair of moral philosophy at Glasgow in 1729. Throughout his writings in moral philosophy, Hutcheson consistently attacks different versions of the selfish hypothesis and argues that disinterested benevolence is a natural motive.[2] The equally disinterested moral sense points out to us that it is benevolence that makes us morally virtuous.

However, as I shall argue in this chapter, these points do not lead Hutcheson into presenting self-love as always a morally problematic, let alone vicious, part of human nature. Rather, in the broader context of Hutcheson's account of the fully virtuous human being, there is an ultimately positive view of self-love. Somewhat against the opposition that Smith draws between Hutcheson and Shaftesbury, I shall argue that, all things considered, the two are closer on questions regarding self-love. I shall first analyse the place of self-love in Hutcheson's moral psychology, discuss some of his arguments against the selfish hypothesis, and then focus on his account of the moral value of self-love, and its role in self-cultivation.

4.1 HUTCHESON ON SELF-LOVE AND THE SELFISH HYPOTHESIS

Self-love in Hutcheson's Theory of the Emotions

To understand Hutcheson's conception of self-love, we need to consider, first, two fundamental axes that mark his moral psychology. In the *Essay on the Nature and Conduct of the Passions and Affections* (1728), Hutcheson introduces what he terms '*Axioms*, or natural Laws of *calm Desire*'. He suggests the following distinction between *self-love* and *benevolence*, or between selfish and benevolent desires: '1. *Selfish Desires* pursue ultimately only the private Good of the Agent. 2. Benevolent or *publick Desires* pursue the Good of others, according to the several *Systems* to which we extend our attention, but with different Degrees of Strength' (Hutcheson, *Essay*: 37). Hutcheson's conception of self-love is best understood broadly in terms of egoistic self-love – his distinction between selfish and benevolent desires, or between interested self-love and disinterested benevolence, corresponds roughly to our present-day distinction between egoistic and altruistic desires, and it is one of the core elements in Hutcheson's moral philosophy.[3] Hutcheson claims that this distinction between 'selfish' or 'private' and 'benevolent' or 'publick' affections and passions has often been overlooked due to the 'confused Use of the Names, *Love, Hatred, Joy, Sorrow, Delight*' (*Essay*: 53). The 'divisions' of the emotions discussed by Hutcheson in the *Essay* – those of the Stoics and of Malebranche – concentrate indeed on another fundamental distinction: that between calm and violent emotions.[4]

Hutcheson combines his distinction between self-love and benevolence with one between *calm affections* and *violent passions*, which constitute two fundamental 'modifications of the mind' or emotions. Calm affections, first, result

> from some *Reflection* upon, or *Opinion* of our Possession of any Advantage, or from a certain Prospect of future pleasant Sensations on the one hand, or from a like *Reflection* or *Prospect* of evil or painful Sensations on the other, either to our selves or others. (*Essay*: 49–50)

Secondly, violent passions are defined as affections which involve, in addition, 'a *confused Sensation* either of Pleasure or Pain' (*Essay*: 31). Affections and passions both require representations of their objects as naturally or morally good or evil. Passions, however, have a tendency to prevent reflection upon the appropriateness of the representation, and upon the consequences of the resulting actions: the 'confused sensation' keeps 'the Mind much employed upon the present Affair, to the exclusion of every thing else, and prolongs and strengthens the Affection sometimes to such a degree, as to prevent all *deliberate Reasoning* about our Conduct' (*Essay*: 31).

This distinction between calm affections and violent passions will be particularly important for Hutcheson's theory of self-cultivation, which is in part a reaction to Mandeville's previously discussed insistence on self-denial as a requirement for moral virtue. Calm affections and violent passions have different scopes and values. Applied to Hutcheson's distinction between benevolence and self-love, this means that benevolence can take the forms of 1) calm and constant universal benevolence (for example, the love of humankind, which is the morally best form of benevolence), 2) calm partial benevolence (for example, calm parental love) and 3) a violent particular passion (for example, pity). The same holds for self-love, which can vary from a calm consideration of one's true interest to a selfish passion (*Essay*: 31–3).

A crucial feature of Hutcheson's moral psychology is his elaborate *hierarchy of the pleasures*. Different kinds of pleasure constitute the natural good, and they can all be the object of self-interested desires. In Chapter V of the *Essay*, Hutcheson elaborates a '*Comparison of the Pleasures and Pains of the several Senses, as to Intenseness and Duration*' (*Essay*: 87). He claims that there are five kinds of pleasure and pain, which form a qualitative hierarchy.[5] This follows his distinction between five different senses, or determinations '*of our Minds to receive Ideas independently on our Will, and to have Perceptions of Pleasure and Pain*' (*Essay*: 17). Human agents are susceptible to experiencing, first, bodily pleasures deriving from the external senses; second, pleasures of imagination of the internal sense, or the sense of beauty; third, social pleasures of the public sense, which is 'our Determination to be pleased with the *Happiness* of others, and to be uneasy at their *Misery*' (*Essay*: 17); and fourth, the pleasures of the sense of honour,

> which makes the *Approbation*, or *Gratitude* of others, for any good Actions we have done, the necessary occasion of Pleasure; and their *Dislike*, *Condemnation*, or *Resentment* of Injuries done by us, the occasion of that uneasy Sensation called *Shame*, even when we fear no further evil from them. (*Essay*: 18)

Fifth, there are the pleasures of the moral sense, 'by which we perceive *Virtue*, or *Vice* in our selves, or others' (*Essay*: 17, 87–8).

Hutcheson argues that pleasurable experiences have different (natural) values, which are a function of their intensity and their duration. The pleasures of the moral sense are the most valuable pleasures in terms of the natural good they provide to us, both in terms of intensity as well as duration. The moral sense, namely, is constant,

> grows more acute by frequent *Gratification*, never cloys, nor ever is sur-feited. We not only are sure never to want *Opportunities* of doing good, which are in every one's power in the highest Degree; but each good Action is Matter of pleasant *Reflection* as long as we live. These Plea-sures cannot indeed wholly secure us against all kinds of *Uneasiness*, yet they never tend naturally to increase them. On the contrary, their general Tendency is to lead the virtuous Agent into all Pleasures, in the highest Degree in which they are consistent with each other. (*Essay*: 106–7)

Unlike the external senses, the frequent gratification of the moral sense does not diminish the pleasures it provides to the agent. Furthermore, the moral pleasures of self-approbation (which is a form of self-love as self-esteem) are not only gained during the performance of a virtu-ous action, but also when we have a reflective awareness of our own past benevolence. The agent's 'true interest', in Hutcheson, can thus be conceived in an hedonistic egoistic manner as the course of action and the state of character in which an agent can be expected, all things considered, to experience the most valuable pleasures. This explains his assertion that 'it is our truest *Interest* to be *virtuous*' (*Essay*: 5), which is ultimately a matter of divine design. It is possible to act in contra-diction to one's true interest, for example when committing a vicious action by following passionate self-love, and then suffering from one's bad conscience.

This discussion on the different kinds of pleasures must be con-nected to another important feature in Hutcheson's moral philoso-phy, namely the distinction between *natural* and *moral goodness*. As pointed out above, pleasure (whether experienced by oneself or some-body else) is a natural good, not a moral good – and this is also true of the highest pleasures of the moral sense. Moral goodness, as opposed to natural goodness, is 'some Quality apprehended in Actions, which procures Approbation, attended with Desire of the Agent's Happiness' (Hutcheson, *Inquiry*: 85, 217).[6] According to Hutcheson, the disin-terested, benevolent intention to promote the good of others for their own sake is reliably identified by the moral sense as moral goodness. Introspection shows that the approval of moral goodness is an experi-ence of a different kind from the approval of natural goodness, and that moral goodness cannot be analysed in terms of natural goodness – one proof is the qualitative difference between our reaction to the benefits we derive from a fruitful field on the one hand, and the reac-tion to an equally profitable gift from a benevolent friend on the other.

Also, we approve of moral goodness even if it has no positive consequences for us in terms of natural good (think of our reaction to the news of a heroic, benevolent action in a distant place), and even if it has negative consequences (compare our reaction to an honest patriot's efforts to further the interests of his country with our reaction to the betrayer of his country) (*Inquiry*: 92, 97). Moreover, we cannot be bribed into proper moral approval of an action with any natural good. Our moral sense, to put it differently, makes a clear distinction between bene*volence*, that is, the ultimately disinterested promotion of the good of others, and bene*ficence*, that is, the ultimately self-interested promotion of the good of others.

The object of self-love is the experience of the different varieties of pleasure, that is, some natural good for the agent herself. Self-love in its different scopes and forms can aim at the bodily and aesthetic pleasures, at the public pleasures of seeing others fare well, at the pleasures of being esteemed or honoured, and at the moral pleasures of self-approbation. This brings into focus several, more specific conceptions of self-love. In Hutcheson, self-love as hedonistic egoism broadly speaking includes what might be construed as the more specific conceptions of, first, self-love as love of praise (which aims at the pleasures of the sense of honour), and second, self-love as self-esteem (which aims at the moral pleasures of self-approbation provided by the moral sense). Note how in Mandeville, love of praise was presented as a form of vanity caused by the insecurities of our self-liking (that is, of self-love as *amour-propre* or excessive pride). For Hutcheson, however, our desire for the 'good Opinion and Love of others' (*Inquiry*: 151) is rooted in our sense of honour. Honour in turn is connected to moral virtue, in that honour is most fundamentally 'the Opinion of others concerning our morally good Actions, or Abilitys presum'd to be apply'd that way' (*Inquiry*: 152). Against Mandeville, both honour itself and love of praise (as the desire for honour) can be appropriate for Hutcheson since they are ultimately connected with the moral sense.

Something similar holds for self-love as self-esteem: Hutcheson distinguishes his discussion of self-approbation by the moral sense from Mandeville's Augustinian paradigm of self-love as *amour-propre*, a comparative and competitive passion. Hutcheson makes room for a conception of *due* pride, even if he is aware that in general, the term 'pride' 'is taken in a bad Sense, when one claims that to which he has no Right' (Hutcheson, *Essay*: 56). However, a good opinion of ourselves *can* be justified, namely if the moral sense approves our morally virtuous actions. Hutcheson here indicates that he might be willing to open the door for the rehabilitation of pride – a door that would be opened more widely by Hume and Smith.

Hutcheson on the Selfish Hypothesis

Throughout his writings, Hutcheson launches numerous attacks on the selfish hypothesis – it seems to be one of his main goals to refute this account of human motivation, and to argue for a more positive account of human nature. We shall see that as far as Scotland in the second half of the eighteenth century is concerned, Hutcheson and Butler seem to have been considered successful in their rejection of the selfish hypothesis: in Smith, Ferguson or Reid, its falsity was taken quite for granted. Subsequent authors instead focused on other themes, such as the nature and workings of sympathy and sociability. In England by contrast, with the emergence of Associationist psychology, explanations of the functioning of the mind in a hedonistic egoistic framework remained fashionable.

Many of Hutcheson's arguments against the selfish hypothesis have been extensively discussed by analytically oriented historians of philosophy, and I shall here restrict myself to mentioning only some that were particularly important to subsequent eighteenth-century debates on self-love.[7] Generally speaking, Hutcheson usually targets claims that reduce our motives to self-love in the broad sense of egoistic desires. Apart from the *Remarks on the Fable of the Bees*, Hutcheson is surprisingly little concerned with Mandeville's more specific and grim version of the selfish hypothesis, which is based on self-love as *amour-propre*. Typically, Hutcheson argues from introspection and thought experiments that are aimed at convincing us that disinterested benevolence is as real and natural a principle in human nature as egoistic self-love (Hutcheson, *Inquiry*: 229). Introspection furthermore shows us that the natural good (pleasures and objects indirectly providing us pleasures) and the moral good (benevolence, in others and ourselves) cause fundamentally different perceptions. Only the latter is approved by the moral sense (*Inquiry*: 89).

More specifically, compassion 'strongly proves Benevolence to be natural to us' (*Inquiry*: 160). Throughout the eighteenth century, defining the nature of pity and compassion was a crucial theme in the debates on the selfish hypothesis: those who rejected the selfish hypothesis typically also attacked Hobbes's and Mandeville's egoistic analyses of pity. For Hutcheson, the object of compassion is not the 'Removal of our own Pain' arising upon the awareness of someone's misery (*Inquiry*: 161). If that were so, then if the Deity offered us the options either of helping the distressed, or of obtaining ease by forgetting the sufferer, we would be indifferent with regard to these options. Introspection shows us, however, that we are not. Similarly, Hutcheson treats parental affections as a proof of the reality of disinterested benevolence. In what is most likely one of

Hutcheson's rare direct attacks on Campbell's *Enquiry into the Original of Moral Virtue* (1733), he writes in the fourth edition of the *Inquiry* (1738) that we do not love our children just because of their likeness to us.[8] Claims about likeness and similarity between individuals are far too unspecific to prove that an affection is self-interested, 'since each one some way resembles each other' (Hutcheson, *Inquiry*: 234). Introspection and experience show us that as parents age, so do they experience a continuous disinterested concern for the future well-being of their children after the parents' demise – a concern that is independent of any self-interested use the parents might derive from them (*Inquiry*: 233–4).

As we shall see below, Campbell was worried that Hutcheson's emphasis on benevolence would make the motive for virtue '*mere Instinct*' (Campbell, *Enquiry*: 334). For Hutcheson, the danger was instead over-intellectualisation in the claim that we are rational, self-interested calculators.[9] If all our affections and passions are analysed in terms of a self-interested calculation of personal benefits, the result is a counterintuitive and overly intellectualised account of human behaviour. It is a fact of human life that we often act upon violent passions, selfish as well as disinterested ones, and do not always calculate: 'And how improbable it is, that Persons in the Heat of Action, have any of those *subtle Reflections*, and *selfish Intentions*, which some Philosophers invent for them' (Hutcheson, *Essay*: 64). An explanation of our behaviour that involves benevolence and a moral sense results in a simpler and more convincing account of human nature. Hume would repeat this point in the *Appendix* to his *Enquiry* (see Chapter 7.1), and similar arguments are presented in the Scottish moral philosopher and theologian George Turnbull's *Principles of Moral and Christian Philosophy* (Turnbull 2005: 155–6).

In this context, it is worth noting that Hutcheson's *Essay* (1728) and the third edition of his *Inquiry* (1729) bear the marks of his debates with John Clarke of Hull.[10] In *The Foundation of Morality in Theory and Practice considered* (1726), Clarke published his objections against Hutcheson's conception of virtue as benevolence. Clarke asserted the selfish hypothesis in combination with a positive view of human nature, as did Campbell just after him. Clarke agreed with Hutcheson on the disinterestedness of moral approbation, but he disagreed about the question of moral motivation, especially about Hutcheson's goal 'to reduce all Morality to Benevolence, or a disinterested Love of others' (Clarke 1726: 47). One of the main points of criticism for Clarke was that according to Hutcheson, an action done in view of divine rewards and punishments did not bear any moral value, since it was not disinterested. Clarke revealed his theological agenda by stating that he wanted to reconcile Hutcheson's doctrine with the Scriptures, where 'the greatest Reward is promised to Virtue, and Vice threatened with the greatest of Punishments, on purpose sure to excite Mankind to the Practice of Virtue [. . .] by making it every Man's greatest Interest to be Virtuous' (1726: 48).

On the level of psychology, Clarke asserted a hedonistic version of the selfish hypothesis and claimed that all our desires ultimately aim at self-interest in the sense of gaining pleasure and avoiding pain (1726: 64). As to moral motivation, he argued that both a desire for the pleasures of the moral sense as well as a regard to sanctions from the Deity can motivate morally virtuous actions – in spite of their being ultimately self-interested. Clarke then quoted Hutcheson's claim that *'the most useful Action imaginable, looses all appearance of Benevolence, as soon as we discern that it only flowed from Self-Love, or Interest'* (1726: 51). Clarke objected that it is a psychological fact that 'no Man can desire, or be under any Concern for, the Happiness of others, but where it makes a part of his own, either by the Pleasure and Satisfaction it naturally and immediately gives him, or the Hopes of future Benefit and Advantage to arise from it' (1726: 55). Desiring the happiness of others requires an identification that makes their interests my own and results in my promoting ultimately my own interests by means of promoting those of others. Accordingly, Clarke analysed benevolence in terms of an ultimately self-interested 'Concern for the Happiness of others, in order to secure our own', which comes 'under the Disguise of a Concern *only* for the Happiness of others' (1726: 55–6). As we shall see in Chapter 6, Campbell used similar arguments to analyse benevolence in terms of self-love.

On the grounds of his psychology, Clarke distinguished different kinds of self-interest and argued that ultimately self-interested motives can give rise to morally virtuous actions. Against Hutcheson's claim that the revealing of any self-interested aspect in a beneficent action takes away its benevolent and thus virtuous appearance, Clarke objects that this holds only for interests in the sense of 'the Advantages and Conveniencies of this Life, exclusive of that Pleasure and Satisfaction, necessarily and immediately attending upon Benevolent Actions, considered in themselves, without Regard to any Beneficial Consequences, that may follow from them' (1726: 67–8). However, desiring the good of others in view of an ultimately self-interested desire for the pleasures of the moral sense, or from an interest in the rewards of a future state does not diminish the moral value of an action.

To counter Clarke's objections, Hutcheson refined some of his theses in the third edition of the *Inquiry* (1729) and in the *Essay* (1728). If he wrote in 1726 that there is no benevolence 'without any desire of, or delight in, the Good of others' (Hutcheson, *Inquiry*: 103), the same phrase now had the word 'ultimate' added before 'desire' (*Inquiry*: 223), and Hutcheson more explicitly excluded the desire for future rewards and the pleasures of self-approbation from possible motives for virtuous actions.[11] These can only make us *desire* benevolent affections, but they are not benevolent affections themselves, and thus do not give rise to virtuous actions in Hutcheson's sense (*Inquiry*: 223). But our moral sense does not deceive us. Hutcheson also more systematically distinguished between bene*volence*, that is, an ultimately disinterested desire for the good of others, and mere 'external Acts of Bene*ficence* [my emphasis]', which is the promotion of the good of others for ultimately self-interested reasons, such as the pleasure of being applauded by others, seeing others happy because one realises that this makes oneself happy, or being rewarded in the afterlife (*Inquiry*: 229). Only genuinely disinterested benevolence is approved by the moral sense as morally good, whereas self-interested beneficence, in spite of its potential good consequences (which are a natural good, but not a moral good), is not.

Hutcheson produces numerous further arguments against the selfish hypothesis. One is based on an attack on Locke's definition of desire as uneasiness (Hutcheson, *Essay*: 24, 40), which strongly resembles what came to be known as 'Butler's Stone' (see Chapter 5). Hutcheson argues against the claim that we can voluntarily choose benevolence because we want to benefit from the pleasures of the moral sense (which is a form of self-love as self-esteem) or from the pleasures of the applause of others (which is a form of self-love as love of praise). Affections cannot be raised by will, and not all forms of benevolence are simply pleasurable (think of the grief involved in pity) (Hutcheson, *Inquiry*: 225). Several of Hutcheson's arguments concern the *public* sense, on account of which we could be said to desire the happiness of others only 'with a View to this private Pleasure' of seeing them happy. The *moral* sense would clearly not approve such a desire, since it is not disinterested (Hutcheson, *Essay*: 23; 27–8). Furthermore, introspection shows us that 'we all often feel Delight upon seeing others happy, but during our Pursuit of their Happiness we have no Intention of obtaining this delight' (Hutcheson, *Inquiry*: 227). Also, upon the approach of our death, we do not lose 'all Concern for our Families, Friends, or Country' (*Inquiry*: 228).

In the context of the present study, one of Hutcheson's crucial (yet often rather neglected) arguments against the selfish hypothesis deserves special attention. It concerns not the presupposed falsity of the selfish hypothesis, but the pernicious psychological and moral consequences of this theory of human motivation. For Hutcheson, moral philosophy is not just concerned with the correct description of our psychologies and with the correct definition of morality. Rather, moral philosophy is a project with the important practical task of helping us to morally improve ourselves – remember how Hume famously associated Hutcheson with a 'Painter' in matters of morality (Hume 2011: I, 32–3). In Hutcheson's view, if we are (mistakenly) convinced of the truth of the selfish hypothesis, we do not merely have a false belief regarding human motivation. Rather, we run the risk of becoming accustomed to mistakenly interpreting the behaviour of others, and ultimately of ourselves, as being motivated by self-love only. This has two problematic consequences. First, by distorting our natural view of others' benevolence, we may block our own responsive benevolence, which naturally arises upon the detection of benevolence in others. Secondly, we will refrain from cultivating and strengthening benevolence in ourselves. In this case, we will miss one of the most important opportunities to morally improve ourselves (Hutcheson, *Essay*: 3–4). If we observe an action which (in reality) is motivated by benevolence, this naturally triggers our moral sense and engenders our responsive benevolence towards the benevolent agent. However, if we are made to believe in the selfish hypothesis, our erroneous 'previous Notions that there are no such Affections in Nature, and that all Pretence to them was only *Dissimulation, Affectation,* or at best some *unnatural Enthusiasm*' (*Essay*: 4) will counteract this providentially designed mechanism. The selfish hypothesis is thus not only a false psychological theory, but one with potentially dangerous moral consequences.[12] Hutcheson's verdict is as follows:

> If any Opinions deserve Opposition, they are such as raise Scruples in our Minds about the Goodness of Providence, or represent our Fellow-Creatures as base and selfish, by instilling into us some ill-natur'd, cunning, shreud Insinuations, 'that our most generous Actions proceed wholly from selfish Views.' This wise Philosophy of some Moderns, after Epicurus, must be fruitful of nothing but Discontent, Suspicion, and Jealousy; a State infinitely worse than any little transitory Injurys to which we might be expos'd by a good-natur'd Credulity. (Hutcheson, *Inquiry*: 143)

The psychological question concerning the source and qualities of our motives has an important moral dimension, for Hutcheson – it is not simply a matter of correctly describing the workings of the human *psyche*. Even the selfish hypothesis in its *prima facie* innocent version of psychological hedonism is, for Hutcheson, inseparable from a pessimistic view of human nature's moral qualities – and this pessimism is even more present in Mandeville's pernicious version of the selfish hypothesis, which is based on self-love as *amour-propre*. Hutcheson's claim that the psychological and moral dimensions are connected (a claim, for that matter, also made by Mandeville) was very influential, but we need to note right away that various contemporary philosophers rejected such a link. Among them, most prominently, were John Clarke, John Gay and Archibald Campbell. As we shall see below, these authors made room for moral motivation as well as self-cultivation *within* the framework of the selfish hypothesis (see especially Chapter 6). Similarly, Hume's distinction between several versions of the selfish hypothesis also tended to undermine the connection claimed by Hutcheson (see Chapter 7.1).[13]

4.2 THE MORAL VALUE OF SELF-LOVE

Hutcheson's numerous attacks on the selfish hypothesis, in combination with his insistence that benevolence is the moral good, might make us assume that he has a negative view of self-love as one of the two main motivational sources in human nature. Adam Smith argues in this direction in his *Theory of Moral Sentiments* when critically commenting that

> Dr Hutcheson was so far from allowing self-love to be in any case a motive of virtuous actions, that even a regard to the pleasure of self-approbation, to the comfortable applause of our own consciences, according to him, diminished the merit of a benevolent action. (Smith, *TMS*, VII.ii.3.13, 2002: 358)

According to Smith, who insists on the differences between Hutcheson and Shaftesbury, Hutcheson's emphasis on benevolence was so strong 'not only to check the injustice of self-love, but in some measure to discourage that principle altogether, by representing it as what could never reflect any honour upon those who were influenced by it' (2002: 358). Present-day commentators often follow Smith in emphasising Hutcheson's critical treatment of self-love, for example by discussing his claims regarding self-love principally in the context of his refutations of the selfish hypothesis.[14] However, this is not the whole story.

If we take into account the full range of Hutcheson's claims regarding self-love as part of human nature, then his rehabilitation of postlapsarian human nature against the Calvinist *topos* of the Fall can be shown to extend occasionally to at least a partial rehabilitation of self-love against the Augustinian condemnation of the passion. Only in part can this be explained by Hutcheson's choice to put at the centre of his account of human nature the morally less charged conception of egoistic self-love, and not the conception of self-love as *amour-propre*. As we shall see in subsequent chapters, Butler and Campbell would be even more positive on self-love in their own ways, and subsequent authors such as Hume and Smith would contribute to self-love's rehabilitation. I shall now discuss the passages that support a critical view of self-love in Hutcheson, and then look at other, less frequently discussed passages, which are more positive.

A Critical View of Self-love: Self-love as the Counterpart to Benevolence

We have seen above that Hutcheson distinguishes different forms of benevolence and self-love according to their emotional characteristics and their scope: both can take the forms of calm universal affections, calm partial affections and violent particular passions (Hutcheson, *Inquiry*: 239; *Essay*: 32–3). Regarding benevolence, Hutcheson suggests that these three forms have different degrees of moral value, calm universal benevolence being

> above all amiable and excellent: 'Tis perhaps the sole Moral Perfection of some superior Natures; and the more this prevails and rules in any human Mind, the more amiable the Person appears, even when it not only checks and limits our lower Appetites, but when it controuls our kind particular Passions, or counteracts them. (Hutcheson, *Inquiry*: 237)[15]

Calm universal benevolence has as its object the good of humankind, and it is the morally best form of benevolence. It is more valuable than calm *partial* benevolence, which has as its object the good of particular groups, and which is again more valuable than *passionate* partial benevolence, for example pity. Still, as a disinterested passion, this latter bears moral value.

Table 4.1 Hutcheson on private and public affections and passions

Emotions (affections and passions)	Private (self-love)	Public (benevolence)
Calm affections	calm self-love	calm universal benevolence (e.g. 'universal calm Good-will toward all sensitive Natures') calm partial/particular benevolence (e.g. parental affections)
Violent passions	selfish passions (e.g. hunger, ambition, etc.)	benevolent passions (e.g. pity)

This moral hierarchy is revealed to us by our moral sense, but it may also be spelled out in terms of explicit criteria. First, the moral value of benevolence is a function of its scope, that is, of its degree of universality. Calm universal benevolence is morally better than calm partial benevolence because it does not depend on the personal relationship between the agent and other persons or groups – it is impartial. Thus, a given quantity of natural good produced by universal benevolence appears more amiable than the same quantity of natural good produced by partial benevolence. Partial calm as well as passionate benevolence could be in conflict with the interests of larger systems (as in the case of nepotism), or with the interests of humanity in general (Hutcheson, *Inquiry*: 126–7). Secondly, calm benevolence is morally better than passionate benevolence, because the latter excludes reflection. Since actions motivated by calm reflective benevolence involve a consideration of the relevant circumstances, they more reliably promote the true happiness of others than actions motivated by passionate benevolence, and they are under considerable control of the agent. Thirdly, Hutcheson points out that there is a difference in the constancy of benevolent affections and passions, which influences their moral value. An action motivated by a benevolent character with calm and constant benevolent dispositions can be more easily cultivated and controlled, and thus appears more virtuous than an action that is provoked by an accidental benevolent passion, however intense (*Inquiry*: 132).

Self-love, like benevolence, can take different forms. In many cases, there are good reasons to follow Smith and attribute a generally critical view of self-love to Hutcheson. This critical view is especially apparent in Hutcheson's discussions of mixed motives, and in his moral mathematics. When talking about mixed motives in the *Inquiry* (*Inquiry*: 104), Hutcheson distinguishes three cases. First, if an agent's benevolence is *strong enough* to motivate an action by itself, then the fact that the action is also intended because of its positive effects for the agent herself (for example, because it provides her moral pleasures) does not diminish the moral value of the resulting action. Secondly, if *additional* considerations of private advantage or self-interest are necessary to motivate the action because benevolence is not a strong enough motivation on its own, then the moral value of the action is diminished. Thirdly, if the action is motivated by benevolence *against* self-love, then the action's moral value increases. In these cases, self-love is treated as a negative factor in the evaluation of the resulting action. This holds even if self-love, which is required for self-preservation, does not seem to have a negative moral value *per se* for Hutcheson.

A similarly critical view of self-love appears in Hutcheson's treatment in his moral mathematics – a methodological innovation later ridiculed by Mandeville in *Part II* of the *Fable*, yet adopted in a modified version by Campbell in his *Enquiry* (Mandeville, *Fable II*: 345; Campbell, *Enquiry*: 276–81). Hutcheson explains again how actions can be motivated by a combination of selfish and benevolent desires, which sometimes motivate jointly, and sometimes oppose each other. If an action is recommended by benevolence yet opposed by self-love or interest, the action's moral value increases, since the action is more demanding. If benevolence and self-love prompt the same action because it produces good for the public as well as for the agent herself, the action's moral value decreases, since it is less demanding. When an action is not only performed in view of the promotion of public interest, but also in view of the promotion of the agent's private interest, it is less virtuous than an action that is performed in spite of the agent's interest.[16] This critical treatment of the agent's egoistic desires to promote her interest (as opposed to her altruistic desires to promote the public interest) is again supported by a subsequent passage where Hutcheson explains the relation between selfish motives and benevolence in more detail. He insists that in the case where the virtuous action brings about advantages for the agent herself, 'the Interest must be deducted to find the true Effect of the Benevolence, or Virtue' (Hutcheson, *Inquiry*: 129). In the case where the virtuous action brings disadvantages for the agent, 'this Interest must be added to the Moment, to increase the Virtue of the Action, or the Strength of the Benevolence' (*Inquiry*: 129).

These points lend support to Smith's interpretation of Hutcheson on self-love, as far as actions are concerned. Two remarks must be made, however. First, even on a critical reading of self-love, Hutcheson's discussion of mixed motives still allows for an action to count as virtuous, to some lesser degree, if it is partly aimed at moral pleasure, and if it includes an intention to promote the public good. This will be of great importance for Hutcheson's account of self-cultivation (see Chapter 4.3), and it opposes Mandeville's rigoristic definition of moral virtue as requiring self-denial or the frustration of one's passions (see Chapter 3.3). Secondly, as we will see shortly, there are several passages that demonstrate that Hutcheson also has an overall less negative and more complex understanding of the relation between self-love and morality – and these passages stand to some extent against his moral mathematics. In these other passages, self-love is presented as a motive that is necessary for the good of the whole, under the condition that it does not engender any negative effects for the good of the public (Hutcheson, *Inquiry*: 187). Furthermore, the moral evaluation of self-love depends considerably on the distinction between affections and passions – calm self-love is preferable to passionate self-love. The mathematical model does not take this distinction into account.

More Positive Views of Self-love in Hutcheson

Hutcheson suggests that under certain conditions, self-love is indispensable for a fully virtuous moral agent. Hutcheson may here be looking at Shaftesbury's conception of the self-affections as necessary for being fully virtuous. As we shall see in Chapter 4.3, Hutcheson also attributes to self-love an important role in the cultivation of virtue, since the pleasures of self-approbation delivered by the moral sense are a crucial support to strengthen benevolence. His positive remarks concern primarily calm, reflective self-love.[17]

For Hutcheson, self-love and benevolence do not necessarily oppose each other. These two distinct principles of action can jointly motivate an action if it is seen as promoting both public and private interest. This typically leads to a less valuable action than one motivated solely by benevolence. Yet Hutcheson also claims that if actions motivated solely by egoistic self-love do not evidence a character deprived of benevolence, and if they do not have a negative impact on the good of others, they can be treated as morally indifferent: 'The Actions which flow solely from Self-Love, and yet evidence no Want of Benevolence, having no hurtful Effects upon others, seem perfectly indifferent in a moral Sense, and neither raise the Love or Hatred of the Observer' (Hutcheson, *Inquiry*: 122). In other words, self-interested actions are not necessarily problematic from the moral point of view.[18] This rich passage continues with some even more positive views of self-love:

> Our Reason can indeed discover certain Bounds, within which we may not only act from Self-Love, consistently with the Good of the Whole, but every Mortal's acting thus within these Bounds for his own Good, is absolutely necessary for the Good of the Whole; and the Want of such Self-Love would be universally pernicious. Hence, he who pursues his own private Good, with an Intention also to concur with that Constitution which tends to the Good of the Whole; and much more he who promotes his own Good, with a direct View of making himself more capable of serving God, or doing good to Mankind; acts not only innocently, but also honourably, and virtuously: for in both these Cases, a Motive of Benevolence concurs with Self-Love to excite him to the Action. And thus a Neglect of our own Good, may be morally evil, and argue a Want of Benevolence toward the Whole. (*Inquiry*: 122)

In this passage, Hutcheson points out, alongside Shaftesbury, not only the potential moral indifference, but the necessity for the good of the whole of self-interested actions that are not in conflict with the public good.[19] Without a minimal degree of self-love, human agents neglect themselves, which is 'universally pernicious', because they then deprive the whole system of their capacity to promote the public good and deprive themselves of the possibility of performing virtuous benevolent actions. This claim is particularly interesting in view of the complementary observation that passionate benevolence could be morally problematic if it is harmful to the agent – for example, in the case of actions motivated by excessive pity.

In the last third of the quoted passage, Hutcheson goes a step further and claims that, under certain conditions, pursuing one's own good can be morally virtuous. The conditions are that the pursuit of the agent's private good neither counteracts her benevolence nor harms others, and that the promotion of one's own interest is done in view of 'serving God, or doing good to Mankind'. This presupposes that self-love is calm and reflective, and that one recognises oneself to be part of a larger system of human beings. Calm self-love can thus be instrumentally useful in furthering an ultimately benevolent goal, namely the promotion of the good of the whole. From this point of view, the lack of calm self-love can be morally vicious and show a want of benevolence in the agent's character.

There are only a few passages in the *Inquiry* where Hutcheson claims explicitly that calm egoistic self-love can be not only morally unproblematic, but also morally virtuous. Yet they suggest that being fully virtuous in Hutcheson, as in Shaftesbury, and thus against Smith's presentation, requires not only acting on benevolent motives and cultivating benevolent dispositions of character, but also being instrumentally self-interested in view of one's larger capacity to be benevolent. This point suggests that Smith's confining the concept of virtue purely to benevolent motivation for actions is an oversimplification of Hutcheson's position, at least when considering passages other than the moral mathematics. A minimal degree of self-love remains a moral requirement, in as much as it is instrumental to maintaining one's capacity for being benevolent.

In the *Illustrations*, there is yet another passage suggesting that self-love is required in a fully virtuous agent. Hutcheson writes that the virtuous life

> consists in sacrificing all *positive Interests*, and bearing all *private Evils* for the publick Good: And in submitting also the Interests of all *smaller Systems* to the Interests of the whole: Without any other *Exception* or *Reserve* than this, that every Man may look upon himself as a Part of this System, and consequently not sacrifice an *important private Interest* to a *less important Interest* of others. (Hutcheson, *Essay*: 194)

This passage suggests that in certain situations, an agent can be morally justified in preferring the promotion of her self-interest over the promotion of the public interest: an important private interest can outweigh a less important public interest. This is supposedly the case if the system as a whole is harmed by the agent's attempt to promote others' interests in place of her own – for example, if she neglects herself or puts herself in unnecessary danger. Again, an appropriate minimal degree of self-love seems to be morally required in view of the promotion of the good of the whole. This is, however, restricted to calm, reflective self-love, which requires that the agent sees herself as a part of a whole and that she reflects on the importance of the different interests.[20]

The points discussed in this section undermine the stark contrast that Smith draws between Shaftesbury and Hutcheson. Smith focuses closely on Hutcheson's moral mathematics, but Hutcheson and Shaftesbury may not be appropriately compared if we take into account only Hutcheson's critical view of the moral value of actions motivated by self-love. Several other passages suggest that Hutcheson has a more complex and, on the whole, less negative view of self-love's moral value than admitted by Smith. In his discussion of the fully virtuous agent, Hutcheson can be seen to rely to quite some extent on the idea found in the Stoics and in Shaftesbury that a natural degree of self-affections is required for virtue. Gill was right to point out that for Hutcheson, human nature is morally good, not only because of the reality of natural benevolence, but also since self-love is not *per se* corrupt. The opposition to the Augustinian condemnation of self-love is important, and it puts Hutcheson at quite some distance from Hobbes and Mandeville. This becomes even clearer in Hutcheson's theory of self-cultivation, which is in stark contrast to Mandeville's claim that genuine moral virtue requires self-denial.

4.3 SELF-LOVE AND SELF-CULTIVATION

The theme of self-cultivation, that is, the moral improvement of oneself, has been an important subject throughout the history of ethics.[21] Specific recommendations concerning moral self-improvement obviously depend on the underlying accounts of human nature. In this section I discuss how Hutcheson treats self-love again quite positively in his theory of self-cultivation, which is influenced by (selected) Stoic ideas as well as by contemporary natural law theories, and which opposes orthodox Calvinist ideas about the impossibility of performing self-cultivation, since genuine moral reform is the effect of grace. Samuel Pufendorf (1632–94) was the most influential European natural law theorist, and subsequent thinkers typically followed him in adopting the traditional distinction between duties to God, to oneself and to others, treating the topic of self-cultivation most extensively in the context of duties to oneself. Jean Barbeyrac (1674–1744) and Gershom

Carmichael (1672–1729) critically engaged with Pufendorf's ideas and developed them further.[22] They emphasised the crucial importance of sound opinions regarding our duties, of right judgements about the values of the objects we desire, and of controlling the passions by right reason. Some of these ideas may indeed have been inspired by Stoic reflections.

Hutcheson takes on board a good number of these ideas, yet the importance he attributes to benevolence and the moral sense in his moral philosophy makes his account of self-cultivation different in interesting ways. As far as Hutcheson's debts to Stoicism are concerned, matters are also complicated. Hutcheson adopts and adapts some Stoic ideas regarding the passions (for example, the general distinction between violent passions and calm affections), yet rejects others (for example, the claim that the agent's virtue is the sole real good, and that the well-being of others should not really affect us).[23]

The perfection of self-cultivation in Hutcheson is to strengthen calm, universal benevolence, the most valuable form, over other emotions – both self-interested *and* benevolent ones: 'the Perfection of Virtue consists in "having the *universal calm Benevolence*, the prevalent Affection of the Mind, so as to limit and counteract not only the *selfish Passions*, but even the *particular kind Affections*"' (Hutcheson, *Essay*: 8). Hutcheson gives a series of more specific recommendations as to how exactly we can cultivate virtue. Some of these are more traditional and concern the distinction between violent passions and calm affections. In accordance with Pufendorf's, Barbeyrac's and Carmichael's discussions of self-cultivation, Hutcheson recommends, for example, that we should avoid actions motivated by violent passions by suspending them while we are under the passion's influence (*Essay*: 110). More generally, we should try to transform our violent passions into calm affections by frequent and habitual reflection upon the value of the objects of our desires, and upon the potentially pernicious consequences of actions 'to which even the *best of our Passions* may lead us' (*Essay*: 110–11). Once we exert control over our violent passions, both self-interested and benevolent, we can direct our calm affections towards the right objects, and give the affection the right strength by making an effort to correctly represent the value of its object (*Essay*: 110).[24]

Further recommendations for the cultivation of virtue are rooted specifically in Hutcheson's distinction between benevolence and self-love – and thus the distinction that he claimed was too often overshadowed by the distinction between calm and violent emotions (*Essay*: 53). Hutcheson recommends that we strengthen benevolence in general by focusing our attention on the relevant features of a situation and of others' motives.

If we think of others as motivated by benevolence rather than by concealed selfish motives, we strengthen our own responsive benevolence. This point explains again why for Hutcheson, the selfish hypothesis is not only false but dangerous: it makes us blind with respect to those features that cause responsive benevolence in us and represents 'our Fellow-Creatures as base and selfish' (Hutcheson, *Inquiry*: 143).

Yet another recommendation by Hutcheson concerns the restriction and frustration of self-love when it opposes benevolence. In such cases, we ought to remind ourselves that universal benevolence has a tendency to promote our own happiness as well, and that selfish passions often have negative consequences (*Inquiry*: 179). Such self-interested considerations will result in calm, selfish affections opposing other selfish affections and passions, and this will allow for natural benevolence to exert itself:

> Let the Obstacles from Self-love be only remov'd, and Nature it self will incline us to Benevolence. Let the Misery of excessive Selfishness, and all its Passions, be but once explain'd, that so Self-love may cease to counteract our natural Propensity to Benevolence, and when this noble Disposition gets loose from these Bonds of Ignorance, and false Views of Interest, it shall be assisted even by Self-love, and grow strong enough to make a noble virtuous Character. (*Inquiry*: 179)

If Hutcheson recommends the frustration of self-love in case it constitutes an obstacle to benevolence, he does not recommend its eradication. Since self-love can come to the support of benevolence, we should benefit from this fact in our efforts to cultivate ourselves. Calm, reflective self-love, given the agent's knowledge about the psychological connections between benevolence and the moral pleasures, provides her with self-interested reasons to strengthen benevolent desires and character traits, and to suppress selfish desires that oppose benevolent ones. Hutcheson claims regularly that calm self-love can support benevolence. In the *Inquiry*, for example, he writes that 'Self-Interest may be our Motive in studying to raise these kind Affections'.[25] He claims that self-love can assist benevolence, if it does not counteract our 'natural Propensity to Benevolence' (*Inquiry*: 179). Self-love supports benevolence, especially when calm and reflective self-love is directed by additional motives, such as honour or advantage (*Inquiry*: 187). And at the end of the *Inaugural Lecture*, Hutcheson asserts that virtue will provide us the 'highest pleasures of life' (*Inaugural Lecture*: 216). Thus, we have self-interested reasons to cultivate virtuous dispositions.

Hutcheson signals awareness of a possible tension between his critical view of self-love in matters of morality on the one hand, and the fact that he emphasises the importance of self-love for self-cultivation on the other. At the beginning of the *Essay*, he writes:

> It may perhaps seem strange, that when in this *Treatise* Virtue is suppos'd *disinterested*; yet so much Pains is taken, by a *Comparison* of our several *Pleasures*, to prove the *Pleasures* of *Virtue* to be the greatest we are capable of, and that consequently it is our truest *Interest* to be *virtuous*. (*Essay*: 5)

Both self-love and benevolence are '*natural Dispositions of our Minds*' (*Essay*: 5). In other words, we have natural desires to promote both our private and the public interest. It is possible that self-love can oppose benevolence, and thus temporarily block it. In these cases, we can help the latter exert itself by removing 'these *Opinions of opposite Interests*, and to shew a superior Interest on their side' (*Essay*: 5). The agent who is informed of the natural connection between benevolence and the moral pleasures knows that she has (non-moral) self-interested reasons, or a 'superior interest', for cultivating the moral good of benevolence, namely the natural good of the pleasures of virtue, which she knows are the highest pleasures she can possibly experience. This knowledge will help the agent resolve possible conflicts between selfish and benevolent desires in favour of benevolence. Thus, benevolence can be supported by calm self-love in that the agent removes selfish desires by endorsing the true belief that there are superior, self-interested reasons to be benevolent.

Hutcheson highlights an interesting problem with the idea that self-love can be used to support benevolence:

> Not that we can be truly Virtuous, if we intend only to obtain the Pleasure which arises from Beneficence, without the Love of others: Nay, this very Pleasure is founded on our being conscious of disinterested Love to others, as the Spring of our Actions. But Self-Interest may be our Motive in studying to raise these kind Affections, and to continue in this agreeable State, tho it cannot be the sole, or principal Motive of any Action, which to our moral Sense appears Virtuous. (Hutcheson, *Inquiry*: 134, 244)

This passage draws attention to a psychological point that has been discussed as the 'paradox of moral motivation' in more recent literature.[26] For Hutcheson, it is a psychological fact that the pleasures of self-approbation depend upon the agent's consciousness of having acted from benevolent motives. Since benevolence constitutes the agent's greatest happiness, she has self-interested reasons to be benevolent. However, if she attempts to be benevolent for the ultimately self-interested reason of experiencing the pleasures of the moral sense, she will fail and will only be bene*ficent*. As a consequence, the agent will not gain the desired pleasures, since they depend on bene*volence*. From the moral point of view, an agent is not truly virtuous if she acts merely (or predominantly) on the ultimately selfish desire to experience the pleasures of self-approbation, which are provided by the moral sense as a result of a benevolent action.

Hutcheson's solution to the paradox is that we treat such cases as actions with mixed motives, where both genuine benevolence and the self-interested desire to gain the moral pleasures are present. He encourages this reading when he qualifies in the quoted passage that we cannot be truly virtuous, 'if we intend only to obtain the Pleasure', and when he writes that the selfish desire for the moral pleasures 'cannot be the sole, or principal Motive of any Action, which to our moral Sense appears Virtuous' (Hutcheson, *Inquiry*: 134, 244). Actions with mixed motives are still virtuous, albeit to a lesser degree than an action motivated purely by benevolence. From the psychological point of view, the agent can still derive moral pleasures from actions with mixed motives. In other words, even if Hutcheson acknowledges the paradox of moral motivation, he can answer it in a way that makes room for self-love to be a support for benevolence.[27]

Another question engendered by these discussions concerns the obligation of being virtuous and cultivating virtue – a question that was important for Hutcheson's treatment of Shaftesbury, and that was touched upon by William Leechman and Hugh Blair (see Chapter 5.4). Why should we be morally virtuous and cultivate ourselves in order to become more virtuous, according to Hutcheson? What has been said previously about the link between self-love and virtue should not be mistaken for an egoistic reduction of the obligation to virtue and self-cultivation. Rather, Hutcheson suggests that the ultimate obligation for virtue lies in the moral sense:

> If any one ask, Can we have any Sense of Obligation, abstracting from the Laws of a Superior? We must answer according to the various Senses of the word Obligation. If by Obligation we understand a Determination, without regard to our own Interest, to approve Actions, and to perform them; which Determination shall also make us displeas'd with our selves, and uneasy upon having acted contrary to it; in this meaning of the word Obligation, there is naturally an Obligation upon all Men to Benevolence. (Hutcheson, *Inquiry*: 177)[28]

Hutcheson rejects egoistic accounts of the obligation to virtue and its cultivation, which he thinks he finds in Pufendorf, Barbeyrac and Carmichael. These theorists can be taken to have claimed that the obligation of self-cultivation, a part of the duty to oneself, is rooted in self-interest. Undeniably, Hutcheson claims that there are sound, self-interested reasons for self-cultivation and for living a moral life – think of the hierarchy of the pleasures, for example, with the supreme place attributed to the moral pleasures. Yet the proper moral obligation of virtue and its cultivation does not lie in self-interested reasons but in the moral sense, which approves of benevolent motives and disapproves of excessive selfishness.[29] Considerations from self-interest only show us egoistic reasons to be virtuous, which are grounded in facts about human psychology, and they can be helpful in cultivating virtue.

A remark is apposite on an interesting comment by Hutcheson on the Stoic theory of self-cultivation.[30] The Stoic conception of virtue as an internal good emphasises the importance of a harmonious state of the soul – the avoidance of *perturbationes* or violent passions is crucial, and apathy is the central aim. For Hutcheson, however, virtue as benevolence necessarily connects us with others – to be virtuous is to have the potentially frustrating intention of promoting the well-being and virtue of others. Moreover, the public sense makes us feel the pains of sympathy, for example if we do not succeed in our efforts to achieve the goal of promoting the well-being of others. Here, Hutcheson points out a tension with at least some of the Stoics:

> This may shew the Vanity of some of the lower rate of Philosophers of the *Stoick Sect*, in boasting of an undisturbed Happiness and Serenity, independently even of the DEITY, as well as of their Fellow-Creatures, wholly inconsistent with the *Order* of Nature, as well as with the Principles of some of their great Leaders: for which, Men of Wit in their own Age did not fail to ridicule them. (Hutcheson, *Essay*: 83)

Some Stoics reduce virtue and its cultivation to a '*private sublimely selfish Discipline*' (*Essay*: 83), which tends to disconnect us from our fellow creatures instead of supporting our natural connections via benevolence and the public sense. But being virtuous, for Hutcheson, entails being vulnerable to the well-being of others. Since our desires to promote this well-being are likely to be frustrated, virtue 'may also be the Occasion of no inconsiderable Pains in this Life' (*Essay*: 83). In self-cultivation, against (some of) the Stoics, we should not aim at suppressing benevolence and the public sense simply so as to remain undisturbed by the unhappiness and vices of others. Rather, we should remind ourselves that the moral pleasures are the most valuable pleasures we can possibly experience, and that they will compensate us for potential pains connected to our own virtue. And on the negative side, we should remember that the lack of benevolence will cause '*Self-Condemnation* and *Abhorrence*' (*Essay*: 83).[31]

4.4 A SIDE-NOTE ON ALEXANDER FORBES'S *ESSAY ON SELF-LOVE*

An illuminating comparison can be made between Hutcheson and Alexander Forbes, fourth Lord Forbes of Pitsligo (1678–1762), with his nowadays almost forgotten *Essay on Self-love*, published in *Essays Moral and Philosophical* (1734).[32] Forbes had travelled to France and there met Fénelon, whom he regularly quotes alongside Pascal and La Rochefoucauld, Henry More, Seneca, Cicero, Augustine, Paul and others. Forbes appears to support Hutcheson's analysis of moral virtue in terms of disinterested benevolence or charity, yet he discusses the question of self-love in a psychological setting which is much inspired by French Augustinian moralists. This leads to interesting overlaps and differences with Hutcheson.

Forbes agrees with Hutcheson that we need to distinguish two fundamental principles of action: 'In rational Creatures there are but two Principles, or two Sources, to which all deliberate Actions are reducible, *viz. Self-Interest* and *Disinterestedness*' (Forbes 1734: 259). These principles also determine the moral value of an action. According to Forbes, and in line with Hutcheson *and* Fénelon, 'virtuous Actions thus derive their Value from their Disinterestedness' (1734: 261). 'Disinterestedness' in Forbes is connected to Fénelonian '*pure disinterested* Love of God' (1734: 247), but insofar as our dealings with other people are concerned, we can understand it in the Hutchesonian sense of the disinterested promotion of the good of others for their own sake. Forbes clarifies that 'Disinterestedness may be considered as the Foundation of that active Principle call'd *Charity*' (1734: 377).

If disinterestedness is the foundation of virtue, then the moral badness or 'Baseness of vicious Actions must be from their Interestedness' (1734: 261). I have argued that Hutcheson would not endorse this conclusion, since for him, depending on the circumstances, self-interest can be neutral or even virtuous. In Shaftesbury, the requirement that a fully virtuous agent should have self-affections is even more explicit. For Forbes, however, in the fallen state of humankind, 'interestedness' is the same as moral corruption. Forbes defines self-love in Augustinian terms, translating La Rochefoucauld, as

> the Love of one's self, and of every thing for the sake of one's self; it makes Men Idolizers of themselves, and would make them Tyrants to others, if Fortune furnish'd them with the means of doing it: it never takes any rest but within itself, or dwells longer on any other Objects, than Bees do upon Flowers, to extract what may be to its advantage.
> (1734: 341)

Such passages are inspired by Augustinian conceptions of self-love as *amour-propre*, a passion that in the postlapsarian state diverts us from loving God. Unsurprisingly, Forbes links his moral psychology with the *topos* of the Fall and with the difficult requirement of self-denial.

More generally, Forbes distinguishes several positions in the 'new Disputes concerning Human Nature'. First, there are those who elevate self-love to a moral principle, since they have recognised that humankind is incapable of honesty or friendship 'without a deliberate Prospect of his own Interest as the prevailing Motive' (1734: 246). Here, Forbes may be thinking of philosophers such as Clarke or Campbell, the latter with his theory that self-love as love of praise motivates us to morally virtuous actions. Secondly, there are those who insist that disinterestedness is the moral principle, but at the same time 'deny the Infirmity and Corruption of human Nature' (1734: 246) – in other words, those philosophers who deny that postlapsarian human nature is corrupt and vicious. Here, Forbes may have in mind Hutcheson, Shaftesbury and Butler with their optimistic accounts of human nature as naturally tending to virtue.[33] Both positions, according to Forbes, are marked by an 'Aversion to reveal'd Religion' (1734: 246).

Forbes, however, quoting an Augustinian passage by Pascal in his support, claims that the Fall has left us with corrupt self-love, and that it has annihilated pure disinterested love of God (1734: 253–4). He insists that in the state of postlapsarian corruption, self-denial is necessary for virtue, since 'that which is easy to Nature in a State of Order, is not so in a State of Disorder; for Nature is one thing, and corrupt Nature another' (1734: 294). For Forbes, this unfortunate fact must make us reconsider the Stoic dictum of virtue as *life according to Nature*, which was so dear to Shaftesbury, Hutcheson and Butler as well as Campbell. Forbes refers to Pascal's *Entretien avec M. de Saci* (1655), where Epictetus is compared to the 'Christian' doctrine (1734: 309). In this illuminating text, the Stoic idea of virtue as something which is ἐφ' ἡμῖν or in our power to cultivate is criticised as a proud neglecting of our deplorable reality after the Fall. For Forbes, the question of whether or not the Fall is accepted as a reality most profoundly opposes Christians on the one hand, and Deists (such as Shaftesbury and, presumably, Hutcheson, according to Forbes) on the other, even if both parties may agree on the fact that disinterestedness is what makes us morally virtuous:

> an uncorrupt Man is the same with an upright Man, and Disinterestedness but another Term for Uprightness. This way of speaking therefore, when the Matter is well consider'd, will pass both with Christians and Deists; for both Parties suppose Man to be originally upright, the latter only denying his Defection from that State. (1734: 277)

Even though Hutcheson is not mentioned by Forbes, this passage can be read as an attack on his moral philosophy. The crucial point is that Forbes accepts Hutcheson's emphasis on disinterested benevolence as the morally virtuous motive, yet Forbes's account of our psychological make-up emphasises the devastating psychological reality after the Fall. To some extent his position resembles that of Mandeville, yet Forbes lacks the provocative emphasis on the beneficial consequences of vice. Forbes is an example of how one could accept a Hutcheson-like definition of virtue, yet insist on a pessimistic view of humankind's present moral state because of the contingent psychological reality after the Fall.

4.5 CONCLUSION

Together with disinterested benevolence, egoistic self-love is at the centre of Hutcheson's moral psychology, and his arguments against the selfish hypothesis can be closely related to our present-day debates on psychological egoism. One point is particularly noteworthy: Hutcheson's strong emphases on the reality of disinterested benevolence and of a disinterested moral sense, his numerous attacks on the selfish hypothesis, and his treatment of the moral value of self-love in his moral mathematics may leave us with the impression that he was quite critical of the moral value of egoistic self-love. Hutcheson promotes an overall very positive view of human nature as naturally virtuous, and as capable of cultivating this virtue to a higher degree – yet is it only disinterested benevolence, and benevolence *qua* principle acting against self-love's tendencies, which makes us virtuous and capable of the cultivation of virtue? Hutcheson's treatment of self-love in his moral mathematics seems to suggest this, and so does his claim that adopting the selfish hypothesis means adopting a negative view of human nature's moral capacities (a claim that still dominates present-day reconstructions of the debates on self-love). Smith, and with him quite a number of present-day commentators, mainly note Hutcheson's critical view of self-love. This view is undoubtedly strongly present, and to some extent it opposes Hutcheson to Shaftesbury's more balanced conception of the fully virtuous human agent.

However, I have tried to show that Hutcheson's negative view of self-love is not the full picture. In his writings, there are passages where he suggests, alongside Shaftesbury, that self-love is a necessary ingredient of a fully virtuous person. On some occasions, Hutcheson even seems to contend that the very principle of self-love, under certain conditions, can be virtuous. Moreover, taking into account Hutcheson's theory of self-cultivation, we understand that the distinction between interested self-love and disinterested benevolence is not the only relevant distinction to be considered in our efforts to morally improve ourselves – the distinction between calm affections and violent passions, and the distinction between different scopes of affections, both interested and disinterested, are of equal importance. Hutcheson clarifies that self-love can not only be a support to virtue, but that it may even be required from the moral point of view: the fully virtuous agent might be morally *required* to sacrifice an unimportant public interest to an important private interest. These points speak for an adjusted picture of Hutcheson's treatment of self-love: his frequent attacks on the selfish hypothesis and his often critical treatment of egoistic self-love should not make us forget that these views of self-love are counterbalanced by some quite positive comments. In sum, I want to suggest that Hutcheson is somewhat closer to Shaftesbury than is admitted by Smith, since Hutcheson's rehabilitation of human nature against the Calvinist *topos* of postlapsarian corruption extends at least occasionally to a rehabilitation of self-love.

NOTES

1. This subtitle disappeared in the second edition (1726), possibly as an attempt by Hutcheson to put some more distance between himself and Shaftesbury. The model of 'Mathematical Calculation' was replaced in the fourth edition (1738) by a textual version.

2. Moore (1990) suggests that we distinguish Hutcheson's philosophical texts into 1) those aimed at a wider public (the letters to the *London Journal* and the *Dublin Weekly Journal*, 1724–25, the *Inquiry*, 1725, and the *Essay*, 1728), and 2) those primarily aimed at an academic audience (*Oratio Inauguralis*, 1730, *Metaphysicae Synopsis*, 1742, *Short Introduction*, 1742, and *System of Moral Philosophy*, 1755). The degree of the distinction between these texts is disputed (see Heydt 2018: 56–7), but in any case, evidence of Hutcheson's efforts to refute the selfish hypothesis can be found in both types. For further information on Hutcheson's biography, Scott (1900) is still worth consulting.

3. Bishop (1996: 283) argues that in his later writings, Hutcheson tried 'to get away from both egoistic and hedonistic theories of motivation and was trying to move towards a faculty based theory'. See also the larger narrative in Scott (1900). To my mind, the rejection of egoistic theories of human motivation is an important theme throughout Hutcheson's writings, but it is correct that especially in the *Inquiry* and the *Essay*, he concentrates on hedonistic versions of egoism, defining the natural good as pleasure.

4. I have discussed this point in greater detail with an interest in Hutcheson's relation to Stoicism in Maurer (2010). In spite of Hutcheson's affinities with Stoic ideas, his interest in the distinction between benevolence and self-love and his focus on benevolence as the moral good render

him very critical with respect to certain fundamental Stoic tenets, most importantly the conception of virtue as a private affair. See especially Hutcheson (*Essay*: 83–4).

5. See also the discussion in Strasser (1987), which focuses on Hutcheson's account in the *System*.

6. I quote the text from the third and fourth editions of the *Inquiry*. In the first and second editions, the passage reads as follows: 'The Word Moral Goodness, in this Treatise, denotes our Idea of some Quality apprehended in Actions, which procures Approbation, and Love toward the Actor, from those who receive no Advantage by the Action.' In the third and fourth editions, Hutcheson drops the condition that the approver receive 'no advantage' from the action in question. This is consistent with the idea that virtuous actions, in spite of being disinterested, have as their consequence to provide the agent with the pleasures of self-approbation from the moral sense. In the third and fourth editions, Hutcheson also replaces the term 'love' with the expression 'desire for the other agent's happiness'. This makes his claim that moral approbation engenders responsive benevolence (which he defines elsewhere as the desire for the other agent's happiness) more obvious.

7. For discussions, see, for example, Jensen (1971: 13–19), Irwin (2008: 401–7), Gill (2006: 147–55) and Tilley (2016).

8. For Campbell's reductive analysis of parental affections, see Campbell (*Enquiry*: 336–44, 25, 311), as well as Chapter 6.1.

9. This comes close to Shaftesbury's objection to the more specific version of the selfish hypothesis, discussed in Chapter 2.1. See Shaftesbury (*Sensus Communis*: 53–4).

10. This paragraph is largely based on Maurer (2013a: 301–2). For further discussions of the debates between Hutcheson and Clarke, see Garrett's introduction in Hutcheson (*Essay*: xiv–xvii), as well as Stewart (1982) and Turco (1999).

11. Strikingly, there are numerous additions of the word 'ultimate' before 'desire' in the *Inquiry* and the *Essay* after 1726.

12. James Harris highlights furthermore the religious dimension of Hutcheson's rejection of the selfish hypothesis: admitting the reality of 'natural benevolence and sociability is better to serve the cause of religion: for that way, "the benevolence towards mankind of the Deity, whom we should always gratefully worship and admire, is obvious from man's very constitution"' (Harris 2005: 147).

13. The Scottish moral philosopher and theologian George Turnbull is often close to Shaftesbury's and Hutcheson's arguments against the selfish hypothesis – see, for example, Turnbull (2005: 174–5). However, he adds an original argument in his discussion of the fact mentioned by Shaftesbury that, in some cases, self-love is too weak and benevolence too strong. Since we do not conclude from such cases that 'self-love had originally no place in our frame; so, by parity of reason, it would

be equally absurd to infer from a few particular instances, where self-love is too strong, and benevolence almost quite extinct, that originally there was no social principle in our nature.' See Turnbull (2005: 1, 221), as well as Chapter 2.2.

14. This is, for example, the case in Gill (2006). To some extent against Gill and Smith, I want to draw attention to more positive moments in Hutcheson's treatment of self-love as egoistic desire which are part of his positive view of postlapsarian human nature.

15. This passage was added to the fourth edition of the *Inquiry* (1738), that is, after the debates with John Clarke of Hull and the publication of Campbell's *Enquiry*. See also Hutcheson (*System*: 69–70).

16. Hutcheson's famous formula stands as follows: '$B = (M \pm I / A)$', where 'B' is the moral good or benevolence, 'M' is the natural good (intentionally) produced by the action, 'I' is self-interest and 'A' the agent's capacities or ability. Jaffro (2013) offers an illuminating discussion of Hutcheson's moral mathematics in comparison with Shaftesbury and Bentham.

17. Darwall (1995: 236–7) emphasises the importance of the distinction between calm and passionate self-love for Hutcheson's claim that calm benevolence and calm self-love are ultimately coordinated.

18. In a similar tone, Hutcheson (*System*: 65) comments on the different forms of self-love in the *System*, claiming that the 'calm desire of private good, tho' it is not approved as virtue, yet it is far from being condemned as vice'.

19. In his discussion of Hutcheson, Hirschman (1977: 65) highlights that self-love in Hutcheson can take the form of a calm desire for wealth, which under the aforementioned conditions is *morally* acceptable. It is essential, however, that Hutcheson's focus in this passage is on natural good in general (most importantly the moral pleasures), and not only on material wealth. Also, I take this passage in Hutcheson to be a counter-example to Heydt (2018: 150).

20. The idea that self-love is morally required in view of the fully virtuous agent's capacity to exert benevolence has an interesting complement. Every rational agent is part of larger systems to which she should extend her benevolence. Calm universal benevolence, which aims at promoting the good of the whole, includes a concern for one's own happiness. In other words, intending to promote the well-being of humanity *also* involves promoting one's own well-being – provided the latter is not in conflict with the former. By being universally benevolent, one is also benevolent towards oneself. Thus, self-interest is interwoven with benevolence in two important positive respects in Hutcheson's moral theory. First, calm universal benevolence, which is the highest form of virtue, extends to a certain degree to the agent's private interests. Secondly, paying minimal attention to one's private interests is a precondition of being able to exercise benevolence on a regular basis.

21. See especially Heydt (2018: 133–79).

22. Pufendorf's remarks on the duties to oneself, and Barbeyrac's and Carmichael's discussions of Pufendorf, are particularly noteworthy in this context. In his extensive commentaries on Pufendorf, Barbeyrac emphasises that the duties to oneself are not to be restricted to those of self-preservation, but must include those of self-perfection. And Carmichael objected of Pufendorf that he 'passes too lightly over the *cultivation of the mind*' (in the Latin, *cultura animi*). See Pufendorf (2003: 69–94) and Carmichael (2002: 59–60). See also Moore and Silverthorne (1984), Haakonssen (1990; 1996) and Heydt (2018: 159–60).

23. See Maurer (2010; 2016c) on Hutcheson's theory of self-cultivation and his critical adaption of selected Stoic tenets.

24. For very similar recommendations, see Carmichael (2002: 59–60).

25. Hutcheson (*Inquiry*: 134, 244). I quote the text from the third and fourth editions.

26. See, for example, the discussion in Bishop (1996: 285).

27. A second interesting case is slightly different. Consider the agent who wants to have a benevolent or virtuous character for *purely* self-interested reasons, that is, exclusively for the advantages she recognises in having a virtuous character. For reasons specified above, the agent must fail in her attempts to become truly virtuous for purely self-interested reasons, as well as in her attempts to perform virtuous actions for purely self-interested reasons. Genuine virtue is disinterested and ultimately aims at promoting the well-being of others. But then again, selfish motives 'may make us desire to have benevolent Affections, and consequently turn our Attention to those Qualities in Objects which excite them; they may overbalance all apparent contrary Motives, and all Temptations to Vice' (Hutcheson, *Inquiry*: 229). The agent who wants to become virtuous for purely selfish reasons must fail, but a psychological consequence of her attempts is that her attention remains focused on the benevolence of others. The moral sense's natural and disinterested approval of these motives then causes genuine benevolent affections, which are independent of the agent's former self-interested motives. Thus, the formerly purely selfish agent may develop genuine benevolent dispositions which have their origin in psychological mechanisms that are independent of her former selfish intentions. In the end, even an entirely self-interested agent may thus successfully develop disinterested virtuous dispositions.

28. On this point, see Darwall (1995: 221) and Gill (2006: 150–1). This theme is also discussed in Hutcheson's *System*, and in Leechman's *Preface* to it (Hutcheson, *System*: xlv–xlvi, 74–9).

29. On this point I contradict Gill, who suggests in his discussion of Hutcheson's analysis of the relation between morality and self-interest that, for Hutcheson, the two 'are on a normative par'. Gill (2006: 185)

writes: 'Rather than claim that the moral sense trumps, or is in some sense superior to or more authoritative than self-interest, Hutcheson tried to show that even though morality and self-interest are on a normative par, morality still will not be threatened.'

30. I have discussed this point more extensively in Maurer (2010; 2016c).

31. Harris (2008: 213–14) highlights furthermore the importance of the religious standpoint, or the belief that in a providentially ordered system the pains of virtue will be outweighed or compensated by its pleasures. This guarantees the stability of the virtuous dispositions of the agent.

32. On Forbes's biography, see Pittock (2006).

33. In a note, Forbes (1734: 324) quotes Shaftesbury's attack on the 'Modern Projectors', and elsewhere mentions Butler, in a slightly obscure context, as someone who 'expres'd himself against *Self-Love* in his Sermons' (1734: 378).

5. Butler on Self-love as Respect of Self

The second and third of Joseph Butler's *Sermons Preached at the Rolls Chapel* have as their added motto a passage from Paul's Epistle to the Romans: 'For when the Gentiles which have not the law, do by nature the things contained in the law, these having not the law, are a law unto themselves' (Rom. 2:14). These and other passages from Romans regarding the law and the light of nature were subject to heated debates in the early modern period. In Chapter 6, I discuss how orthodox Calvinists interpreted this passage alongside Rom. 2:15 and Rom. 1:19–20 primarily to stress postlapsarian inexcusability: natural conscience, that is, the light of nature unaided by divine revelation, reveals still enough concerning God and his moral law to render us all guilty for our sins, but not enough to reach salvation.

With a very different interest, Butler uses Paul's Epistle to the Romans to suggest that by understanding our psychological make-up, we can find out more about the moral law of God in us, and thereby morally improve ourselves. Given the often critical attitude towards self-love in the eighteenth century, one of Butler's claims looks particularly surprising: According to him, there is no 'reason to wish self-love were weaker in the generality of the world, than it is [. . .] Upon the whole, if the generality of mankind were to cultivate within themselves the principle of self-love [. . .] it would manifestly prevent numberless follies and vices' (Butler, *Sermons*, Preface: 13–14). Hutcheson is famous for having emphasised that we should cultivate and strengthen universal benevolence for moral self-improvement – but self-love? Much of the present chapter is dedicated to explaining more precisely how Butler's conception of self-love differs from that of most thinkers before him, and how he could thus make the quoted claim.

Joseph Butler (1692–1752) is most famous for his *Sermons Preached at the Rolls Chapel* (1726) and for *The Analogy of Religion* (1736) with the appended 'A Dissertation of the Nature of Virtue'. Butler was originally educated in a dissenting academy, but then converted to Anglicanism. Towards the end of his life, in 1750–52, he was Bishop of Durham.[1] Butler is quite well known to present-day philosophers, but often through a narrow selection of decontextualised passages from the *Sermons*, which mostly concern his arguments for the authority of conscience and his rejection of psychological egoism and hedonism.[2] In this chapter, I shall neither focus on assessing Butler's arguments anew, nor provide a fully contextualised account of his moral philosophy, but offer a relatively focused reading of his claims regarding self-love in comparison with Hutcheson.

5.1 THE 'INWARD FRAME OF MAN': BUTLER'S MORAL PSYCHOLOGY

The Principles of Human Nature

Butler's account of self-love is one part of his larger project to prove that human nature is 'plainly adapted' (Butler, *Sermons*: 1, 17) to virtue – which is a reference to the Stoic dictum *vita secundum naturam*. More generally, Butler claims that his *Sermons* 'were intended to explain what is meant by the nature of man, when it is said that virtue consists in following, and vice in deviating from it' (*Sermons*, Preface: 5). Butler can often be seen to combine an interest in Stoicism with Christianity. It is not inappropriate to term this combination 'Christian Stoicism', but I argued in Chapter 1.3 that it is essential in the case of both broad categories to look more deeply into which doctrines were adopted and adapted, and which were not.

Methodologically speaking, Butler chooses not to inquire 'into the abstract relations of things' (*Sermons*, Preface: 5), but to inquire into 'a matter of fact, namely, what the particular nature of man is, its several parts, their economy or constitution; from whence it proceeds to determine what course of life it is, which is correspondent to this whole nature' (*Sermons*, Preface: 5). It cannot be emphasised enough that in his inquiry, Butler strongly relies on a theistic teleological account of human nature as the product of divine design.[3] The study of our 'real nature' (*Sermons*: 2, 26) reveals a system designed by God, which is fully adapted to virtue – in contrast to Calvinist orthodoxy, Butler does not emphasise the Fall at this point. If on his interpretation of Rom. 2:14, the 'inward frame of man is considered as [a] guide in morals' (*Sermons*: 2, 26), this does not, of course, exclude the possibility of vicious actions – yet neither does this possibility falsify the claim that human nature is designed for virtue.

For Butler, human nature is a system composed of different parts which stand in hierarchical relations to each other, 'the chief of which is the authority of reflection or conscience' (*Sermons*, Preface: 6). The distinction between the 'authority' and the 'strength' of a principle allows Butler to claim that 'to follow nature' neither means to follow merely any principle the agent is aware of, nor simply to follow only the most strongly felt principle. Rather, 'following nature' requires taking into account the moral hierarchy of the principles, and thus respecting the judgements of conscience:[4]

> It is by this faculty, natural to man, that he is a moral agent, that he is a law to himself: by this faculty, I say, not to be considered merely as a principle in his heart, which is to have some influence as well as others; but considered as a faculty in kind and in nature supreme over all others, and which bears its own authority of being so. (*Sermons*: 2, 29)

In his moral psychology, Butler introduces several important ideas that are also essential for understanding his concept of self-love. First and foremost, Butler distinguishes between what he calls 'particular' and 'general principles'. The former are particular passions, appetites and affections. Among the latter, he counts the 'general affection or principle of self-love' (*Sermons*: 1, 25) and the general principle of reflection or conscience. Benevolence Butler seems to count occasionally among the general principles, yet more often he treats it as a particular principle.[5] The distinction between general and particular principles remains notoriously unclear, and Butler offers various ways of characterising the two. In a more extensive passage juxtaposing the general principle of self-love to the particular principles (*Sermons*: 11, 94–5), he points to two central distinctions.

First, the *general* desire for one's happiness has an object which is in some sense 'internal' to the self, and it seeks 'external' objects (or states of affairs) only as a means for happiness. *Particular* principles or desires, by contrast, have 'external' objects, which they seek as ends in themselves. It seems to me that this distinction is best understood as stipulative: there is one and only one internal object, namely the agent's happiness. Butler's point is that we cannot satisfy the general desire for happiness directly, but only by means of the satisfaction of particular principles. This point will play a major role in Butler's famous arguments against the selfish hypothesis in the form of psychological hedonism.

The second feature that distinguishes general and particular principles is that general principles are *reflective*, whereas particular principles are *non-reflective*, according to Butler. Only rational human beings are endowed with the reflective general principles of self-love and conscience. These evaluate and endorse or oppose non-reflective particular principles in view of the agent's true happiness or interest (in the case of self-love), and in view of morality (in the case of conscience). From the point of view of authority, general principles are designed to have a governing function, whereas particular principles are designed to be governed by general ones. General principles might thus be understood as second-order principles, that is, as authoritative volitional structures with first-order principles as their objects.

The general principle of conscience occupies the central position in Butler's moral philosophy. Conscience is characterised as 'a principle of reflection in men, by which they distinguish between, approve and disapprove their own actions' (*Sermons*: 1, 19). Butler encourages the view that conscience motivates actions not directly, but only indirectly by endorsing and stabilising, or by opposing and stopping, particular principles. As in the case of Hutcheson's moral sense, Butler's moral agent cannot prevent her conscience from passing judgement, and in 'all common ordinary cases we see intuitively at first view what is our duty, what is the honest part' (*Sermons*: 7, 65). As mentioned above, conscience is the principle with the highest authority, or with what he terms a 'natural supremacy' (*Sermons*: 2, 32). It exerts its function effectively unless it is 'forcibly stopped' (*Sermons*: 2, 29) by excessively strong principles of lower authority. This is, however, unnatural and a sign of 'wantonness', that is, of being determined by lower principles, which is against divine design (*Sermons*: 2, 32). If an action is in accordance with an agent's self-love, yet in conflict with her conscience, the action is judged 'unnatural'. However, Butler claims that conscience and true self-love always recommend the same actions – a claim we will investigate in greater detail in Chapter 5.2. If due to the supreme moral faculty of conscience, man can be said to be by his nature 'a law unto himself' (*Sermons*, Preface: 10), then self-cultivation must aim at securing the supreme position of conscience as the most authoritative principle, and at being motivated only by the combination of first-order principles that conscience endorses. Conscience furthermore has a role in the discovery of the design of our nature: it is 'pointing out to us in some degree what we are intended for' (*Sermons*: 1, 20).

Among the *particular* principles that make the 'inward frame of man', Butler distinguishes somewhat loosely between appetites, passions and affections. Crucially, and in accordance with his theistic teleological conception of human nature, Butler rejects the generally negative view of these principles put forward by certain versions of Christianity – as well as by certain versions of Stoicism. Particular principles 'no way imply disease: nor indeed do they imply deficiency or imperfection of any sort; but only this, that the constitution of nature according to which God has made us, is such as to require them' (*Sermons*: 5, 48). They pose problems only if they become excessively strong and if they are gratified in opposition to the general principles of conscience or self-love.

Benevolence is crucial to Butler's moral philosophy, as it is to Hutcheson's. In the *Sermons*, Butler puts benevolence at the very centre of his conception of virtue and claims that 'to love our neighbour as ourselves includes in it all virtues' (*Sermons*: 12, 109). Butler more often than not includes benevolence among the particular principles and describes it as 'an affection to the good and happiness of our fellow-creatures' (*Sermons*: 12, 103). Crucially, his argument that there is no conflict between self-love and benevolence (which I will discuss below) depends on the juxtaposition of self-love, a general principle, to benevolence as a particular principle. Sometimes, however, Butler also encourages the interpretation of benevolence as a general principle, for example when he treats particular principles such as compassion and parental affections as proofs of the reality of benevolence in general, or when he contrasts benevolence and self-love jointly with particular principles (*Sermons*: 1, 19). In any case, benevolence is a disinterested or altruistic affection, and it is presented as one of the pillars of virtue in human nature.

The Selfish Hypothesis and the Distinction between Private and Public Particular Principles

Without having properly introduced Butler's conception of self-love, we are already in a position to look at his rejection of two versions of the selfish hypothesis. If Hutcheson distinguishes between disinterested benevolence and self-love generally speaking, Butler distinguishes between public and private *particular* principles. The object of public particular principles, for Butler, is the promotion of the good of others, and it is as natural for human agents to have such public principles as it is to have private principles. The reality of affections and passions such as friendship, familial affections, compassion and pity prove the reality of *public* particular principles, and thus of the claim that we are not merely motivated by *private* particular principles.

One of Butler's most famous arguments for the reality of public particular principles is his rejection of Hobbes's analysis of pity or compassion in terms of a self-interested passion. Butler claims that Hobbes's analysis of pity as an ultimately self-interested concern for one's own well-being does not take into account that 'real sorrow and concern for the misery of our fellow-creatures' which is the core ingredient of pity (*Sermons*: 5, 52). Here emerges a first significant difference between Hutcheson and Butler. For Hutcheson, the rejection of the selfish hypothesis relies on the distinction between self-love (in the conception of self-love as egoistic desire) and benevolence. Demonstrating the reality of the 'benevolent', 'publick' or 'disinterested' passion of pity means refuting the claim that self-love is the only motive for our actions. Butler's argument, however, is expressly concerned with the distinction between public and private *particular* principles, and since he treats self-love as a *general* principle, he does not need to make reference to it at this point. Demonstrating the reality of public particular principles such as pity, compassion, parental affections and benevolence means rejecting the selfish hypothesis in the formulation that we are always motivated by private particular principles.

There is a second important argument by Butler, namely his rejection of psychological *hedonism* (the hedonistic version of psychological egoism), which is one variety of the selfish hypothesis. Psychological hedonism consists essentially in the claim that every human action ultimately aims at procuring pleasure for the agent herself. (Crucially, a refutation of psychological hedonism is not a full refutation of psychological egoism, since the hedonistic egoistic claim that all actions ultimately aim at pleasure for the agent is more specific than the egoistic claim that all actions ultimately aim at some kind of benefit for the agent.) Butler's famous attack on psychological hedonism, in a short passage in *Sermon* 11, has been discussed by an entire series of commentators, and has become known as 'Butler's Stone'.[6] In the context of the aforementioned distinction between internal and external objects, Butler argues that particular desires are directed towards the external objects themselves and not towards the pleasure arising from their gratification:

> That all particular appetites and passions are towards *external things themselves*, distinct from the *pleasure arising from them*, is manifested from hence; that there could not be this pleasure, were it not for that prior suitableness between the object and the passion: there could be no enjoyment or delight from one thing more than another, from eating food more than from swallowing a stone, if there were not an affection or appetite to one thing more than another. (*Sermons*: 11, 94)

In a similar vein to Hutcheson's objection against Locke on uneasiness (Hutcheson, *Essay*: 24, 45; see Chapter 4.1), Butler claims that no particular principle can possibly have as its ultimate object the pleasure that arises from its own gratification.[7] Unless there is a previous desire for some particular external thing (which, for Butler, cannot be pleasure), no pleasure can be gained from 'obtaining' that thing. I shall not assess the strengths and weaknesses of Butler's argument against psychological hedonism, but emphasise again that the argument relies on the notion of private particular principles, and not on what Butler terms 'self-love'. Here, Butler differs from Hutcheson, who attacks both psychological hedonism and psychological egoism by arguing that not only self-interested self-love, but also disinterested benevolence motivate our actions.

5.2 BUTLER ON SELF-LOVE AS RESPECT OF SELF

Butler's conception of self-love differs greatly from those previously analysed – he is the first British thinker to fully elaborate a conception of self-love as respect of self, and on this point he will exert quite some influence on subsequent authors. In this section, I suggest that Butler is best understood as developing a conception of self-love as a second-order affection that reflectively controls the gratification of first-order principles in view of the agent's happiness. Butler remains quite ambiguous in his description of what the 'object' of self-love is. He lists happiness, interest, private good and the self: 'The object of self-love is expressed in the term, self' (*Sermons*: 11, 97). I want to suggest the following interpretation of the connection between self-love, the self and happiness: self-love is a general affection with the agent's 'true' self as its object (that is, the divinely designed self as opposed to the actual existing self). Self-love can be understood as the principle that 'respects' this true self by making its realisation its goal, and it promotes the realisation of one's true self in view of the promotion of the agent's happiness. Happiness is the natural consequence of the realisation of the agent's 'real' self.

In the following central passage, Butler opposes the particular affections to self-love by drawing upon the abovementioned distinction between internal and external objects:

Further, private happiness or good is all which self-love can make us desire, or be concerned about: in having this consists its gratification: it is an affection to ourselves; a regard to our own interest, happiness, and private good: and in the proportion a man hath this, he is interested, or a lover of himself. Let this be kept in mind; because there is commonly, as I shall presently have occasion to observe, another sense put upon these words. On the other hand, particular affections tend towards particular external things: these are their objects: having these is their end: in this consists their gratification: no matter whether it be, or be not, upon the whole, our interest or happiness. An action done from the former of these principles is called an interested action. An action proceeding

> from any of the latter has its denomination of passionate, ambitious, friendly, revengeful, or any other, from the particular appetite or affection from which it proceeds. Thus self-love as one part of human nature, and the several particular principles as the other part, are, themselves, their objects and ends, stated and shewn. (*Sermons*: 11, 95)

Butler is aware of the fact that his terminology differs from common (and, for that matter, Hutchesonian) language – a point to which I shall come back below, especially regarding his use of the adjectives 'interested' and 'disinterested'. He states again that particular principles involve desires for particular external objects or states of affairs. Self-love, on the other hand, even if it makes us desire 'private happiness or good', does not make us desire any particular external objects or states of affairs. Instead it endorses or opposes desires for particular objects in view of the promotion of the agent's happiness (*Sermons*: 11, 94–5). If the agent has a particular private or public desire – say, to eat a sandwich, or to help a child – then self-love endorses or opposes this particular desire in view of the agent's happiness, depending on whether satisfying this particular desire is an appropriate means to promote happiness. Since self-love is a *general* principle, it could not make her desire to eat the sandwich merely for the sake of eating the sandwich, according to Butler. The satisfaction of particular principles provides the agent with pleasure. Still, the gratification of particular principles can be against the true interest of the agent, and prevent her from achieving a state of happiness.

Butler claims that self-love involves a general desire for the agent's happiness. At times, he suggests a specific view of the relation between happiness and the general affection of self-love on the one hand, and the particular principles on the other:

> Happiness consists in the gratification of certain affections, appetites, passions, with objects which are by nature adapted to them. Self-love may indeed set us on work to gratify these: but happiness or enjoyment has no immediate connection with self-love, but arises from such gratifications alone. (*Sermons*: 11, 99)

Here, Butler encourages the view that the satisfaction of the general desire for happiness depends on the satisfaction of particular principles. Without the gratification of particular principles, self-love cannot be gratified either: 'Take away these affections [i.e. the particular principles], and you leave self-love absolutely nothing at all to employ itself about' (*Sermons*, Preface: 12). Self-love promotes happiness indirectly, via the gratification of particular principles – without these latter, it has nothing to exert itself upon. Like conscience, self-love does not directly motivate actions on its own. If Butler occasionally suggests that an action is motivated by self-love, this is best interpreted as an elliptical way of claiming that the action has been motivated by a particular principle endorsed by self-love.[8]

Happiness is not reached by means of the satisfaction of just *any* series of particular principles. Rather, it must be a combination of particular principles that is adapted to the (divinely designed) nature or self of the agent. For example, the combination must respect the hierarchy between the different kinds of principles in that none of the particular principles rises above its natural degree of strength. Butler claims elsewhere in *Sermon* 11: 'Self-love then does not constitute *this* or *that* to be our interest or good; but, our interest or good being constituted by nature and supposed, self-love only puts us upon obtaining and securing it' (*Sermons*: 11, 95). The agent's designed nature constitutes what is in her interest, or – to put it differently – which combination of particular principles is such that their gratification procures happiness for the agent. Indulging in just one kind of particular principle, and neglecting all others, for example, is against the agent's nature and opposes her happiness. The same holds for the unreflective gratification of merely the strongest particular principle. Self-love controls the gratification of the particular principles by endorsing a combination that is appropriate to the agent's nature, the gratification of which will promote her happiness because it respects her real self.

Butler calls self-love a 'reflective' principle. The general desire for one's happiness 'seems inseparable from all sensible creatures, who can reflect upon themselves and their own interest or happiness, so as to have that interest an object to their minds' (*Sermons*: 11, 94). Self-love controls the satisfaction of particular principles in view of the realisation of human nature, and this control is based on reflecting on one's nature and the corresponding interests. Butler's frequent characterisation of self-love as a 'cool' or 'reasonable' principle indicates that self-love controls first-order principles on the basis of reflection on the agent's interests, which is different from a blind following of one's selfish instincts. Butler's self-love must thus not be mistaken for a self-interested particular or first-order principle, the satisfaction of which is not guided by reflection and could turn out to be in conflict with the agent's true interest. Even if such a principle were gratified and would provide pleasure, it would fail to promote the agent's happiness. Again, happiness does not consist in the experience of just any kind of pleasure, but is based on the pleasures that stem from the gratification of a combination of first-order principles that is in accordance with the agent's nature, or adapted to her divinely designed self.

One of the core features of Butlerian self-love is captured in the idea that it is a second-order concern to be motivated by a combination of particular principles that promotes one's happiness. In this sense, Butlerian self-love can be qualified as 'egoistic' – but it is strongly linked with benevolence and other public principles. Benevolence is a part of human nature, and unless benevolence is in conflict with the agent's true self (for example, because it leads to the agent's self-destruction), self-love endorses benevolence. Butler writes about his contemporaries' tendency to conceive of self-love as bringing about a conflict with other-directed principles that 'such positive exclusion, or bringing this peculiar disregard to the good of others into the idea of self-love, is in reality adding to the idea, or changing it from what it was before stated to consist in, namely, in an affection to ourselves' (*Sermons*: 11, 97).[9] We will take a closer look at this point when discussing Butler's claims about the relation between self-love and benevolence below, and compare it to Hutcheson's claims.

Given these features, self-love in Butler may rightly be called self-love as respect of self – especially given Butler's own statement that it is the part in human nature 'which respects *self*' (*Sermons*: 1, 22). A Butlerian agent who loves herself in the right way has a conception of her real self, of her divinely designed nature. She evaluates this self positively, and 'respects' it in the sense of having a regard for her own real interests, accepting her true nature as a guide for decisions about endorsing or opposing first-order principles. The Butlerian lover of self is concerned about the realisation of her true self during the course of her life. She respects the hierarchy of authority between the different principles that are part of her nature; she cultivates these principles to have them in their natural degree; and she is concerned about being motivated by a combination of first-order principles that is suitable to her nature. Here, we might see a strong similarity between Butler's self-love and Aristotle's recommended kind of φιλαυτία, which is also based on a conception of the self as a hierarchical structure. In sum, Butler has a strikingly positive account of self-love, which is part of a very positive view of human nature in general.

By analogy with his treatment of particular principles, Butler suggests that the general affection of self-love can take different degrees. We saw at the beginning of this chapter that, in his opinion, self-love is in general too weak rather than too strong:

> Neither does there appear any reason to wish self-love were weaker in the generality of the world than it is [. . .] The thing to be lamented is, not that men have so great regard to their own good or interest in the present world, for they have not enough; but that they have so little to the good of others. (*Sermons*, Preface: 13–14)

And elsewhere he claims that 'Upon the whole, if the generality of mankind were to cultivate within themselves the principle of self-love [. . .] it would manifestly prevent numberless follies and vices' (*Sermons*, Preface: 14). If we read these passages with the dominant eighteenth-century conceptions of self-love as some kind of self-interested first-order affection or passion in mind, they sound rather puzzling. Yet given Butler's concept of self-love as respect of self, they are perfectly compatible with his attacks on the selfish hypothesis in its different forms, and they emphasise his positive account of self-love as one part of the 'inward frame of man'. What Butler sees as a problem is not that human beings love themselves too much, in the sense that they have too much regard for their real nature and for the interests that are constituted by it. Self-love in Butler's sense is often too weak in that human agents have too little regard for their true interest – for example, if they do not reflectively control the gratification of their first-order principles in view of what is appropriate to their real nature. For Butler, as opposed to Hutcheson, it is not a paradox to say that having too strong first-order self-directed principles is to have too weak self-love. Our interpretation of Butler's concept of self-love in terms of a second-order affection allows us to understand his remarks in the appropriate way.

Towards the end of the *Preface*, Butler refers to a passage in *Sermon* I which states that 'men in fact as much and as often contradict that *part* of their nature which respects *self*, and which leads them to their *own private* good and happiness; as they contradict that *part* of it which respects *society*, and tends to *public* good' (*Sermons*: I, 22). To contradict the 'part of nature which respects self' is to be motivated by a combination of first-order principles, the gratification of which is 'against our nature', and thus not in our true interest. If an agent is thus motivated, her self-love is too weak, since it does not prevent the excessive first-order principle from motivating action. Interestingly, however, Butler also states that self-love can be *too strong*, but this has a different meaning than in Hutcheson:

> So that if self-love wholly engrosses us, and leaves no room for any other principle, there can be absolutely no such thing at all as happiness, or enjoyment of any kind whatever; since happiness consists in the gratification of particular passions, which supposes the having of them. (*Sermons*: II, 95)

Butler does not think of the case of too violent self-interested first-order principles. Rather, he thinks of the hypothetical case of an agent who focuses all her attention on reflecting upon her interest or happiness, and who thus wholly neglects the satisfaction of first-order principles – benevolent as well as self-interested ones. Since happiness can only be gained by means of the (reflectively controlled) gratification of first-order principles, the agent who only reflects on how to promote her happiness, and who only intends to satisfy her self-love as respect of self, has a problem: if for all this she does not gratify any of her first-order principles, she cannot gain happiness. Her self-love as respect of self is too strong.[10] Compare this with Hutcheson, who relies on a hedonistic concept of self-love: this is said to be too strong if the satisfaction of self-interested first-order desires is given more weight than the satisfaction of benevolent first-order desires. If Butler's self-love as respect of self is said to be too strong, however, the gratification of *both* self-directed and benevolent first-order principles is rendered impossible.

For Butler, thus,

> *Disengagement* is absolutely necessary to enjoyment; and a person may have so steady and fixed an eye upon his own interest, whatever he places it in, as may hinder him from *attending* to many gratifications within his reach, which others have their minds *free* and *open* to. (*Sermons*: 11, 95–6)

Self-love as respect of self is too strong if it keeps the agent from gratifying particular principles – self-directed *and* benevolent ones. It is on this basis that Butler gives a negative answer to the question of 'whether private interest is likely to be promoted in proportion to the degree in which self-love engrosses us, and prevails over all other principles' (*Sermons*: 11, 93).

5.3 A COMPARISON BETWEEN BUTLER AND HUTCHESON ON SELF-LOVE

In this section, I want to compare some of Butler's claims regarding self-love with some of Hutcheson's. Surprisingly, such comparisons have rarely been made. Again, this is a problem with philosophers: in some important philosophical monographs on Butler, for example, Hutcheson is not mentioned at all, and there is a widespread tendency to reconstruct Butler's arguments in almost complete isolation from their eighteenth-century context. Intellectual historians and philosophical commentators working on Hutcheson more often highlight the influence of Butler's concepts of conscience and benevolence on the development of Hutcheson's thought, yet a proper comparison of their approaches to self-love is often missing. However, the differences in their conceptions of self-love can be demonstrated to have fascinating consequences for our understanding of claims that Butler and Hutcheson seem to defend together, for example the claim that benevolence cannot be reduced to self-love, or the claim that self-love is not the sole motive for human actions. Here, the problems of interpreting eighteenth-century debates on self-love within a framework based on our present-day notion of egoism appear most strikingly.

On the Relation between Self-love and Benevolence

Butler's claims concerning the relation between self-love and benevolence have attracted a good deal of attention from commentators.[11] In light of my previous remarks on Butler's concept of self-love, it is particularly interesting to investigate these claims and to compare them with Hutcheson's account of the relation between self-love and benevolence. At the beginning of *Sermon* 11, *Upon the Love of Our Neighbour*, Butler states that

> there is generally thought to be some peculiar kind of contrariety between self-love and the love of our neighbour, between the pursuit of public good and of private good; insomuch that when you are recommending one of these, you are supposed to be speaking against the other; and from hence arises a secret prejudice against, and frequently open scorn of all talk of public spirit, and real goodwill to our fellow-creatures. (*Sermons*: 11, 93)

Butler notices that the prevailing opinion among his contemporaries is that the principles of self-love and benevolence are 'contrary' to one another – supposedly, they mutually exclude one another's satisfaction and cannot be pursued together. Note that Hutcheson claims that self-love and benevolence can be gratified together, even if his treatment of self-love (as egoistic desire) in the moral mathematics is critical. We have also seen that for Mandeville, human nature is dominated by self-liking (self-love as *amour-propre*) and other kinds of self-love, which makes genuinely disinterested benevolence rare or even impossible.

Alongside Hutcheson, Butler declares that the view that there is a contrariety between self-love and benevolence is not only false but also dangerous: it puts benevolence in an unfavourable light, which might negatively affect our cultivation of it. Therefore, Butler argues against the supposed contrariety between self-love (as respect of self) and benevolence. He writes in the *Preface* that

> whoever will consider all the possible respects and relations which any particular affection can have to self-love and private interest, will, I think, see demonstrably, that benevolence is not in any respect more at

variance with self-love, than any other particular affection whatever, but that it is in every respect, at least, as friendly to it.

If the observation be true, it follows, that self-love and benevolence, virtue and interest are not opposed, but only to be distinguished from each other; in the same way as virtue and any other particular affection, love of arts, suppose, are to be distinguished. (*Sermons*, Preface: 13)

How does Butler argue for the claim that self-love and benevolence are not opposed? Self-love and benevolence are obviously two distinct principles. Yet this implies neither that they mutually exclude one another's gratification, nor that the agent would always have to choose between following either private or public interest. In the two *Sermons* entitled *Upon the Love of Our Neighbour* (*Sermons* 11 and 12), Butler spells out his earlier claim that 'the greatest satisfactions to ourselves depend upon our having benevolence in a due degree' (*Sermons*: 1, 19). Butler's main point here is the characterisation of self-love (as respect of self) in terms of a second-order affection. If benevolence is a first-order affection (and in *Sermon* 11 he clearly presents it this way), then there is no 'contrariety' between self-love and benevolence in the sense that they could not be gratified together. Benevolence is a natural first-order affection. In view of the realisation of the agent's true self, self-love thus naturally endorses benevolent character traits, affections and actions. There might be rare occasions on which self-love has to oppose the gratification of benevolence – for example, if a public passion such as pity engenders the risk of self-destruction. These occasions, however, are rare and in no way justify the general claim that self-love and benevolence are in conflict.

The question of the relation between self-love and benevolence reflects the differences between Butler's and Hutcheson's moral psychologies. On the surface, both claim that self-love and benevolence are *not* necessarily in conflict and can indeed be satisfied together, yet their arguments for this point differ. In Hutcheson, self-love and benevolence, which are presented as first-order principles with different scopes, emotional attributes and degrees of reflection, are distinguished from each other according to their objects. The object of Hutchesonian hedonistic egoistic self-love is the agent's experience of natural good, namely of different kinds of pleasure, and the object of benevolence is the promotion of the good of others. Self-love he calls the 'interested' principle, and benevolence the 'disinterested' principle, a terminological point that I will discuss in the next subsection. Again, for Hutcheson self-love and benevolence can be said to be in conflict in situations in which they cannot be gratified together (for example, if benevolence appears very costly). Yet there are other situations in which both direct the agent to the same action (for example, if benevolence can be expected to be immediately rewarded by bystanders' applause, or later by the moral pleasures of self-approbation). Self-cultivation can make us see more clearly the advantages of benevolence. Even in cases where the agent cannot directly gratify her self-love by acting benevolently, she can see that she will still be able to derive some natural good for herself, as a consequence of having acted for the well-being of others. In this sense, thanks to providential design, self-love and benevolence converge even in cases where benevolence may require, at first, acting against self-love.

Butler's discussion of the relation between self-love and benevolence is based on his conception of self-love as respect of self. Self-love is charged with the reflectively controlled satisfaction of first-order desires in view of one's happiness. As a second-order principle, self-love has to assure that both private self-directed *and* public other-directed first-order principles (which correspond to Hutchesonian self-love and benevolence) are duly gratified. Butlerian self-love is thus neither opposed to natural first-order self-interested principles, nor to natural first-order benevolent principles (under the condition that they occur in their natural degree). Therefore, self-love (as respect of self) and benevolence in their natural degree cannot be in conflict. Rather, since benevolence is generally endorsed by self-love as a natural principle that accords with the agent's true self, they are generally gratified together.

'Interestedness' and 'Disinterestedness'

Butler's treatment of self-love has far-reaching consequences for his understanding of the widespread distinction between 'interestedness' and 'disinterestedness'.[12] Butler ties the notion of 'interested action' to his concept of self-love: 'An action done from the former of these principles [i.e. self-love] is called an interested action' (*Sermons*: 11, 95). I have argued above that this means that the action is motivated by a combination of first-order principles endorsed by the second-order principle of self-love. The first-order principles in play can be both egoistic and altruistic.

Again, on a superficial reading, Butler's claim that an action is interested if it is done from self-love seems to be supported also by Hutcheson. However, given Butler's conception of self-love as respect of self, we need to reconsider this point. In Hutcheson, an action is labelled 'interested' if and only if it is motivated by self-love in the sense of a desire for pleasure for the agent. An action that is interested in this sense can turn out to be contrary to the true interest of an agent, for example when it turns out that it renders the gratification of some more important, long-term interest impossible, or that it is based on an incorrect representation of the relevant state of affairs and leads to the agent's misery. Nonetheless, the action is said to be 'interested' since it aims at pleasure for the agent. Interested actions differ from disinterested actions in that the latter ultimately aim at promoting the well-being of other agents. We have seen several arguments in Hutcheson for the claim that the agent has good self-interested reasons to perform disinterested benevolent actions, since these have as their consequence the moral pleasures of self-approbation, which are the highest pleasures we can experience.

Butler, on the other hand, neither claims that all actions motivated by first-order self-interested desires are 'interested' (in the sense of being endorsed by self-love as respect of self), nor that all actions motivated by first-order other-directed desires are 'disinterested'. Compassion and benevolence, for example, are said to be 'interested' only if endorsed by self-love (as respect of self). Furthermore, Butler argues – only apparently in contradiction to Hutcheson – that it is absurd to speak of virtue as 'disinterested' (*Sermons*: 11, 97). Self-love as respect for the divinely designed self clearly supports the virtuous way of life, for Butler. Thus, there are actions that are motivated by first-order self-interested principles, but that cannot be called 'interested', since they are not endorsed by the reflective principle of self-love. Also, actions that are motivated by other-directed first-order principles are not necessarily 'disinterested', since they can be endorsed by self-love. Both points conflict with Hutcheson's terminology.

This background explains the following remark by Butler:

Hence arises that surprising confusion and perplexity in the Epicureans of old, Hobbes, the author of *Reflexions, Sentences, et Maximes Morales*, and this whole set of writers; the confusion of calling actions interested which are done in contradiction to the most manifest known interest, merely for the gratification of a present passion. Now all this confusion might easily be avoided, by stating to ourselves wherein the idea of self-love in general consists, as distinguished from all particular movements towards particular external objects; the appetites of sense, resentment, compassion, curiosity, ambition and the rest. (*Sermons*, Preface: 12)

Explicitly against Hobbes and La Rochefoucauld, but possibly also against Hutcheson and his terminology (rather than against Hutcheson's claims), Butler holds that an action deserves to be called 'interested' if and only if it is endorsed by the reflective higher-order principle of self-love. Actions merely motivated by selfish first-order desires can be in conflict with the agent's true interest.

As to the concept of disinterestedness, Butler remains rather vague, connecting 'disinterested' with 'not interested'.[13] While arguing in *Sermon* 11 that there is no 'peculiar contrariety' between self-love and benevolence, since the former is a second-order affection and the latter is a first-order affection, he states that

> every appetite of sense, and every particular affection of the heart, are equally interested or disinterested, because the objects of them all are equally self or somewhat else [. . .] The most intelligible way of speaking of it seems to be this: that self-love, and the actions done in consequence of it [. . .] are interested; that particular affections towards external objects, and the actions done in consequence of those affections, are not so. (*Sermons*: 11, 97)

Butler seems to suggest that actions are 'disinterested' or 'not interested' if they are motivated by first-order principles without the endorsement of self-love as respect of self. In Hutcheson, by contrast, the distinction between interestedness and disinterestedness concerns the question of whether first-order principles aim at promoting the good of the agent herself or the good of others.

Butler's terminology thus has interesting consequences for his arguments against the selfish hypothesis. In Hutcheson, the claim that self-love as egoistic desire is not the only motive of human actions contains a rejection of the selfish hypothesis. Hutcheson argues for its falsity by arguing for the reality of benevolence, or of 'disinterested' first-order motives. When Butler asserts that self-love as respect of self, which is a second-order principle, cannot be the only motive for human actions, this does not contain a rejection of the selfish hypothesis, which concerns first-order affections and passions. Against Butler, the psychological egoist could still argue that human agents are motivated only by self-directed or egoistic *first*-order desires, whether or not they are endorsed by second-order self-love. The situation is similar in Butler's use of the terms 'interestedness' and 'disinterestedness'. When Butler argues that there are other than 'interested' principles of action, this does not imply an assertion of the reality of first-order other-directed principles – rather, it implies the assertion that there must be some instances of first-order principles of action, egoistic *or* altruistic. Butler, like Hutcheson, attacks the selfish hypothesis when he claims that there are not only first-order particular principles that aim at the private good, but also first-order particular principles that aim at the *public* good (such as benevolence, friendship, parental affections and pity).

The Convergence of Conscience and Self-love

Butler insists regularly that self-love and conscience, both of which are second-order reflective principles, 'always lead us the same way' (*Sermons*: 3, 36). This claim is best taken to mean that they ultimately endorse the same combination of first-order principles. Self-love does so in view of their conduciveness to the agent's happiness, conscience does so in view of their moral rightness, and divine design assures that they ultimately coincide. Butler depicts the relation between self-love and conscience as follows:

> Reasonable self-love and conscience are the chief or superior principles in the nature of man: because an action may be suitable to this nature, though all other principles be violated; but becomes unsuitable, if either of those are. Conscience and self-love, if we understand our true happiness, always lead us the same way. Duty and interest are perfectly coincident; for the most part in this world, but entirely and in every instance, if we take in the future, and the whole; this being implied in the notion of a good and perfect administration of things. (*Sermons*: 3, 36)

In what sense do self-love and conscience converge? Or, in other words, why is it in the agent's interest to be virtuous? Consider again that, for Butler, the agent's interest is constituted by her divinely designed nature. Only a combination of principles that is adapted to this nature will promote the agent's true happiness. Self-love's function, then, is to secure the agent's happiness by endorsing an appropriate combination of principles. Following one's nature in this sense promotes the agent's interest. Now, to follow one's nature means also to respect the supreme authority of conscience. Since the agent's self-love prompts her to follow her nature in order to gain happiness, self-love (indirectly) prompts the agent to respect the authority of conscience and to live the virtuous life. We might say that self-love recommends indirectly what conscience recommends directly. Ultimately, divine design guarantees that there is a convergence between true self-love (as opposed to erroneous self-love that does not aim at true happiness) and conscience. The fact that they lead us in the same way has its roots in the design of human nature. In spite of occasional *apparent* conflicts between self-love and conscience, if we consider the future state, for Butler, they 'entirely and in every instance' coincide (*Sermons*: 3, 36).

I have argued above that, for Hutcheson, the agent has self-interested reasons to be virtuous because this provides her with the highest pleasures she can experience. The proper obligation of virtue, however, lies in the moral sense's approval of benevolence and not in the pleasure that can be gained from it – a fact he explains again as rooted in divine design. Butler gives a more directly theistic teleological argument for the claim that it is in the interest of the agent to be virtuous: it is in the design of her nature to follow the supreme principle of conscience, even if it is also true that being virtuous provides the agent with happiness. In a similar vein, Butler specifies in the *Preface* to the *Sermons* against Shaftesbury that the obligation to virtue does not lie in the happiness that virtue provides the agent, but in conscience's authority. 'For the natural authority of the principle of reflection, is an obligation the most near and intimate, the most certain and known' (*Sermons*, Preface: 9).

5.4 THE INFLUENCE OF BUTLER'S CONCEPTION OF SELF-LOVE AS RESPECT OF SELF

In the previous sections, I have shown how Butler's conception of self-love as respect of self differs from other widespread conceptions of self-love, especially the conceptions of self-love as egoistic desire and as *amour-propre*. Comparing Hutcheson and Butler has allowed us to highlight various points that were already considered by eighteenth-century thinkers. Over the course of the century, Butler's conception of self-love as respect of self was less widespread than the conception of egoistic self-love, yet several authors relied on his contributions to the debates on self-love, most prominently Henry Home, Lord Kames, and Thomas Reid, on whom I shall say something in Chapter 7. But there is evidence also that Hutcheson considered Butler's notion of self-love very carefully.

Hutcheson's *System of Moral Philosophy* was published in 1755, but most likely drafted in the 1730s for the purposes of university teaching. In Book 1, Chapter III, Hutcheson shows interest in the Butlerian idea of self-love as a second-order principle. The chapter is entitled *Concerning the Ultimate Determinations of the Will, and Benevolent Affections* (Hutcheson, *System*: 38), and it deals, roughly, with questions concerning self-love and benevolence as the two 'leading' principles of action. As elsewhere in his writings, Hutcheson rejects the selfish hypothesis by defending the reality of disinterested benevolence. However, there is an interesting additional discussion that shows his reflection on Butler's conception of self-love as respect of self. The point Hutcheson now treats as central is not the general question whether we are ever motivated by disinterested benevolence, but the more specific question whether there is something like an 'original calm determination toward a public interest' (*System*: 50–1) which would be distinct from a 'calm general determination toward personal happiness of the highest kind' (*System*: 50). In other words, Hutcheson specifically juxtaposes calm universal benevolence and calm universal self-love, and not benevolence and self-love in general.

Hutcheson lists several versions of the selfish hypothesis and discusses how they account for our motives for virtuous actions. Following his hierarchy of the pleasures, he mentions 'worldly advantage' and bodily pleasures; personal safety and prosperity; the pleasures of sympathy; and the 'pleasures we enjoy in being honoured' (*System*: 39) for our virtuous actions. All these answers reduce our motives for virtuous action to some kind of self-interested desire. Hutcheson then introduces yet another answer, which is different from the selfish hypotheses:

> But there is still an higher scheme; allowing indeed no other calm setled determination of soul but that in each one toward his own happiness; but granting that we have a *moral faculty*, and many particular kind affections truly disinterested, terminating upon the happiness of others, and often operating when we have no reference of it in our minds to any enjoyment of our own. (*System*: 39–40)

According to this 'higher scheme', there are indeed 'particular', that is, first-order benevolent affections – the 'higher scheme' is thus *not* a version of the selfish hypothesis properly speaking. However, this new theory only allows for a '*calm selfish determination*' on a second-order level. Accordingly, all attempts to *cultivate* benevolent first-order affections would be motivated by the desire to 'experience the sublimest joys of self-approbation in gratifying these generous motions' (*System*: 40), which are first-order benevolent affections. Hutcheson himself insists, however, on the reality of an 'original calm determination toward a publick interest', connected to our moral faculty and to a desire for moral excellence (*System*: 51).

The idea raised by Hutcheson is interesting for several reasons. First, because in some sense Hutcheson himself prepared this, say, 'meta-egoistic' point by presenting an elaborate account of a hierarchy of the pleasures, according to which the moral pleasures are classified as the highest possible. Secondly, Hutcheson's idea is a reflection of his interest in Butler's treatment of self-love and benevolence. I have argued above that Butler presents self-love as something very different from first-order self-interested affections, arguing that self-love (as respect of self) is not contrary to benevolence (because self-love is a second-order principle, and benevolence a first-order one), and that it is not possible for us to be motivated by self-love only (since self-love, as a second-order principle, does not motivate actions directly). In his discussion in the *System*, Hutcheson thus takes very seriously Butler's conception of self-love as a second-order principle, and he uses it to answer a potential objection to his own claim that there is a calm benevolence of a higher order. This is, of course, not Butler's objection, but it is one that presupposes an understanding of self-love in terms of Butler's self-love as respect of self.

Hutcheson does not make explicit whom he may have had in mind as a potential adherent to this 'higher scheme' position, but two sources writing on his *System* clearly point at Shaftesbury: William Leechman, in his *Preface* to the *System*, and Hugh Blair in his *Review* of Hutcheson's *System*.[14] Blair raises the following question: 'For what reason we ought to pursue virtue, and to cultivate the friendly and benevolent affections, rather than the selfish?' (Blair 1755: 14). According to Blair, Shaftesbury insists on the fact that virtue is the chief happiness, and there sees our *only* obligation for virtue.[15] Hutcheson, however, would have thought that

> the desire of our own happiness is not the supreme principle in the soul. But, independent of this, and independent of all particular affections, there is a calm desire of the happiness of all rational beings, which is not only co-ordinate with, but even of superior authority to, the desire of our own happiness. (Blair 1755: 14)

To be fair, there are different possible interpretations of Shaftesbury, who, like Hutcheson and Butler themselves, insists on the natural advantages of virtue. Blair insists on the interpretation that, for Shaftesbury, personal happiness is the only source of moral obligation. However, Gill points out that we can also find a teleological account of moral obligation in Shaftesbury, according to which 'virtue is the end or telos for which [humans] were designed' (Gill 2006: 118). Given the providential ordering of the universe, being virtuous will *also* make humans happy, but the reason we have for being virtuous, according to this account, is that it is in the design of our nature.[16] If this is a plausible interpretation, at least of certain passages in Shaftesbury, then the difference between Hutcheson and Shaftesbury is smaller than admitted by Blair, Leechman and Hutcheson himself. Without attempting to settle the question here, I want to highlight that the structural features and the language with which Blair frames the opposition between Shaftesbury and Hutcheson is strongly reminiscent of Butler's discussion of self-love and conscience as superior principles, with conscience bearing the highest authority. Butler here clearly encouraged reframing some of the problems that continued to occupy eighteenth-century thinkers.

5.5 CONCLUSION

I started this chapter with Butler's claim that there is no 'reason to wish self-love were weaker in the generality of the world, than it is' (*Sermons*, Preface: 13). By now, it is clear how this is to be understood. For Butler, 'self-love' means respect of self, that is a second-order affection with the agent's divinely designed, true self as its object. Aiming at happiness, self-love endorses a combination of particular principles suited to realising this self. Since we are providentially equipped with private affections and passions (Hutcheson's 'self-love' in the sense of egoistic desires, which are particular principles in Butler's sense), and with public affections and passions (Hutcheson's 'benevolence' – again particular principles in Butler's sense), the general principle of self-love as respect of self will endorse the gratification of both. When reconstructing Butler's arguments, it is crucial to note that some of his most famous attacks on the selfish hypothesis (or, in present-day terminology, 'psychological egoism' and 'psychological hedonism') are *not* based on what Butler calls 'self-love' (namely self-love as respect of self), but on his distinction between private and public particular principles.

In comparison to other contributors to the debates on self-love, most notably Hutcheson, Butler's claims are based on a strikingly positive conception of self-love, which in some respects comes close to Aristotle's commendable form of φιλαυτία. This explains the claim quoted at the beginning of this chapter, as well as a series of other points that might surprise us when we think of the central claims regarding self-love in Hutchesonian terms. What Butler terms 'self-love' is not in conflict with benevolence because self-love is a second-order and benevolence a first-order principle. This argument is very different from Hutcheson's point that, under certain circumstances, self-love can come as a support to benevolence. If Butler claims that self-love (as respect of self) cannot and should not be the sole principle in human nature, this is not because as a matter of fact benevolence is a real motive in human nature (as Hutcheson would argue), but because if self-love as a second-order principle were the only principle in human nature, we could not perform any actions at all, neither altruistic nor egoistic. Butler's claim that virtue is not disinterested, then, is in some sense not simply an attack on Hutcheson's claim that virtue is based on disinterested benevolence, but rather an assertion that self-love as respect of self will support the cultivation of benevolent principles, because they are part of human nature as designed by God. Such points highlight once more that Butler's arguments on self-love need to be carefully analysed: in contrast to Hutcheson's case, most of Butler's arguments about what he terms 'self-love' are not arguments concerning what we call 'egoism' today. Trying to reconstruct Butler's arguments with our present-day broad category of egoism makes us blind to many of their finer points.

Butler's conception of self-love as respect of self left its traces in the subsequent eighteenth century. I have already pointed out how in Hutcheson's *System* we find a reflection of Butler's conception of self-love. In Chapter 7, I shall add some more remarks on Thomas Reid's and Dugald Stewart's conceptions of self-love, which were heavily influenced by Butler's conception of self-love as respect of self. Here, I want to end with a brief remark on Henry Home, Lord Kames. Home discusses Jean-Baptiste Dubos's and Locke's theories of motivation in his *Essays on the Principles of Morality and Natural Religion* (1751) in the wider context of explaining our enjoyment of representations of the misery of others in tragedies – a point on which Dubos famously referred to our self-interested desire to avoid *ennui*, or a state of emotional inactivity (Dubos 1770: 10). To counter this explanation, Home relies on Butler's distinction between general and particular principles of action, and attacks Locke and Dubos, who 'acknowledge no motive to action, but what arises from self-love; measures laid down to attain pleasure, or to shun pain' (Home 2005: 16). For Home, by contrast, 'self-love operates by means of reflection and experience' (2005: 15). Since this is not the case with our appetites and passions, and since we are clearly 'more frequently influenced by these than by self-love' (2005: 16), the claim that we are only motivated by self-love must be false. Home then continues to argue that compassion and sympathy are further important ingredients of human nature, and that they must figure in an explanation of our enjoyments of tragic representations of others' misery. Crucially for the present study, we see Home resting his case on Butler's rather than on Hutcheson's conception of self-love, which is only one evidence for the impact of Butler's ideas.

NOTES

1. For more biographical information on Butler, see especially Tennant (2011).
2. Darwall (1995: 244–83), Irwin (2008: 507–57) and Heydt (2018) offer analyses of Butler which are more comparative. For introductions to Butler's philosophy, see Duncan-Jones (1952), Broad (1971), Roberts (1973), Penelhum (1985) and Garrett (2012). There are a number of interesting studies by analytically minded historians of philosophy on topics related to the debates on self-love, for example Sturgeon (1976), Millar (1988; 1992), Henson (1988), Sober (1992), Phillips (2000) and Tilley (2018).

3. See Millar (1988), Darwall (1995), Gill (2006: 178–9) and Irwin (2008: 476–88) for more extensive discussions of the expression 'following nature' in Butler.

4. Butler's notion of conscience and his arguments for its authority have attracted a lot of attention from commentators. See, for example, Duncan-Jones (1952), Sturgeon (1976), Darwall (1995) and Garrett (2012).

5. On the relation between self-love and benevolence in Butler, see, for example, Frey (1992) and Garrett (2012).

6. See especially Duncan-Jones (1952: 95ff.), Penelhum (1985: 50ff.), Henson (1988) and Sober (1992).

7. Sober (1992: 99–100) points out that the universal claim that *no* particular principle can have pleasure as its object is not really supported by Butler's claims.

8. Here I suggest a different interpretation from Phillips (2000: 425).

9. This point might be directed against Mandeville, but Butler might also be thinking of Hutcheson's occasional tendency to treat (egoistic) self-love and (altruistic) benevolence as opposed principles, for example in the moral mathematics. I have argued, however, that in Hutcheson's theory of self-cultivation, the emphasis is on the fact that calm egoistic self-love can support benevolence.

10. Butler also claims that self-love as respect of self *cannot* be our only motive. Henson points out that what is shown here is rather that 'if self-love *is* one's only motive it can never be gratified' (Henson 1988: 38). Crucially, refuting the claim that Butlerian self-love is the only motive is *not* a refutation of psychological egoism, since the latter is a claim about first-order principles, not second-order principles.

11. See, for example, Duncan-Jones (1952: 112–13), Henson (1988: 41–2, 51–2), McNaughton (1996: 216–17) and Penelhum (1985: 47–8).

12. See also Scott-Taggart (1968), Phillips (2000) and Maurer (2006).

13. See also Scott-Taggart (1968).

14. See also the discussion in Grote (2006).

15. This is also the interpretation of Shaftesbury adopted in Leechman (1755: xlv) and in Butler (*Sermons*, Preface: 9).

16. Gill discusses the differences between these two accounts with regard to the question of extreme scepticism about morals (2006: 123–32).

6. Campbell on True Self-love and Virtue

In the *Preface* to his *Enquiry into the Original of Moral Virtue* (1733), Archibald Campbell (1691–1756) writes that Hutcheson and others 'make the Virtue of moral Actions to depend entirely on their arising from a *mere Instinct* in our Nature, that leads us to promote the Happiness of other Beings, without our being at all mov'd to it by any secret Impulse of Self-interest' (Campbell, *Enquiry*: ii). Campbell may here downplay Hutcheson's elaborate account of the pleasures of virtue and self-cultivation, in which reflection plays a significant role. Campbell wants to prove that we have an interest in being virtuous, and that this can be rationally demonstrated within the psychological framework of the selfish hypothesis, putting self-love at the centre both of his moral psychology and his moral theory. From this perspective, the theories of Hutcheson and Campbell appear fundamentally different: Hutcheson is probably one of the strongest opponents of the selfish hypothesis, and Campbell one of its strongest defenders. However, their differences appear considerably smaller once we shift attention to the question of the moral status of postlapsarian human nature. The conservatively orthodox Calvinist Committee for Purity of Doctrine was well aware of Campbell's very positive view of humankind's natural tendencies to virtue. At this point we should recall that Hutcheson and Campbell were both students of the theologian John Simson (1667–1740), who was condemned for several heresies in 1717 and 1727. Considering the general emphasis on benevolence and sociability in the mainstream of Scottish Enlightenment moral philosophy, Campbell's 546-page treatise defending the selfish hypothesis appears, at first glance, to be rather awkward. However, a second and broader consideration must take in his optimistic anthropology, along with the fact that many English philosophers, for example John Gay, John Clarke of Hull, David Hartley, Joseph Tucker and Joseph Priestley, also adopted the selfish hypothesis.

The works of Archibald Campbell have received almost no attention from historians of philosophy, and little attention from intellectual historians. Campbell studied in Edinburgh, and then in Glasgow with Simson. After Simson's condemnation for heresy, they continued their friendly relationship, as various letters demonstrate. Campbell's treatise on self-love was first published in 1728 in a plagiarised edition by the Scotsman Alexander Innes in London under the title of *Aretê-Logia*. Some remarks at the beginning of Mandeville's second volume of *The Fable of the Bees* show his awareness of Campbell's work, then still attributed to Innes (Mandeville, *Fable II*: 23–8). In 1731 Campbell was appointed Regius Professor of divinity and church history at the University of St Andrews. His publications on various theological and philosophical issues caused tensions with the Committee for Purity of Doctrine of the Church of Scotland, leading to a fascinating episode that lasted from 1735 to 1736, during which Campbell had to defend himself against various charges of heresy.

Campbell presents his *Enquiry* as a rejection of both Mandeville's *and* Hutcheson's moral philosophies. To understand and assess this move, it is essential to investigate which aspects of Mandeville's and Hutcheson's moral philosophies Campbell rejected, and which he accepted. Campbell is not a philosopher with the systematic capacities of Hume, Smith or Reid, and his writings often suffer from imprecisions, repetitions and ambiguities. However, his contributions to the debates on self-love, especially when considered in the context of Hutcheson's and Mandeville's writings, and in light of the reactions to Campbell by the Committee for Purity of Doctrine, reveal crucial facets of the intellectual atmosphere in the first half of the eighteenth century. This draws our attention to the theological background of the debates and to hitherto overlooked aspects of them.

6.1 CAMPBELL ON SELF-LOVE, THE SELFISH HYPOTHESIS AND SOCIABILITY

Campbell's *Enquiry* is marked by frequent assertions of the selfish hypothesis. For Campbell, self-love is the motive for all our actions, and he wants to build a moral philosophy entirely on this one principle. At first glance, one might think that this puts him in proximity to Mandeville and Hobbes, and at a distance from Hutcheson, yet I shall argue that ultimately it is rather the opposite – Campbell is closer to

Hutcheson than one might think, and Hutcheson's condensed historiography is quite misleading (see Chapter 1.3). This teaches us something important about the different roles of the selfish hypothesis, and about the importance of distinguishing different conceptions of self-love. Hume would perceptively comment on this point when distinguishing two versions of the selfish hypothesis (see Chapter 7.1).

Self-love and the Selfish Hypothesis

At the very beginning of the *Enquiry*, in the first *Treatise*, Campbell asserts that

> 'Tis very certain, that all Men have implanted in their Nature a Principle of *Self-love* or Preservation, that irresistibly operates upon us in all Instances whatsoever, and is the great Cause, or the *first Spring* of all our several Motions and Actions, which Way soever they may happen to be directed. (Campbell, *Enquiry*: 4)

Later he writes that 'it is thus evident, that all rational Agents are irresistibly, in all Instances, under the prevailing Power of *Self-love*' (*Enquiry*: 101). 'Self-love' Campbell defines as 'the very same with our *natural Desire after Pleasure or Happiness*' (*Enquiry*: 5), or as an

> original Turn of the Mind, whereby we are made *susceptible* of *Pleasure* and *Pain* [so that] we must necessarily *delight in*, and approve of our having *pleasing Perceptions*, and seek and *pursue* after them; but on the other Hand, *hate Pain* and *avoid* it: Which is what I understand, in general, by *Self-love, Self-preservation*, or *Self-interest*. (*Enquiry*: 274)

In spite of occasional ambiguities (for example, when not clearly distinguishing between self-love and self-preservation), Campbell is best read as sticking to a hedonistic egoistic conception of self-love – like Hutcheson. In contrast to the latter, however, Campbell asserts the selfish hypothesis and insists that self-love is the *sole* principle of action. Like Hutcheson, but unlike the Augustinians, Campbell treats self-love in the first place as a morally neutral motive – it is part of divine design that we seek to procure ourselves pleasure and to avoid pain, thereby naturally preserving ourselves. Note how the resulting picture is different from Mandeville, who strongly emphasises the problematic dimensions of self-liking, that is, self-love as *amour-propre*. Thus, even if Campbell may be said to join Mandeville in asserting the selfish hypothesis, their actual moral psychologies look very different, in spite of Campbell's rejection of Hutcheson's claims about the reality of disinterested benevolence.

At the very beginning of his *Enquiry*, Campbell presents a lengthy translation of Aristotle's discussion in the *Nicomachean Ethics* of the laudable and reproachable forms of φιλαυτία, associating the former with the English 'self-love', the latter with 'selfishness'. Campbell uses Aristotle's authority with the express intention of preventing 'any Prejudices that may arise from introducing *Self-love* as a laudable Principle, in the Business of moral Virtue' (*Enquiry*: 5). Similarly, he warns against 'narrow and contracted Notions of Self-love or Interest' (*Enquiry*: 259). As we shall see later in the reaction of the Committee for Purity of Doctrine, Campbell's sense that there might be a problem with his presentation of self-love as a 'laudable principle' was accurate – this very point led to a confrontation between theological orthodoxy and philosophical innovation. Another point that caused tensions was Campbell's assertion that 'all rational Agents' (*Enquiry*: 101) are under the influence of self-love. Campbell counts God among these rational agents, with the argument that this makes it transparent to us what we should do in order to please him. Again, the Committee would comment on this point in their *Remarks*.

Campbell's most vigorous assertion of the selfish hypothesis is backed by (more or less convincing) attempts to analyse all seemingly benevolent or altruistic motives in terms of ultimately self-interested ones. Especially in the chapter entitled *Treatise II* of the *Enquiry*, which is essentially an attack on Hutcheson's ethics of benevolence, Campbell proposes a series of such analyses – of benevolence in general, pity, parental love, marital love, friendship etc. Benevolence, for Campbell, 'is not *disinterested*, but manifestly springs from *Self-interest*' (*Enquiry*: 351). In a somewhat similar vein to Hume in his *Treatise*, Campbell attacks Hutcheson's argument that there is disinterested benevolence towards rational agents even if we have no social connections with them at all. Campbell argues that 'we always consider them as our *Fellow-men*, or as *intelligent Beings*, like ourselves, susceptible of the same Joys and Sorrows' (*Enquiry*: 347). Only if there is a minimal form of identification, or representation of similarity, can there be any concern for the other, which will take the form, ultimately, of a self-concern. Since it is

> impossible for us not to apprehend the Objects of our Benevolence under some particular *Ideas* or other; so I am well perswaded, that every Man, who attends to what passes in his own Breast, will easily discern, that those *Ideas* in which they appear to us, and whereby our Benevolence towards them is excited, refer directly to *Self-interest*. (*Enquiry*: 367)

It seems that, ultimately, Campbell thinks that this mechanism boils down to the experience of seeing oneself in others who on some account resemble oneself. The agent sees a '*Second-self*, or its own Likeness' (*Enquiry*: 25), and thereby expands the circle of concern and starts to love 'himself in another' (*Enquiry*: 309). In his analysis of parental love, Hutcheson's response to which we have discussed previously (see Chapter 4.1), Campbell writes that 'Parents look upon their Children as *Parts of themselves*, and that 'tis from this View they have of them, that they love them so tenderly as they do' (*Enquiry*: 336). Parental love is based on resemblance, and is a love of oneself in one's child. This is strengthened by the 'sincere Good liking and Friendship' between the parents – friends respect not only the other person, but everything that belongs to her, which includes children (*Enquiry*: 342–3).

Crucially, for Campbell, and in striking contrast to Hutcheson, asserting the selfish hypothesis and analysing the paradigm examples of benevolent affections and passions in terms of self-love does not result in a pessimistic view of human nature as incapable of moral virtue. Against Hutcheson, Campbell makes great efforts to distance his own version of the selfish hypothesis from that of Mandeville, who emphasised the role of deception, flattery and self-delusion. One aspect of this is Campbell's account of sociability.

Natural Sociability and the Selfish Hypothesis

Considering Campbell's attempts to analyse all instances of benevolence as instances of self-love, it may come as a surprise to find him also arguing against Hobbes that we are, indeed, naturally sociable. Campbell tackles the argument in Hobbes's *De Cive*, which was summarised in Chapter 1.3. Hobbes argued against the Aristotelian claim that 'man is a creature born fit for society'. Rather, we are *made* fit for society by education and self-interest (Hobbes 1991: 110), and we seek honour and profit primarily, and companions only secondarily (1991: 111). Glory or honour is, however, a tricky good, the quest for which causes conflicts and undermines the foundations of society. Thus, 'the original of all great and lasting societies consisted not in the mutual good-will [*benevolentia*] men had towards each other, but in the mutual fear [*metus*] they had of each other' (1991: 113). Hutcheson argued, against Hobbes's position, that benevolence is a natural ingredient of human nature, which makes us sociable in a primary, not only a secondary sense. It is indeed companions we seek, not only the possibility of gratifying our desires for honour or pleasure.

Campbell, with a moral psychology built on the principle of self-love as hedonistic egoism, cannot simply follow Hutcheson's attack on Hobbes – he must suggest an argument compatible with the selfish hypothesis. In accordance with virtually every author on the subject of sociability (including Hobbes and, most often, Mandeville), Campbell states that solitude is a problem for the human being. In contrast to authors such as Hobbes and Pufendorf, however, he claims that the reason for this is not our 'imbecility' or our incapacity to survive alone. Rather, it is the fact that there is

> so irresistible a Desire in the Mind of Man to have *Companions* of his own Make, or to *associate* himself with other rational Beings, that all the other Sweets and Enjoyments of Life, even the Contemplation of the Nature of Things, with all the inward Transports of Mind it can afford to us, would without *this* be quite tasteless and insipid. (Campbell, *Enquiry*: 13)

In other words, by divine design there is a deep desire in human beings to associate with other members of their species – a desire that can be satisfied only in society. In allusion to Shaftesbury, Campbell also names this desire 'friendly' and 'natural' affection (*Enquiry*: 15–16), 'Disposition to Society', '*social Appetite*' (*Enquiry*: 17–18), and 'Propension to associate' (*Enquiry*: 14–15). In these passages, he quotes extensively from Cicero, Aristotle, Seneca, Arianus and Marcus Aurelius in his support. Obviously, Campbell understands his claims about our natural social tendencies to be supported by Stoic authors – an understanding that must surprise a reader taking for granted Hutcheson's opposition of the Stoics to the Epicureans based on the criterion of the selfish hypothesis.

But is Campbell's claim that there is a natural desire for society not in conflict with his obsessive assertion of the selfish hypothesis? Would a natural desire for society not be irreducible to self-love? Campbell seems to think that the natural desire for society can be embedded in his egoistic psychology: it is self-love that makes us flee solitude, since we understand that we can gratify the desire for companions in society only (*Enquiry*: 18). It seems that this idea has solved the potential conflict for Campbell.

He then offers a causal explanation for the natural attraction we feel towards other members of our species: it is because of their general similarity with us, because we see a '*Second-self*' (*Enquiry*: 25) in them:

> So far as I can understand Things, it appears to me, that our *first Propension* to Society springs directly from our viewing of one another under the Notion of Men, or as Individuals of the same Species, whom our *Self-love* immediately prompts us to embrace with kind tender Affections. (*Enquiry*: 33)

If we look at this passage from a Hutchesonian point of view, the language sounds quite bizarre, yet it is consistent with Campbell's attacks on Hutchesonian benevolence as an ultimately self-interested love for oneself in the other.[1] For Campbell, there are affections that we can qualify as kind and tender, even if they are not disinterested in Hutcheson's sense. Campbell offers a teleological explanation of why we feel naturally attracted (in ultimately self-interested ways) to other members of our species: God has given us this desire to make a peaceful life in society possible. Crucially, Campbell claims against Hobbes that it is not mutual fear that makes us form and join societies, but the desire for companions – which involves the evaluation of others as lovable members of our own species, rather than as potential dangers. If there is ultimately a reduction of this 'kind affection' to some self-interested mechanism, this does not affect the qualification as 'kind', for Campbell, which makes his position look very different from Hobbes's. He emphasises not the competitiveness in human nature, but its kindness, even if he spells it out in an unusual way.

After these reflections, Campbell focuses on Hobbes's account of the desire for honour in *De Cive*: 'Mr. *Hobbes* must talk most absurdly, when he affirms, that we desire Honour *primarily*, or from a Propension of Nature, and Companions only *secondarily*, or by Accident' (*Enquiry*: 35). Campbell agrees with Hobbes on the basic psychological point that honour or esteem 'lies in the Mind or Affections of other People, who bear a kind respectful Sense of our *Worth* and Merit' (*Enquiry*: 34). Fundamentally, honour concerns their opinion about us, and desiring honour means desiring their goodwill. Campbell also agrees with Hobbes that the desire for honour is natural. But he disagrees on the nature of these desires. Against Hobbes, Campbell ultimately holds that honour is *not* a positional good that engenders competition and conflict.

Campbell defines honour as follows: '*Honour* lies in the friendly Affections of intelligent Minds' (*Enquiry*: 34). For Campbell, then, the naturalness of this desire for honour 'necessarily implies that all Men have naturally a *Good-liking* for one another' (*Enquiry*: 35–6). This is because we only desire honour from people whom we esteem ourselves. Hence, the fact that we desire to live in society cannot be explained by a primary desire for honour (as suggested by Hobbes), but is based on a desire for companions (as suggested by Campbell and Hutcheson). If there were no such primary desire for companions, we could not explain the reality of the desire for honour. Campbell must understand this point as backing his claim that society is *not* based on mutual fear, but on reciprocal natural affections, and thus as a refutation of Hobbes.

Ultimately, these psychological and social mechanisms are the work of a wise and caring providence (*Enquiry*: 63). Campbell's systematic challenge is to make an attack on Hobbes's account of sociability compatible with his own thoroughly egoistic moral psychology, without subscribing to Hobbes's view of human nature as aggressive and competitive. Campbell's optimistic view of human nature and self-love within an egoistic psychological framework becomes even more obvious from his analysis of moral motivation, to which I shall now turn.

6.2 CAMPBELL ON MORALITY AND MORAL MOTIVATION

Campbell begins his *Enquiry* by announcing that he wants to defend 'the moral Virtues' against Mandeville, who made them 'all a *Chimera*, an idle Fancy, a mere Trick impos'd upon the World by designing Lawgivers and Philosophers' (Campbell, *Enquiry*: 1). The title page states that Campbell wants to demonstrate '(Against the Author of the *Fable of the Bees*, &c.) That VIRTUE is founded in the *Nature* of Things, is *unalterable*, and *eternal*, and the *great Means* of private and publick HAPPINESS' (*Enquiry*: title page). From a Hutchesonian point of view, this goal cannot be reached from within the psychological framework of the selfish hypothesis: denying the reality of benevolence also means denying the reality of virtue, and the possibility of cultivating it. For Campbell, however, things look utterly different. He wants to stick to the selfish hypothesis, according to which all our actions are motivated by self-love as hedonistic egoistic desire, and therefore he wants to show that self-love also motivates morally virtuous actions.

For Campbell, a specific kind of self-love, namely the desire for esteem from all other rational agents (in other words, a version of self-love as love of praise), is the natural motive for our virtuous actions: '*Self-love*, as it exerts it self in the Desire of universal unlimited *Esteem*, is the *great* commanding Motive that determines us to the Pursuit of such [virtuous] Actions' (*Enquiry*: 257–8). Campbell is not alone in defending this point: John Clarke of Hull and John Gay, for example, also make room for morally virtuous motives within the framework of the selfish hypothesis (see Chapters 4.1 and 7.3).

Campbell distinguishes the desire for '*universal unlimited Esteem*' (*Enquiry*: 76), that is, the desire to be esteemed by all rational agents, including God, from more restricted and defective forms of desire for esteem such as '*Vain-glory*, or popular Applause', which exclude God and great parts of humankind, and which are restricted to 'that particular Commonwealth to which we immediately belong' (*Enquiry*: 75). Again, if both Mandeville's and Campbell's psychologies could be broadly qualified as 'egoistic', it is crucial to highlight that, for Campbell, there are very different kinds of self-interested motives and very different scopes of self-love as love of praise.

Self-love as desire for universal unlimited esteem is connected to what Campbell terms 'true' self-love. True self-love more generally

> signifies our embracing and pursuing those Perceptions, whether pleasing or painful at present, which, after we have look'd into the Nature and Consequences of Things, and fairly balanc'd them together, we judge to be most valuable, with relation to the Mind the only Seat of all our Pleasures, and properly one's Self. (*Enquiry*: 290)

Campbell argues for a version of reflective hedonism: true self-love is provident as opposed to short-sighted, and it prefers the higher pleasures to the pleasures of the senses. True self-love gives preference to intellectual and social pleasures, which are both pleasures of the mind, over bodily pleasures. This does not mean that true self-love would entail renouncing all bodily enjoyments, which would be damaging for the agent, but rather renouncing them where they conflict with the higher pleasures (*Enquiry*: 274–87). In his description of true self-love, Campbell quotes Marcus Aurelius' *Meditations* (Book 5, §1), which is yet another sign that he sees the Stoics and other 'antient Moralists' as supporting his claims (*Enquiry*: 290–1).

Remember that in his *Inquiry*, Hutcheson wanted to introduce 'Mathematical Calculation in Subjects of Morality', with the goal of comparing the moral value of different motives (see Chapter 4.2). In the *Essay*, he demonstrated great interest in comparing different experiences of pleasure in terms of their value. In a comparable effort, Campbell suggests a mathematical model to compute the value of different experiences of pleasure. This should help determine more precisely the direction of true self-love. 'In all our pleasing or painful Perceptions, there are three Things which every reasonable Man ought carefully to attend to, viz. the *Degrees* of Pleasure or Pain, the *Duration*, and the *Consequents* of these Perceptions' (Campbell, *Enquiry*: 275). For Campbell, one of the most important outcomes of this model is that true self-love necessarily involves an (ultimately self-interested) concern for the well-being of others – we cannot exert true self-love when we neglect others. The pleasures of being esteemed by other rational agents, including God, are crucial. Since these pleasures are the most valuable an agent can experience, and since we are esteemed for virtuous actions, self-love in the form of the desire of esteem will motivate us to perform morally virtuous actions, according to Campbell. (As we shall see shortly, a morally good action is one that gratifies the self-love of other agents.) The desire for universal, unlimited esteem is the principle of action that motivates the morally best actions.

This last idea resembles Hutcheson's point that universal benevolence is the best form of benevolence – but now it is formulated within the framework of the selfish hypothesis. Still, the claim that morally virtuous actions are motivated by a self-interested desire for esteem is in fundamental opposition to Hutcheson's view of moral motivation. Hutcheson argues, too, that it is in our best interest to be virtuous, yet for him only bene*volence*, that is, the disinterested doing good to others, is approved as morally virtuous by others and our own moral sense. Actions motivated by a desire for esteem, that is, by self-love as love of praise, can be bene*ficent*, but they are not disinterested and thus not morally virtuous. For Mandeville, too, Campbell's desire for esteem would not count as a motive for morally virtuous actions – true moral virtue (as opposed to mere *social* virtues such as politeness and honour) requires self-denial in the sense of a voluntary frustration of our natural passions.

Given these contrasts, it is interesting to note that Campbell claims several times that, ultimately, he and Hutcheson defend very similar views (*Enquiry*: 327–8). If we focus solely on the selfish hypothesis, this claim is confusing. But if we shift to other themes, the situation may look different – and this is the point where stepping into Campbell's shoes and reflecting upon a historiography dominated by Hutcheson's emphasis on benevolence becomes particularly interesting. When claiming proximity to Hutcheson, Campbell may have in mind the most important corollary of his theory of moral motivation, which is rendered invisible by an exclusive focus on the question of the selfish hypothesis – Campbell's generally optimistic view of postlapsarian human nature as naturally virtuous is perfectly compatible with Hutcheson's, in spite of their disagreement regarding the selfish hypothesis. For Campbell, even if our psychology is ultimately determined by self-love, we nevertheless naturally tend to virtue: the desire for esteem is natural, and it has been given to us by God with the providential purpose of making a peaceful life possible. Hutcheson and Campbell may disagree on questions of psychology, yet they agree on the fundamental point that human nature naturally tends to virtue.

Again, if instead of comparing Hutcheson and Campbell on their positions regarding the selfish hypothesis, we compare their views of the moral status of postlapsarian human nature, Campbell is much closer to Hutcheson than to Hobbes, Mandeville and Augustinians such as the Calvinists. In the Confession of Faith, we famously read that human nature is 'dead in Sin, and wholly defiled in all the Faculties and Parts of Soul and Body' (Church of Scotland 1728: VI.1). In addition, the ability of human agents 'to do good Works, is not at all of themselves, but wholly from the Spirit of Christ' (Church of Scotland 1728: XVI.3). For Campbell, by contrast, human nature is such that '*Virtue* leaves every Man in the full Possession of all his natural Desires and Appetites, to be indulg'd and gratified within the Limits of the *Self-love* of those intelligent Beings among whom we are mixed' (Campbell, *Enquiry*: 534). This claim became one of the main points of attack for the Committee for Purity of Doctrine – in their eyes, Campbell was downplaying postlapsarian corruption.

One corollary of Campbell's distinction between true and mistaken forms of self-love is that there is room for an account of self-denial and self-cultivation.[2] Campbell makes this explicit in reaction to one of the charges of the Committee, which insisted on 'the divine Commands to Self-denial' (Campbell, *Remarks*: 9). Campbell relies on his distinction between true and mistaken self-love and states that following true self-love does not mean giving oneself 'to the Entertainments and Gratifications of Sense, that are no other but the Lust of the Flesh, the Lust of the Eyes, and the Pride of Life' (*Remarks*: 21) – a reference to 1 John 2:16. True self-love consists in the voluntary frustration of mistaken forms of self-love, and it 'necessarily determines us to pursue our own Fortunes, in the Good and Prosperity of others, as we are rational eternal Minds, associated to God and to one another' (*Remarks*: 21). Like Hutcheson, according to whom we ought to cultivate universal benevolence, Campbell suggests that for moral self-improvement, we ought to cultivate a desire for universal, unlimited esteem (Campbell, *Enquiry*: 106). At this point, yet another interesting difference between Campbell and Mandeville emerges: according to Mandeville, we are almost or entirely incapable of genuine self-denial, and therefore incapable of performing genuinely virtuous actions and improving our moral status – these points are clearly rejected by Campbell.

We have seen that, according to Campbell, self-love in the form of the desire for esteem is our motive for morally virtuous actions. But what exactly renders an action morally virtuous as opposed to vicious? In other words, what is Campbell's criterion of morality? For Hutcheson, to be virtuous is to be motivated by disinterested benevolence – this answer Campbell cannot accept because he adheres to the selfish hypothesis as the fundamental element of his psychology. For other authors, it is accordance with divine law – an answer that Campbell does not endorse either. Rather, Campbell argues that the criterion of morality is an action's conformity with the self-love of other agents: 'I make Virtue, or *moral Goodness*, to consist in the Proportion and *Agreement*, which any Action of a rational Mind bears to the *Self-love* of all those other intelligent Beings, to whom she is naturally associated' (*Enquiry*: 257). In other words, gratifying the self-love of others by promoting their interests or by procuring them pleasure is what makes an action virtuous. The motive for this is self-love as desire for esteem.

Here, we should note two important points. First, Campbell may be a *psychological* egoist, but he is no *ethical* egoist: he does not claim that an action is virtuous because it gratifies the agent's own self-love. Rather, it is the gratification of *others'* self-love that makes it virtuous. Campbell is clearly aware of this point: against one of the charges of the Committee, Campbell specifies that according to some philosophers, 'the Self-love or Happiness of the Agent himself, is both the Motive and Standard of Moral Virtue' (Campbell, *Report*: 47). This, he adds, is very different from his own position. However, he admits that it is true that in our providentially ordered world, and under the condition that we restrict this claim to *true* self-love, both views 'naturally agree and consist together, and seem equally to answer all the Ends and Purposes of Religion' (*Report*: 47). In our providentially ordered world, every virtuous action (that is, every action that procures pleasure to other rational agents) *also* gratifies the self-love of the agent by causing esteem in the person who benefits from the action towards the agent.

Secondly, Campbell's criterion of morality is an early eighteenth-century formulation of a consequentialist position. What is of import for the moral value of an action are its consequences, namely the pleasure it provides to other agents. Campbell's mathematical model to 'determine the true *Moment* or *Value* of any Perceptions' of pleasure and pain is first of all meant to be a hedonistic quantitative model to determine which action to perform in order to best gratify one's own true self-love. However, it also shows that Campbell thinks that his approach to pleasure and pain could be used to quantify the moral value of actions.

On the basis of his claim that 'that Action is best, which procures the greatest Happiness for the greatest Numbers' (Hutcheson, *Inquiry*: 125), Hutcheson is occasionally presented as a 'precursor' to utilitarianism.[3] However, for Hutcheson the motives, not the consequences, bestow moral value on an action – we can fail to accomplish a benevolent action, but our benevolent intentions still make us morally praiseworthy. Due to his insistence on the importance of the consequences of an action, Campbell seems a better candidate as a precursor to utilitarianism than Hutcheson.

And in comparison with Mandeville, it is again Campbell who is closer to utilitarian ideas properly speaking. Remember that Mandeville strictly distinguishes between genuine moral virtue, which requires self-denial, and the social virtues, such as politeness, honour and the Stoic virtues, which all function on the basis of the passion of self-liking. Mandeville's claim that private vices are public benefits indeed draws our attention to the consequences of actions as opposed to their motives. However, he strongly insists against Shaftesbury that moral virtue and the social virtues are two very different things.

One other important feature concerns Campbell's moral epistemology. Campbell opposes Hutcheson's influential idea that there is a disinterested moral sense and claims that moral approbation is self-interested. For him, '*Self-love* is the Standard whereby we can only judge of the *Virtue* or *Value* of any Action whatsoever' (Campbell, *Enquiry*: 440). In other words, 'it manifestly appears, that we love the Beneficent from *Self-interest*. And it is very certain, that the same Principle determines us to love not only those Persons that are beneficent to ourselves, but such likewise as are beneficent to others' (*Enquiry*: 382). According to Campbell, if we experience pleasure as a consequence of someone's action, we necessarily love or esteem the agent in accordance with the amount of pleasure her action has procured us – this is again part of the providential order. If we are only the observers of an action, but not the person (B) who benefits, we still love the agent (A), since

> we secretly put ourselves in *B*'s Circumstances, and in our Minds conceive ourselves the Objects of *A*'s Kindness or Bounty: And after this Manner do we take Part in all the Concerns of our Fellow-men. So that there can be no *beneficent Action* done in any Part of the World, which, when it occurs to our Observation, does not affect us, and tend to our *own private Interest*, or serve to give us *Pleasure*. (*Enquiry*: 440)

In this case, moral approbation depends on the observer's successful visualising of being in the place of the person who benefits directly from the action, and on the consequent pleasure of imagination.[4] Thanks to God's providential order, our true self-love correctly represents the moral value of an action – whether we directly benefit from it or not. Obviously, these claims are strictly incompatible with those of Hutcheson, according to whom moral approbation is not concerned with the well-being of the observer – we approve of unsuccessful attempts to be benevolent, and we may even morally approve of benevolent actions that are to our disadvantage, and morally disapprove of actions that are beneficial to us.

We are now in a position to reconstruct Campbell's account of what happens when a morally virtuous action is performed. An agent is naturally motivated by self-love in the form of the desire for esteem and performs an action that gratifies the self-love of someone else by procuring her pleasure. For Campbell, this makes the action virtuous. As a result of divine design, the beneficiary (and any potential observer) will necessarily esteem the agent. This esteem or approbation depends on the pleasure experienced (directly by the beneficiary, via imagination by an observer), and is thus self-interested. This in turn gratifies the agent's desire for esteem and provides her the highest pleasure. According to Campbell, this mechanism demonstrates the reality of a providential order: God arranged the world using these self-interested mechanisms with the goal of promoting morality; they naturally and very effectively guide us to virtue.

6.3 CAMPBELL'S ATTACKS ON MANDEVILLE: VICE, LUXURY, FASHIONABLE CLOTHING AND VIRTUE

In the third *Treatise* of the 1733 edition of Campbell's *Enquiry* (which was the second *Treatise* in the plagiarised 1728 edition by Alexander Innes), he focuses on a theme inspired by Mandeville's notorious subtitle 'Private Vices, Publick Benefits', announcing that he will demonstrate 'That *Moral Virtue* promotes *Trade*, and aggrandizes a *Nation*' (Campbell, *Enquiry*: 469).[5] The chapter contains lengthy quotations from the first volume of *The Fable of the Bees* and a series of attacks by Campbell on Mandeville's comments on moral virtue and vice, on their respective relation to economic prosperity, on luxury and on self-denial.[6] On several occasions Campbell uses his attacks on Mandeville to put forward views regarding the moral status of human nature that were highly controversial in early eighteenth-century Calvinist Scotland.

Almost at the beginning of the *Treatise*, having drawn attention to Mandeville's statement that 'Religion is one Thing, and Trade is another', Campbell discusses Mandeville's definition of luxury in *Remark L*. Mandeville had defined luxury as 'every Thing [. . .] that is not immediately necessary to make Man subsist, as he is a living Creature' (Campbell, *Enquiry*: 473, quoting Mandeville, *Remarks*: 107). Campbell rephrases Mandeville's concession that this is a rigorous definition, '*But*, says he, *if we are to abate one Inch of this Severity, I am afraid we shan't know where to stop*' (Campbell, *Enquiry*: 474, quoting Mandeville, *Remarks*: 107). Based on this definition, Mandeville produces examples for his claim that certain vices, in particular pride and luxury, would under certain circumstances produce beneficial effects for society, such as employment for the poor (Mandeville, *Remarks*: 107ff.). In *Remark M*, Mandeville discusses one particular example of luxury, namely the purchase and wearing of fashionable clothing, which he ties to the passion of pride: we desire ornaments in the form of fashion to gratify our vanity and ultimately because we attempt to display our superiority over others (*Remarks*: 127–8). For Mandeville, fashionable clothing and luxury are connected to self-liking, that is, to self-love as *amour-propre* – they are ways of expressing this corrupt passion that are commonly judged acceptable in civilised societies.

In his reaction, Campbell first attacks Mandeville's definition of luxury as far too rigorous – 'we may very well abate a good many Inches of this Severity' (Campbell, *Enquiry*: 474). Not even Mandeville claims that it is luxury to pursue those things that are necessary for our subsistence. Accordingly, our being determined by the principle of self-preservation cannot count as luxury (*Enquiry*: 475ff.). Appealing to our intuition, Campbell then claims that even Mandeville, 'upon second Thoughts', must concede that not 'every Thing is *Luxury*, that is not absolutely necessary to keep a Man alive' (*Enquiry*: 477). As examples, Campbell discusses the pleasures of sex, the pleasures of thought and reflection, and the pleasures arising from experiencing the beauties of nature – for example, landscapes, colours, flowers and perfumes. A man opening his eyes cannot but 'enjoy numberless other pleasing Perceptions, besides what he has from those Things that are immediately necessary to make one subsist, as he is a living Creature' (*Enquiry*: 481). These enjoyments are in no way vicious or luxurious, and the beneficent Deity would never lay a prohibition upon them (*Enquiry*: 479).

Campbell then discusses the question of whether we are guilty of vicious luxury when we form things we find in nature into something new, for example when we craft textiles from products based on plants and animals. The answer is negative, since we only 'imploy our own Art and Labour' for the production of further enjoyments, using again the powers and faculties God has given us (*Enquiry*: 482). Campbell writes:

> I hope, there is no Guilt in exerting my natural Powers, and making Use of my own Labour, Skill, and Industry, in procuring for myself those Pleasures which I have a natural Taste to enjoy, or in applying Things to those Purposes, to which, not sinful Man, but the Deity himself has so well adapted them. (*Enquiry*: 483)

Campbell's underlying point can be summarised as follows: we have been created by a benevolent God, who gave us faculties to enjoy innocent pleasures prepared more or less directly by that same God. Enjoying these pleasures cannot be vicious luxury, even if they are not immediately necessary for self-preservation. Whether this is convincing or not, Campbell strongly relies on a teleological account of human nature, similar to those of Hutcheson and Butler, for whom human nature is designed by God and equipped with natural tendencies to virtue. And even if the subject of luxury would offer plenty of opportunities to speak about postlapsarian corruption, Campbell does not address this subject, choosing instead a very positive outlook.

Campbell then reacts to Mandeville's discussion in *Remark M* regarding fashionable clothing as one particular dimension of luxury:

> To set this Matter in a fair Light, I shall here briefly remark, that our Clothes are then judged to be ornamental, when, besides their answering the two first Ends which our Author mentions [to hide our nakedness and protect against the influence of weather], they serve likewise to entertain our Minds with pleasing or beautiful Ideas; and derive the like delightful Perceptions to those that are about us, so as to make our Appearance among our own Species the more agreeable. And since *Providence* has prepared Variety of Pleasures, which (if you will forgive the Expression) we may always carry about us on our *Backs*, not only for our own, but for other Peoples Entertainment; where is the Excess of stupid Vanity in our wearing those Ornaments, or in our shewing ourselves under such agreeable Perceptions? I don't think that I discover any boundless Pride, or that I overvalue myself excessively, and as much underrate other People, when I only make use of those Gratifications, which the *Author* of Nature has provided for my Entertainment, which he has given me Taste to enjoy, and Skill to improve, and whereby I make myself more agreeable to the rest of my Species. (*Enquiry*: 487)

Campbell's discussion of fashion is set in the wider anthropological and theological context indicated above: if we derive pleasure from clothing that in addition to hiding nakedness and providing shelter has ornamental aspects, then this is in no way morally problematic. On the contrary, it is in accordance with the intentions of the author of nature, who gave us a faculty to derive pleasure beyond mere subsistence. Wearing fashionable clothes is thus far from being a sign of boundless pride, vanity or over-valuation of oneself – Campbell rejects the competitive aspect that Mandeville attributes to fashion. And a few pages later, Campbell comes to the following more general conclusion against Mandeville:

> I conclude, That the *Author* of Nature having so settled the Constitution of Things, that it is impossible for us not to perceive numberless other

Satisfactions, besides those that arise from such Objects as are absolutely necessary to keep us alive; we may all cheerfully indulge to ourselves those Gratifications, without the least Degree of *Vice* or *Luxury*;
and having our Breasts warmed with a grateful Sense of his unbounded
Goodness, joyfully adore that beneficent Being, who has poured out so
much Gladness all over the visible Creation, and given us the Skill and
Power, above other Animals, to apply so many delightful Objects to our
Entertainment. (*Enquiry*: 493)

In the context of his attack on Mandeville, Campbell puts forward a
very positive view of those activities that Mandeville labels 'luxury' – it
seems that Campbell goes so far as to encourage the view that some
of these can be seen as a form of veneration for God, of 'having our
Breasts warmed with a grateful Sense of his unbounded Goodness'
(*Enquiry*: 493).

Campbell also sets limits to our pursuit of pleasing enjoyments,
beyond which they turn into vicious luxury. In the previous *Treatises*,
Campbell had already emphasised that the moral value of an action
is determined by its impact on the self-love of others. In the context
of luxury, he uses this criterion to draw the line between the innocent
gratification of one's self-love and vicious luxury, by stating that 'every
Pursuit, every Pleasure that carries us beyond the *Self-love* or Interest
of those Beings to whom we are associated, or that inspires us with any
Affection, or determines us to any Action that is contrary to their Good
or Happiness, is *Luxury*' (*Enquiry*: 495). Luxury in the vicious sense
is problematic from the moral point of view because it renders the
gratification of others' self-love more difficult or impossible.[7] As long
as this is not the case, however, we may innocently indulge our desire
for pleasures of different sorts, including many classified as vicious
luxury by Mandeville. On the basis of these definitions and arguments,
Campbell asserts that moral virtue, not vice, makes a nation stronger,
since the desire for esteem incites us to trade (*Enquiry*: 523).[8]

Following his discussion of luxury, Campbell attacks more generally Mandeville's conception of moral virtue as requiring self-denial.
He does not address the question of whether Mandeville is serious in
his rigorism, which is not surprising when we keep in mind the general insistence on self-denial in orthodox Calvinism. For Mandeville,
according to Campbell, 'Virtue consists wholly in *Self-denial*; by which
he understands Peoples *combating* themselves, and undergoing all imaginable Austerities, even refusing what one should think absolutely necessary to keep them alive' (*Enquiry*: 525). Mandeville's 'Sort of Virtue is
a mean, starving, idle, dreaming Thing, that reduces People to a State of

stupid Innocence and slothful Ease' (*Enquiry*: 527). Campbell opposes this with his own view of virtue, which does not insist on self-denial but asserts, on the contrary, the controversial point that '*Virtue* leaves every Man in the full Possession of all his natural Desires and Appetites, to be indulg'd and gratified within the Limits of the *Self-love* of those intelligent Beings among whom we are mixed' (*Enquiry*: 534). Most examples brought into play by Mandeville are, in the eyes of Campbell, innocent economic activities that give no offence to others' self-love, and thus should be morally rehabilitated.

All in all, Campbell puts forward a very optimistic view of human nature and its fundamental principles of action – self-love in particular. This is clearly reflected in his discussion of luxury and fashionable clothing. Providence has equipped humankind with faculties the gratification of which is morally innocent when kept within the limits of the self-love of others. Most importantly, Campbell objects to Mandeville's ambiguous position that moral virtue does not require self-denial and that providence wants us to communicate and have commerce with each other. Campbell's teleological conception of human nature as designed by God shares many features with Hutcheson's, despite their disagreement about the psychological question of egoism. The crucial message in both is that there are natural desires, the gratification of which is perfectly compatible with morality – there is no necessity to 'deny' or frustrate them. For both Campbell and Hutcheson, virtue is in some important sense part of our nature, and following our nature means living a virtuous life. Of course, there are aberrations by excess of natural principles, but this does not mean that our nature itself is corrupt. All this is in stark contrast to the Calvinist emphasis on post-lapsarian corruption and the necessity of grace, as the Committee for the Purity of Doctrine's reaction demonstrates.

6.4 CAMPBELL AND THE COMMITTEE FOR PURITY OF DOCTRINE ON SELF-LOVE

The Committee's First Charges in 1735

In the Scottish Enlightenment, Campbell's obsessive insistence on the selfish hypothesis and the often unsystematic presentation of his ideas rendered his writings less appealing to thinkers who focused on questions concerning sociability, sympathy and the moral sense.[9] For us, however, studying the reception of Campbell's philosophy is most fruitful for rediscovering and understanding some of the issues at stake in the early Scottish Enlightenment. In 1735 a Committee for Purity of Doctrine of the Church of Scotland was charged with investigating Campbell's writings for potentially heretical statements. This episode shows how moral philosophy was seen from a theological perspective, and we need to take this into account if we want to understand the debates on the selfish hypothesis. Considering Campbell's focus on *philosophical* opponents in the *Enquiry*, and given his alleged Presbyterian convictions and opposition to Deism, one might ask whether he either overlooked or strategically tried to hide the tensions between some of his philosophical ideas and orthodox Calvinist theological principles. In any case, he was forced to reconsider his relation to Calvinist orthodoxy when facing the Committee, as the *Remarks* from 1735 show.[10]

Two rather short sections of this pamphlet contain the Committee's charges against Campbell's views in the *Enquiry* and other writings: the section *Note of some Passages in Professor Campbell's printed Treatises* (Campbell, *Remarks*: 5–7) and the section *Some further Notes in Mr. Campbell's Prints* (*Remarks*: 8–10). They provide a detailed list of those points in Campbell's different works that the Committee considered to be in conflict with Presbyterian orthodoxy. The list of 17 points contains a broad range of statements concerning self-love, suspected Deist ideas about the laws of nature and claims about the Apostles.[11] Each charge is supported with passages from the Scriptures, the *Confession of Faith*, and the *Larger and Shorter Catechisms* – the pillars of Scottish Presbyterian orthodoxy.

In her study of Campbell's conflict with the Committee, Anne Skoczylas summarises that the Committee 'criticised Campbell's description of the nature of self love and its relationship to moral virtue' (Skoczylas 2008: 95). Leaving aside other interesting aspects of the pamphlets, I shall here focus on moral philosophy and moral psychology and dissect some of the doctrinal issues at stake. In their first *Note*, the members of the Committee begin by quoting a series of statements concerning self-love from the *Enquiry*. These statements emphasise the crucial role of self-love in different domains of Campbell's moral philosophy: they give evidence of Campbell's assertion of the selfish hypothesis, highlight the importance of self-love in his theory of moral motivation, and show how he treats the gratification of the self-love of others as the criterion for the morality of an action.

The Committee's respective criticisms are summarised as follows: 'From these Expressions it appears, that he makes Self-love or Self-interest the Origine, the first Spring, the leading Principle, the only Standard and great Cause; yea, the sole and universal Motive to all virtuous and religious Actions' (Campbell, *Remarks*: 6). This is followed by a list of references to passages in the Scriptures and in the *Confession of Faith*, mentioning in particular the *Larger Catechism*'s first and central point that 'Man's chief and highest End is to glorify God, and fully to enjoy him for ever' (Church of Scotland 1728: 167), and emphasising that 'Self-love and Self-seeking are mentioned amongst the Sins forbidden in the first Commandment' (Campbell, *Remarks*: 6). The context encourages the interpretation that self-love is seen in the Augustinian manner as a passion that elevates one's self as another God, aiming at one's own glory instead of God's. Alexander Moncrieff, a secessionist minister, may have expressed the Committee's worries when he objected to Campbell in the same year that 'the Self-love of Mankind in their present Circumstances is corrupted and depraved', that it is 'a most vitious Passion, and cannot possibly be the Principle of any virtuous Action whatsoever' (Moncrieff 1735: 14–15). Self-love is a corrupt principle, and it is an essential facet of humankind's postlapsarian corruption – Campbell appears to deny both of these points.

Attacking Campbell's view that we are indeed capable of moral virtue, the Committee refers to a passage in the *Confession of Faith* concerning good works, which emphasises the necessity of grace and states that

> Works done by unregenerate Men, although, for the Matter of them, they may be Things which God commands, and of good Use both to themselves and others: Yet, because they proceed not from an Heart purified by Faith; nor are done in a right Manner, according to the Word; nor to a right End, the Glory of God; they are therefore sinful, and cannot please God, or make a Man meet to receive Grace from God. (Church of Scotland 1728: 95–6, XVI.7)

This is an interesting move: the Committee does not attack Campbell's most dominant psychological claim, the selfish hypothesis.[12] This was probably seen as compatible with the Calvinist *topos* of postlapsarian corruption. However, what attracts the Committee's attention is Campbell's theory of moral motivation with its positive presentation of self-love, in particular his assertion that self-love motivates genuinely virtuous actions. This is seen as contradicting Calvinist orthodoxy and the emphasis on postlapsarian corruption, since it gives self-love a very different status than being a corrupt principle of action, supports the view of human nature as naturally tending to virtue, and diminishes the importance of grace. A connected Calvinist worry lurking in the background is that Campbell's moral philosophy might open the gates for justification by works, as in the case of his former teacher Simson.

Note that the view of human nature as naturally tending towards virtue also marks a fundamental difference between the Committee and

Hutcheson. Hutcheson might reject Campbell's assertion of the selfish hypothesis, yet he also develops an optimistic account of human nature. Mandeville, by contrast, might be taken to argue for a negative view of human nature as incapable of genuine moral virtue on the basis of his version of the selfish hypothesis – a position that in its peculiar way approaches the orthodox Calvinist perspective.

To come back to the theological side of the debate: the Calvinist view of postlapsarian corruption that is in the background of the debate is famously presented in an aforementioned passage of the *Confession of Faith*, namely chapter VI, *Of the Fall of Man, of Sin, and of the Punishment thereof*:

> Our first Parents, being seduced by the Subtilty and Temptation of Satan, sinned in eating the forbidden Fruit [. . .] II. By this Sin they fell from their original Righteousness and Communion with God, and so became dead in Sin, and wholly defiled in all the Faculties and Parts of Soul and Body [. . .] IV. From this original Corruption, whereby we are utterly indisposed, disabled, and made opposite to all Good, and wholly inclined to all Evil, do proceed all actual Transgressions. (Church of Scotland 1728: 51–3, VI)

And chapter IX, *Of Free-will*, states regarding our capacity to overcome this corruption that 'a natural man, being altogether averse from that [spiritual] Good, and dead in Sin, is not able, by his own Strength, to convert himself, or to prepare himself thereunto' (Church of Scotland 1728: 69, IX.3). The Committee's criticisms of Campbell's positive account of the natural principle of self-love are tied to this conception of postlapsarian human nature: in the present state of corruption, only unmerited grace can make us truly virtuous. The cultivation of natural principles such as Campbellian self-love (or Hutchesonian benevolence, for that matter) will not allow us overcome our corruption. To claim that we have this ability would be a heresy.

In its *Further Note* 3, the Committee criticises a more specific point concerning Campbell's self-love-based psychological framework, namely that 'the divine Commands to Self-denial, are thereby made altogether impossible to be obeyed' (Campbell, *Remarks*: 9).[13] The question of self-denial was indeed not extensively treated in the *Enquiry*, and Campbell presents a more elaborate account in his first defence in the *Remarks*. The frustration of our corrupt passions was a major theme in Augustinianism. The theological assumptions concerning postlapsarian corruption encouraged the view that, in some sense, we need to deny our degenerate nature, since it corrupts the moral value of all actions.Motivation by self-love in particular is associated with moral corruption.

Furthermore, Campbell's claim that conformity with the self-love of others is the criterion for virtue did not go unnoticed. In its *Further Note 2*, the Committee insists that this claim is unorthodox because it does not make 'the Nature of Virtue to ly in a Conformity to, or keeping of the Law of God, while the Nature of Sin or Vice, opposite thereto, is any Want of Conformity unto, or Transgression of the Law of God' (Campbell, *Remarks*: 8). In the *Further Note 8*, it criticises Campbell's conception of virtue since it entails that 'not the Will of God in his Law, but the Self-love of others, is made the Rule and Bounds of our natural Desires and Appetites' (Campbell, *Remarks*: 10).[14] The words of Moncrieff may again summarise the Committee's worries about Campbell's potentially heretical position: 'The Morality which Mr. *Campbell* would have the Students of Divinity instructed in [. . .] bears no Relation to *Christ*, and the Grace and Operations of the Divine *Spirit*' (Moncrieff 1735: 15).

The Committee also attacks Campbell's objections to Mandeville. It focuses on Campbell's claim that 'Virtue leaves every Man in the full Possession of all his natural Desires and Appetites, to be indulged within the Limits of the Self-love of others; And there is neither Vice nor Luxury in desiring whatever may make our Life easy and comfortable' (Campbell, *Remarks*: 10; *Enquiry*: 534). Remember that this claim is presented by Campbell as an attack on Mandeville, and that it is in line with Hutcheson's views in its rejection of the obligation to self-denial. The Committee makes the following objection to Campbell's claim:

> The first Part of this Position seems not to hold in the present State of corrupt Nature, and gives too great Countenance to Uncleanness and Bestiality: And the latter Part seems to allow Men too unbounded Liberty in seeking after the Things of Life, against the 8th and 10th Commandments, as explained in our Catechisms; as also, appears against *Jer.* xlv. 5. *Mat.* vi. 19. *John* vi. 27. I *John* ii. 15. And as to both, thereby not the Will of God in his Law, but the Self-love of others, is made the Rule and Bounds of our natural Desires and Appetites. (Campbell, *Remarks*: 10)

Campbell's views about virtue could not possibly be valid in the present state of corruption, where we are 'utterly indisposed, disabled, and made opposite to all Good, and wholly inclined to all Evil' (Church of Scotland 1728: 52–3, VI.4). Again, it is quite striking that in the Committee's discussion of Campbell's moral philosophy, motivational egoism is not really an issue. Rather, the issue is the fundamental Calvinist point about postlapsarian corruption and the total inability to perform morally virtuous actions without the never-merited influence of divine grace. This is confirmed by the further development of the Campbell episode. In a second charge in 1736, Campbell's position was attacked as '*too high* on the Side of Self-love (particularly by his asserting it to be the *sole Principle, Standard* and *Motive* of all religious Actions)' (Campbell, *Report*: iv). In a very peculiar way, then, it would seem that many of Mandeville's claims and his (ambiguous) treatment of motivational egoism as a sign of moral corruption must have seemed more in line with Calvinist orthodoxy than Campbell's claims.

Campbell's First Defence

The remaining sections of the *Remarks*, entitled *Professor Campbell's Explications upon Seventeen Articles*, contain Campbell's first defence. With regard to the themes that are the focus of the present chapter, Campbell concentrates on moral motivation, self-denial and the criterion of morality (Campbell, *Remarks*: 19). Defending his view of moral motivation, Campbell insists on the psychological claim that self-love is the only motive for all human actions – self-love being 'our natural Desire after Happiness' (*Remarks*: 23). Attempting to reconcile his psychology with orthodox Calvinist doctrines, he asserts that this holds true in the corrupt state after the Fall as well as under the influence of divine grace: 'it is still the same Power, having a different Relish and a different Direction, that powerfully operates in a gracious Soul, towards its everlasting Peace and Happiness' (*Remarks*: 24). Following the theory of moral motivation outlined in the *Enquiry*, Campbell then reiterates his controversial claim that self-love 'is the constant, the universal, and the supreme Motive that animates us in all our virtuous and religious Actions' (*Remarks*: 26). As a reaction to the Committee's charge that he neglects the glory of God, he introduces a formal distinction between end and motive, which he stresses in the later pamphlets as well. Adhering to his psychological presuppositions, he specifies that

> the Glory of God, or God in his glorious Excellencies and Perfections, is our chief and our ultimate End; and our prevailing Desire after Happiness in this Glory of God, or God an infinite Good, the great Fountain of all Life and of all Perfection, is the supreme Motive that excites us, and that animates our vigorous Endeavours to attain him. (*Remarks*: 28–9)

This may be a concession to the Committee, yet Campbell's main point remains unchanged and contrasts with the Calvinist view of postlapsarian corruption: the principle of self-love exerting itself in the form of desire for esteem naturally motivates morally virtuous actions. By extension, human nature can be said to be disposed towards morality.

Campbell does not deny the reality of vice – there are vicious motives and actions, and we have to avoid them. A crucial part of Campbell's defence of the self-interested theory of moral motivation is thus to make room for a notion of self-denial – a point that was the focus of the Committee's first criticisms. As I have suggested above, Campbell's argumentative strategy relies essentially on the distinction between true and mistaken self-love. Sticking to the psychological claim that self-love is the motive for all actions, he quotes from the *Enquiry*, in which he explained that true self-love properly understood is provident as opposed to short-sighted, aims at the higher and long-term social pleasures instead of the lower and short-term bodily pleasures, and thus 'necessarily determines us to pursue our own Fortunes, in the Good and Prosperity of others, as we are rational eternal Minds, associated to God and to one another' (*Remarks*: 21). It is only mistaken or corrupt self-love that leads us to seek 'the Entertainments and Gratifications of Sense, that are no other but the Lust of the Flesh, the Lust of the Eyes, and the Pride of Life' (*Remarks*: 21).[15] Properly understood, however, 'the Principle of Self-love [. . .] is in no Sort contradictory to the great Christian Duty of Self-denial' (*Remarks*: 19), but rather does 'necessarily imply our renouncing all corrupt Lusts and Appetites; wherein we certainly obey the great Christian Duty of Self-denial' (*Remarks*: 21).[16] The underlying tone is that we can live according to our nature and need not frustrate our natural inclinations, which is a sign of God's providential order.

Concerning Campbell's objections against Mandeville, his reaction to the charges in the 1735 *Remarks* is quite provocative. Campbell insists on his view that postlapsarian human nature is inclined to virtue as a result of the natural desire for esteem and ultimately because of providence. When defending his claim against the Committee that 'Virtue leaves every Man in the full Possession of all his natural Desires and Appetites', he again attacks Mandeville's conception of virtue as requiring self-denial, 'entire Abstinence from all pleasing Enjoyments' and 'severe Exercise of all Sort of Austerities that can be mortifying and afflicting to human Nature'. This is a 'most ridiculous Account of Moral Virtue' and an 'extravagant Opinion' (*Remarks*: 86). He then directs his attack at the Committee:

> May I not have Leave to ask these three Reverend Members, What is it that seems not to hold in the present State of corrupt Nature? Does not Virtue leave every Man in the full Possession of all his natural Desires

and Appetites, the Workmanship of God, and essential Ingredients to our Constitution? No Doubt their Philosophy will agree to it: And if we are left in the full Possession of all our natural Desires and Appetites, does it not hold, that we may lawfully indulge and gratify every one of 'em? Neither, I suppose, will this be controverted. But the Question is, How must these natural Appetites be gratified? We must not suffer them to lash out into Excesses, but keep them within due Bounds. I have affirmed, That we may virtuously indulge them within the Limits of the Self-love of those intelligent Beings to whom we are associated, or in a Consistency with the Self-love of God and our own Species. (*Remarks*: 87–8)

In the vein of his attack on Mandeville, Campbell rejects the conservatively orthodox Calvinist view of complete postlapsarian corruption. He furthermore puts forward the view that even after the Fall, reflection and consciousness are the rules by which 'a Man can judge what particular Appetites are natural to his own Species' (*Remarks*: 90) – a point that again strongly reminds us of the positions of his contemporaries Butler and Hutcheson. Campbell thus explicitly defends human nature against both Mandeville *and* the Committee – his criticisms are bound together.

Further Developments

Not surprisingly, Campbell's defence was not acceptable to conservative orthodoxy. Thus, a second report by the Committee from 1736 concentrates on four remaining problematic themes in the *Remarks*, one of them '*Self-love's being the sole Principle and Motive of all virtuous and religious Actions*' (Campbell, *Report*: iii). In view of that point, the Committee's members

> judge, that the Expressions objected against are *too high* on the Side of Self-love (particularly by his asserting it to be the *sole Principle, Standard* and *Motive* of all religious Actions) and cannot approve of *several other too high* Expressions he uses on this Subject, and are of Opinion it may be recommended to him to *abstain* from using such high Expressions in Time coming; Yet they hope, from what is above-mentioned, he has had *no unsound* Meaning in them. (Campbell, *Report*: iv)

Did Campbell's rehabilitation of self-love go too far? Clearly, the Committee considers his reaction as still problematic. It complains again that the Glory of God, instead of being at the very centre, has only a subordinate position in Campbell's theory of the motivation for moral and religious actions. His view of self-love is judged too positive, and the Committee's members indicate that they are not persuaded of his strategy to distinguish between true and mistaken self-love.

In 1736 Campbell replied to the Committee's second report in the two pamphlets *Further Explications* and the *Report*. In the *Further Explications*, Campbell summarises the Committee's worry that 'this Assertion looks to the *Committee* as an Exclusion of the Glory of God from *being our chief End*, or at least a *subordinating of it to our own Happiness*; or, which come much to the same Thing, *Loving ourselves in the first and highest Degree, and God only for our own Sakes*' (Campbell, *Further Explications*: 66). Campbell insists on his motivational theory and argues that self-love in the form of love of God is the '*supreme Motive*' for virtuous and religious Actions, and that 'God *alone* is our *chief and ultimate End*' (*Further Explications*: 75), thus taking up a point already made in the *Remarks*. He stresses his conformity with the Committee when concluding that '*the Glory of God, or God in his glorious Excellencies and Perfections, is our chief and our ultimate End*' (*Further Explications*: 79).

In the *Report*, however, Campbell's reaction boils down to a rather self-confident opposition regarding the value of self-love. He clarifies that he is not an ethical egoist, according to whom it would be true that 'the Self-love of the Agent himself, as it terminates and coincides with his Happiness, or his chief End, as they apprehend it; is the Standard of Moral Virtue' (Campbell, *Report*: 47). Yet he asserts again that the criterion for virtue is the self-love of others, or the 'common Happiness of the rational System, which is the Will of God in the Nature of Things' (*Report*: 47). Given the providential order of God's creation, both opinions 'naturally agree and consist together, and seem equally to answer all the Ends and Purposes of Religion' (*Report*: 47). In other words: what makes an action virtuous is that it gratifies the self-love of others. In God's creation, an agent who makes her own true self-love instead of the self-love of others the standard of moral virtue will perform the same virtuous actions, because she wants to gain the esteem of other rational agents, especially God's, by gratifying their self-love.

Interestingly, Campbell now focuses on the more philosophical dimension of the debate and refers to several passages in Shaftesbury – an author who had repeatedly come under attack for being too critical of the Christian religion, and who was suspected of Deism. Campbell quotes the passage from *Sensus Communis* where Shaftesbury raised the possibility of distinguishing different ways of loving oneself or serving one's interest. Attacking Hobbes and the French Augustinians, Shaftesbury emphasises that even if their egoistic psychological assumptions were correct, 'The Question wou'd not be, Who lov'd himself, or who not; but, *Who lov'd and serv'd himself the rightest, and after the best Manner?*' (Campbell, *Report*: 50, quoted after Shaftesbury, *Sensus Communis*: 56). Campbell sees his distinction between true and mistaken self-love as an answer to this question, even if he does not comment on Shaftesbury's rejection of the selfish hypothesis. Quoting Shaftesbury and Butler's *Sermon* 11 on the beneficial consequences of virtue and benevolence, Campbell stresses the close connection between true self-love and virtue, and emphasises that there are other philosophers attributing positive elements to self-love, even if they may disagree with him concerning questions of psychology and moral motivation (Campbell, *Report*: 51). It is obvious that, for Campbell, the main point is the rehabilitation of self-love as a potentially virtuous principle.

The Committee's reactions demonstrate that Campbell's quoting Aristotle on φιλαυτία in an attempt to protect himself against 'prejudices' against introducing self-love in the 'Business of moral virtue' (Campbell, *Enquiry*: 5) was well grounded. In the *Report*, Campbell ultimately insists in a self-conscious tone not only on his positive view of human nature as naturally tending to virtue, but in particular on his optimistic view of self-love. Thus, to some extent he may be said to continue and surpass the neo-Stoic and anti-Augustinian rehabilitation of the self-affections in Shaftesbury, who already had declared that 'the affections towards private good become necessary and essential to goodness' (Shaftesbury, *Inquiry*: 197).

The Committee may have been powerful enough to cause problems for Campbell, yet the General Assembly of the Church of Scotland declared on 21 May 1736 that they 'are of opinion, that the examining and stating the matter, as has been done by the committee for purity of doctrine, is sufficient for cautioning against the errors that some at first supposed Mr Campbell was guilty of, without giving any judgment or formal sentence upon the report; and therefore do resolve and appoint that the matter rest here' (Church Law Society 1843: 639).[17] And unlike Simson, Campbell could continue his teaching. This reflects the changing theological climate at the beginning of the Enlightenment, and at the beginning of the rise of the Moderates – maybe not yet a change in terms of doctrine, but at least a change in an institutional dimension.

6.5 CONCLUSION

Campbell's admittedly not always systematically presented ideas have hitherto received little attention from intellectual historians, and almost none from historians of philosophy – yet especially in the context of a study on the history of the debates on self-love, they deserve our attention.

Campbell's claims, their relation to Hutcheson's and Mandeville's ideas, and the noteworthy episode between Campbell and the Committee for Purity of Doctrine teach us some important lessons about eighteenth-century British moral philosophy. Campbell is probably the clearest example of how one can combine a vigorous defence of the selfish hypothesis with a positive view of postlapsarian human nature – or, in other words, that one can be a 'psychological egoist' *and* argue for a very positive view of the moral status of human nature. We must acknowledge that this point undermines Hutcheson's influential claim that asserting the selfish hypothesis (or adopting an 'egoistic' moral psychology) equals adopting a pessimistic view of human nature as unsociable and incapable of virtue and its cultivation. Furthermore, Campbell's episode with the Committee for Purity of Doctrine demonstrates that the selfish hypothesis was often considered less intrinsically connected with a pessimistic view of human nature than suggested by Hutcheson. Rather than criticising Campbell's egoistic moral psychology, the members of the Committee focused on Campbell's unorthodox positive view of postlapsarian humans as perfectly capable of cultivating virtue, on his not insisting on self-denial, and on his positive view of the principle of self-love in particular.

Even if Campbell asserts, like Mandeville, *some* version of the selfish hypothesis, the two authors differ fundamentally in their moral psychologies more generally, and in their accounts of the moral status of human nature more specifically. With his positive view of the moral status of postlapsarian human nature, Campbell comes much closer to Hutcheson than this latter's 'historiography' of philosophy would allow. This must make us see Hutcheson's story in perspective – the selfish hypothesis is less in the centre of philosophico-theological debates than the overarching question of the moral status of postlapsarian human nature.

In addition, Campbell's efforts (convincing or not) to make sense of sociability within the framework of the selfish hypothesis are quite different from the Hobbesian and Mandevillian conceptions of sociability. These latter are based on competition, with society seen merely as a convenient context for the gratification of our self-interested desires. Society is the response to the fearful attitude we reasonably adopt towards others. For Campbell, by contrast, sociability involves the evaluation of others as lovable because of their similarity to ourselves, a point that he tries to back up with his own reading of the Stoics. This is worth noting since it shows the problematic aspects of too ready an association of the selfish hypothesis with the Epicurean tradition, in opposition to Stoicism. For Campbell, the main question is indeed how to be rightly selfish – the very question Shaftesbury asked in the *Sensus Communis*, in a passage quoted by Campbell against the Committee's charge that his moral psychology does not allow for self-cultivation. Campbell's answer to this question, and his explanations of what true self-love is and how it requires some weak form of self-denial, show how seriously he attempts to fit into the psychological framework of the selfish hypothesis some of the themes that were at the core of Hutcheson's contributions to the debates on self-love.

NOTES

1. See also Stewart (1996: 280).
2. In this context, it is essential to emphasise that even if it is true that Campbell adopts a 'hedonistic motivational theory' (Heydt 2018: 165), he is not a 'pessimist' regarding self-cultivation. Also, the 'hope and fear generated by God's eternal sanctions' play a minor role in his theory of self-cultivation (Heydt 2018: 159, 165, 170). The essential element in Campbell remains our natural desire for esteem. These and similar points highlight aspects of Campbell's quite peculiar position, which may be aptly summarised as follows: 'Campbell focused on the love in self-love' (Garrett and Heydt 2015: 93).
3. See, for example, Irwin (2008: 421), with the depiction of Hutcheson as 'accepting a version of utilitarianism'. See, however, the illuminating objections in Jaffro (2013).
4. One of Hutcheson's additions in the fourth edition of his *Inquiry* might also be a reaction to this point in Campbell. Hutcheson (*Inquiry*: 219–20) points out that we also approve of 'brave unsuccessful Attempts' to promote the happiness of others. Note that on the question of moral approbation, Campbell differs from John Clarke and John Gay, in spite of their shared view that even if human beings are determined by self-love, they are still capable of morally virtuous actions (see also Chapters 4.1 and 7.3).
5. The argument in this section is largely based on Maurer (2014: 8–12).
6. For other analyses, see Skoczylas (2008: 90ff.) and Sagar (2013). My focus here is specifically on Campbell's use of Mandeville, and on the subsequent attacks on Campbell by the Committee.
7. It is noteworthy that Mandeville's discussion of fashionable clothing is based on the assumption that it necessarily causes offence to others' self-liking or pride. Campbell relies on the idea of a providentially ordered universe where envy, jealousy and similar passions appear only as excesses of natural principles.
8. See also the discussion in Sagar (2013: 798–801).
9. The argument in this section is largely based on Maurer (2016a: 360–4; 2014: 12–14).
10. For further details on the historical context of the debates between Campbell and the Committee, see Skoczylas (2008: 93–4) as well as Maurer (2016a; 2016b).

11. This chapter focuses on the debates on moral philosophy and self-love in particular. Maurer (2016b) analyses the debates on more theological topics.

12. More precisely, the Committee does criticise Campbell's assertion of the selfish hypothesis in the *Further Notes*, but only insofar as he extends it to God by stating that '*Self-love determines the Deity to reward the Virtuous, and to be studious of the Good of his Creatures*' (Campbell, *Remarks*: 9). 'This seems to say', the Committee objects, 'that God's rewarding the Good is not an Act of his voluntary Condescension' (Campbell, *Remarks*: 9). Yet as far as human agents are concerned, the selfish hypothesis is criticised in neither of the pamphlets.

13. See also my discussion in Maurer (2012: 21ff.).

14. Scott (1900: 84) suggests that a similar point caused tensions between Hutcheson and the Presbytery of Glasgow, namely that according to Hutcheson, 'the standard of moral goodness was the promotion of the happiness of others'. See furthermore Moore (2013).

15. See also Campbell (*Enquiry*: 186ff.) and Church of Scotland (1728: V, 47, note s, and 242).

16. See also Maurer (2012: 21ff.; 2014: 12ff.).

17. One year later, on 24 May 1737, the General Assembly itself had to insist against a secessionist attack that 'they gave no judgment or formal sentence upon the report of the committee, and therefore could not be constructed to adopt any of [Campbell's] expressions' (Church Law Society 1843: 644–5). It is furthermore noteworthy that the University Minutes of the University of St Andrews mention that there were protests against Campbell's election as commissioner of the University to the General Assembly in 1736 due to his tensions with the Committee (*University Minutes of the University of St. Andrews*, vol. 4: 203).

7. *Hume, Smith and Beyond*

General statements generally carry the risk of oversimplification. Nevertheless, they may still serve as interesting starting points for more refined reflections. Thus, towards the middle of the eighteenth century, a general shift seems to have taken place in the debates on self-love. It looks as though the selfish hypothesis was somewhat less heatedly debated and was more or less tacitly considered either as refuted, which is mostly the case in Scottish philosophical debates on different facets of sociability, or as confirmed, which is mostly the case in English philosophico-psychological debates connected to Associationism. Compared to the space and energy that the partisans and adversaries of the selfish hypothesis dedicated to their arguments in the first half of the century, somewhat different issues about human psychology and society seem to have attracted attention in the second half.

In Scottish debates, the reality of a minimal degree of disinterested sociability was generally presupposed, and the claim that all facets of sociability should be analysed as ultimately self-interested came to be considered an unfruitful and false hypothesis. Rather than spending much time and effort defending the reality of minimal sociability, discussions concerned its mechanisms, its development, and its workings and consequences on psychological, social, political and moral levels. If discussing the selfish hypothesis in general lost some of its attraction, this was not, however, the case with more specific passions from the cluster of self-love, in particular those of pride and vanity. Thus, if Campbell may be said to have lost the battle against Hutcheson in Scotland as far as the selfish hypothesis is concerned, Campbell and Hutcheson together advanced alternatives to the negative Calvinist view of postlapsarian human nature. And, insofar as Campbell was clearly more enthusiastic about the moral value of self-love than Hutcheson, the reinforced interest in the conception of self-love as love of praise (that is, Campbell's 'desire of esteem') in the second half of the eighteenth century may count as a victory for Campbell. Self-esteem and due pride, too, saw increasingly positive evaluations, as we shall see shortly.

In English debates, and in contrast to the Scottish ones, the selfish hypothesis seems to have been quite generally accepted as a basis for a psychological theory in the context of Associationist psychology, developing from John Gay to David Hartley and Abraham Tucker. The analysis of the workings of the mind in terms of one original principle seems to have offered an attractive basis for more systematic and technical discussions regarding human psychology. Again, we need to emphasise right away that against Hutcheson's view, the selfish hypothesis was not necessarily coupled with visions of human nature as morally corrupt – John Clarke of Hull and Archibald Campbell were not the only figures to point this out. In the following sections, I shall first look at the Scottish part of the debates on self-love, and then continue with the English.

7.1 HUME ON SELF-LOVE, PRIDE AND VANITY

In *Appendix II* to his *Enquiry*, entitled 'Of Self-Love', David Hume (1711–76) makes a telling remark on the selfish hypothesis, and on the attempts to reduce all our motives to self-love with the help of complex explanations: 'I shall not here enter into any detail on the present subject. Many able philosophers have shown the insufficiency of these systems' (Hume, *Enquiry*: 298). Does Hume himself think that enough has been said on the matter? Indeed, Hume's treatment of the selfish hypothesis often follows Hutcheson's arguments rather closely. Yet Hume's approach, and especially his treatment of the conceptions of self-love, also differs from Hutcheson's in interesting ways. For example, Hume famously rejects Hutcheson's claim that investigating our nature and rediscovering its ruling principles helps us discover the intentions of a benevolent deity, which in turn gives us more indications about how to cultivate moral virtue and reach earthly happiness. Unlike the 'painter' Hutcheson, Hume the 'anatomist' presents his arguments against the selfish hypothesis less as connected to the theme of moral improvement through self-cultivation, where according to Hutcheson the false belief in the selfish hypothesis could have grave practical consequences.[1] In quite similar terms to Mandeville, Hume claims that his primary goal is to give a truthful account of human nature, not an agreeable one.

Hume does not need much introduction as a philosopher.[2] He is undoubtedly one of the intellectual giants of eighteenth-century philosophy, and his ideas have received so much attention over the last decades that few aspects of his work have not been thoroughly studied. This also holds for his contributions to the debates on self-love. Still, situating Hume's treatment of self-love and of the selfish hypothesis in the broader context of eighteenth-century conversations on these themes provides an additional perspective. With the previous analyses, we are in a good position to highlight his connections and differences with other thinkers, and his innovations. I shall begin with Hume's discussion of the selfish hypothesis, and then look more specifically at his treatment of self-love, pride and vanity.

Hume on the Selfish Hypothesis

The vast majority of present-day commentators agree that Hume cannot be labelled an 'egoist' – most agree on this point regarding the *Enquiry*, somewhat fewer regarding the *Treatise*.[3] Hume indeed consistently rejects the selfish hypothesis, both indirectly by arguing in line with previous thinkers such as Hutcheson and Butler that there are disinterested or benevolent motivational principles in human nature, and directly by attacking it as a false and unsatisfactory theory of human behaviour. However, it seems important to note right away that Hume does not go as far as Hutcheson in his assertion of the reality of natural benevolence: Hume regularly draws attention to the limitations in strength and scope of our natural benevolent affections – a point that famously has consequences for Hume's theory of justice as an artificial virtue in the *Treatise*. In contrast to Hutcheson, Hume explicitly claims in the *Treatise* that there is no such principle in human nature as universal unlimited benevolence, that is, benevolence with the extensive scope of humankind – a claim that Hume does not, however, repeat in this form in the *Enquiry*. Generally speaking, Hume's account of human nature does not have the same optimistic flavour as Hutcheson's – which may be just another way of repeating Hutcheson's claim that Hume lacked 'Warmth in the Cause of Virtue' (Hume 2011: I, 32). In any case, in these discussions the notion of self-love plays an essential role. It makes Hume's conversations with other thinkers more transparent, most importantly those with Mandeville and Hutcheson.

Hume rejects the selfish hypothesis *indirectly* by frequently suggesting, in both the *Treatise* and the *Enquiry*, that there are disinterested motivational principles that are irreducible to self-love – principles such as benevolence, friendship, compassion, kindness and parental affections. In *Appendix II* to the *Enquiry*, quoted above, he writes that 'to the most careless observer there appear to be such dispositions as benevolence and generosity; such affections as love, friendship, compassion, gratitude' (Hume, *Enquiry*: 298). As long as there are no convincing analyses of these dispositions in terms of self-love (and we can assume that, for Hume, hitherto there have been none), they must be supposed genuinely disinterested. Benevolence is one of Hume's most important examples of a disinterested motivational principle, which is not surprising considering the Hutchesonian background from within which – and against which – Hume constructs his arguments. However, his frequent emphases on the limitations of benevolence, especially in the *Treatise*, mark the systematic differences with Hutcheson and others.

In his analysis of the passions in Book II of the *Treatise*, Hume presents benevolence as an instinct 'originally implanted in our natures' (Hume, *Treatise* 2.3.3: 417). He speaks of the disinterested desire of 'happiness to our friends' as a 'natural impulse or instinct' (*Treatise* 2.3.9: 439). His discussion of why we approve of '*generosity, humanity, compassion, gratitude, friendship, fidelity, zeal, disinterestedness, liberality,* and all those other qualities, which form the character of good and benevolent' (*Treatise* 3.3.3: 603) presupposes the reality of affections and passions that are irreducible to selfish motives. In Book III of the *Treatise*, Hume claims that 'tho' it be rare to meet with one, who loves any single person better than himself; yet 'tis as rare to meet with one, in whom all the kind affections, taken together, do not over-balance all the selfish' (*Treatise* 3.2.2: 487). This is quite a characteristic move in Hume: like Hutcheson, Hume presupposes the reality of benevolence, but then he puts this point immediately into a more fine-grained and, possibly, less optimistic picture of human psychology. Certainly, 'the representations of this quality [selfishness] have been carried much too far' (*Treatise*: 486), yet the force of this passion opposing benevolence should nevertheless not be underrated.

In the *Enquiry*, Hume presupposes again the reality of disinterested benevolence in his discussion of the high merit we bestow on that passion:

> Upon the whole, then, it seems undeniable, *that* nothing can bestow more merit on any human creature than the sentiment of benevolence in an eminent degree; and *that* a *part*, at least, of its merit arises from its tendency to promote the interests of our species, and bestow happiness on human society. (Hume, *Enquiry* 2.2: 181)

There is a somewhat puzzling story related to this passage. In one of his last letters, Hume asked his editor to change its first sentence, which contained in the editions published during Hume's lifetime, just after the word 'undeniable', the additional clause '*that there is such a sentiment in human nature as benevolence*' (Hume 2011: II, 331). I do not think that the fact that Hume ordered his most explicit assertion of the reality of benevolence to be erased is to be taken as evidence that, according to Hume, there is, after all, *no* benevolence in human nature – there are simply too many other passages in the *Enquiry* and the *Treatise* in which Hume presupposes or argues for the reality of disinterested benevolence in the sense of Hutcheson. But it shows at least how Hume artfully puts shades of distance between himself and Hutcheson.

Hume names grief, love, gratitude and further affections as proofs for the reality of disinterested affections in human psychology:

> These and a thousand other instances are marks of a general benevolence in human nature, where no *real* interest binds us to the object. And how an *imaginary* interest known and avowed for such, can be the origin of any passion or emotion, seems difficult to explain. (Hume, *Enquiry*, Appendix II: 300)

If there is no '*real* interest' opposing it, general benevolence shows its presence, and reductions of benevolence (and other affections) to imagined or subconscious self-interested processes are unsatisfactory. Again and again, Hume rejects attempts to 'account for the origin of the benevolent from the selfish affections, and reduce all the various emotions of the human mind to a perfect simplicity' (*Enquiry*: 299). To reduce benevolence to self-love is not a serious philosophical aim, since it is too much in tension with common experience, but it is simply part of 'that vulgar dispute concerning the *degrees* of benevolence or self-love, which prevail in human nature; a dispute which is never likely to have any issue' (*Enquiry* 9.1: 270–1). Instead of entering into that dispute, Hume simply insists on

> what surely, without the greatest absurdity cannot be disputed, that there is some benevolence, however small, infused into our bosom; some spark of friendship for human kind; some particle of the dove kneaded into our frame, along with the elements of the wolf and serpent. Let these generous sentiments be supposed ever so weak; let them be insufficient to move even a hand or finger of our body, they must still direct the determinations of our mind, and where everything else is equal, produce a cool preference of what is useful and serviceable to mankind, above what is pernicious and dangerous. (*Enquiry*: 271)

Often, Hume joins Hutcheson (and thus contradicts thinkers such as Mandeville, Campbell, John Clarke of Hull and others) in asserting that benevolence is a real and frequently met motive in human nature.

But the quoted passages demonstrate again how Hume differs from Hutcheson by insisting on the limitations of benevolence, especially when it comes to Hutcheson's universal benevolence to humankind. As a result, the differentiation between proximate and distant relationships with other people becomes systematically much more significant in Hume's moral and political philosophy.

In *Appendix II* of the *Enquiry*, we find one of the most extensive discussions of the selfish hypothesis in Hume. In a footnote, he distinguishes between 'general benevolence, or humanity, or sympathy' on the one hand, and particular benevolence on the other – a distinction based on the different scopes of benevolence. The reality of general benevolence, that is, the desire to promote the well-being of persons with whom 'no friendship or connexion or esteem' links us, is more disputed, according to Hume. Still, in the *Enquiry* he suggests that we can assume that this form of benevolence is 'real, from general experience, without any other proof' (*Enquiry*, Appendix II: 298). Both general and particular benevolence 'must be allowed real in human nature: but whether they will resolve into some nice considerations of self-love, is a question more curious than important' (*Enquiry*: 298). Once more, Hume has a tendency to avoid the question that kept Shaftesbury, Mandeville, Hutcheson, Clarke, Butler and Campbell so very busy. Especially compared to Hutcheson, Hume expends less effort to demonstrate the reality of disinterested benevolence – more often he simply presupposes it.

Further evidence for Hume's not being an 'egoist' in any relevant sense comes from his *direct* attacks on the selfish hypothesis. Hume claims that the selfish hypothesis is both a *false* account of human nature and a *useless* one. This is most obvious in *Appendix II* to the *Enquiry*. There, Hume puts forward the epistemological point that the selfish hypothesis, or the attempt to explain all behaviour from the sole principle of self-love, originally started out from the 'love of *simplicity*' (*Enquiry*: 298). But ultimately, this reductive strategy forces us into far too complex and counterintuitive explanations of human behaviour. This is useless and against available evidence, since there are numerous 'marks of a general benevolence in human nature', and since 'the hypothesis which allows of a disinterested benevolence, distinct from self-love, has really more *simplicity* in it' (*Enquiry*: 301). This point was already raised in Shaftesbury and Hutcheson, in combination with the claim that the proponents of the selfish hypothesis rarely use their vocabulary with the conceptual clarity that would make their theory empirically verifiable.[4] But with Hume's more general criticism of the debates on the selfish hypothesis, it acquires new strength.

Yet another argument is developed in Hume's 'Essay of the Dignity or Meanness of Human Nature' (1741).[5] In order to defend a balanced view of the moral qualities of human nature, Hume compares the underlying strategies of different representations of these. We can make comparisons with inferior or superior species, which leads to cheerful or, respectively, depressing results, neither of which are really appropriate. We can also look more closely into our own species and compare how 'different motives or actuating principles of human nature' are represented (Hume, *Essays*: 84). In this context, Hume writes the following about the selfish hypothesis: 'Were our selfish and vicious principles so much predominant above our social and virtuous, as is asserted by some philosophers, we ought undoubtedly to entertain a contemptible notion of human nature' (*Essays*: 84). Here, he seems to accept Hutcheson's suggested linkage between the selfish hypothesis and a pessimistic outlook on human nature's moral status. In the *Enquiry*, however, he will put this point in perspective, as we shall see shortly.

In subsequent passages of his 'Essay on the Dignity and Meanness of Human Nature', Hume furthermore rejects the weaker, somewhat more credible claim that selfish principles are merely the 'predominant', but not necessarily the *sole* principles in human nature. Here, Hume tackles a point that may have become more pressing due to his strategy in the *Treatise* of presenting himself as the more reasonable middle ground between Hutcheson and Mandeville. In Hutchesonian-Shaftesburian terms, Hume argues for the reality of 'private friendship, if no interest or self-love intermix itself' (*Essays*: 84), and against a reduction of 'natural affection' to 'self-love', 'vanity' and similar principles. (I shall make some further comments on Hume's use of the term 'self-love' below.) Moreover, the fact that there are pleasures that accompany virtue and friendship should not make us think that these principles are self-interested. Like Shaftesbury, Hutcheson and Butler before him, Hume argues that these accompanying pleasures are only a *consequence* of the very fact that the motivating principles are disinterested. In a similar vein, our being not indifferent to praise must not lead us to think that all virtuous actions are done out of a desire for praise or vanity (*Essays*: 86). Remember how Mandeville has often been presented as claiming that morally virtuous actions are motivated by some corrupt desire for praise (an interpretation that is not supported by his distinction between moral virtue, singular, and the social virtues, plural). From a different angle, Campbell claimed that self-love as love of praise, or self-love in the form of a desire for esteem, is the motive for morally virtuous actions. Defending the moral value of love of praise against one interpretation of Mandeville, and arguing in a similar direction as Campbell, Hume claims that 'to love the glory of virtuous deeds is a sure proof of the love of virtue' (*Essays*: 86). Smith would take this point on board in *The Theory of Moral Sentiments*.

Hume's arguments against the selfish hypothesis, and for the reality of disinterested benevolence in human nature, can be put into fruitful conversation with his more general views on the moral status of human nature. In the *Treatise*, Hume often takes the reality of disinterested benevolence for granted, and sometimes he argues for it. However, he does not fully adopt Hutcheson's optimistic view regarding the psychological strength and moral dimension of benevolence. As mentioned above, Hume frequently emphasises the psychological limitations of benevolence, particularly when it comes to what Hutcheson terms 'universal' benevolence. Here Hume follows Butler, who refrained from putting too much emphasis on universal benevolence in his recommendations concerning self-cultivation. Since 'man is so much limited in his capacity' (Butler, *Sermons*: 12, 103), benevolence should primarily be focused on 'that part of the universe, that part of mankind, that part of our country, which comes under our immediate notice, acquaintance and influence, and with which we have to do' (*Sermons*: 12, 104).

Seen from the point of view of Hume's theory of justice in the *Treatise*, his view of universal benevolence is even more critical. Extensive benevolence is not only very rare, but there is also no such thing as Hutchesonian universal unlimited benevolence: Hume writes that 'we perceive, that the generosity of men is very limited, and that it seldom extends beyond their friends and family, or, at most, beyond their native country' (Hume, *Treatise* 3.3.3: 602). And in his discussion of the artificiality of the virtue of justice, he claims that 'there is no such passion in human minds, as the love of mankind, merely as such, independent of personal qualities, of services, or of relation to ourself' (*Treatise* 3.2.1: 481). This last passage might contradict what Hume writes in the *Enquiry* on general benevolence, but it points to one of his most crucial arguments in the *Treatise*: there is an important distinction between the close circle of an individual, made up of more intimate relations, and a remote circle. This is the basis for his claim that the mechanisms of sympathy are required for the agent to consider the interests of the wider circles, or to support an 'extensive concern for society' (*Treatise* 3.3.1: 579).[6] Against Hutcheson, Hume claims that there is no original or natural instinct of universal benevolence for the good of society *as such* – as opposed to the benevolence we experience towards particular close persons. The interest of humankind 'is a motive too remote and too sublime to affect the generality of mankind' (*Treatise* 3.2.1: 481), and if there was something like a Hutchesonian benevolence that extended to all humankind and was strong, the virtue of justice would be superfluous (*Treatise* 3.2.2: 494–5). The psychological mechanisms of sympathy will, however, make us care not only for the good of ourselves and of close people with whom we are connected by intimate bonds, but also for the good of remote people and of society in general. This is the beginning of the artificial virtue of justice.

As far as the selfish hypothesis is concerned, Hume distinguishes two versions in *Appendix II* of the *Enquiry*. This point brings us back to the different conceptions of self-love present in eighteenth-century British moral philosophy. Since there are several profoundly different conceptions of self-love, general claims such as 'self-love is the only motive for human actions' may result in a broad range of accounts of human psychology. Traces of a distinction between several versions of the selfish hypothesis can be found in Shaftesbury and Hutcheson, but Hume is the first to spell this out clearly. For Hume, one version of the selfish hypothesis insists

> that all *benevolence* is mere hypocrisy, friendship a cheat, public spirit a farce, fidelity a snare to procure trust and confidence; and that while all of us, at bottom, pursue only our private interest, we wear these fair disguises, in order to put others off their guard, and expose them the more to our wiles and machinations. (Hume, *Enquiry*, Appendix II: 295)

This first version of the selfish hypothesis obviously puts self-love as *amour-propre* or excessive pride at the centre of human psychology. Mandeville's account of human psychology with its emphasis on self-liking or self-love as *amour-propre* is the paradigmatic example in eighteenth-century Britain – but there are also French Augustinian moralists and Scottish Calvinists whom Hume could have had in mind. For Hume, asserting such a view of human nature is evidence of either a 'corrupted heart' on the part of those who represent humankind in this base way, or at least of a 'most careless and precipitate examination' in which no 'degrees of good or bad' are admitted (*Enquiry*: 295–6).

The second hypothesis, then, is that

> whatever affection one may feel, or imagine he feels for others, no passion is, or can be disinterested; that the most generous friendship, however sincere, is a modification of self-love; and that, even unknown to ourselves, we seek only our own gratification, while we appear the most

> deeply engaged in schemes for the liberty and happiness of mankind. By a turn of imagination, by a refinement of reflection, by an enthusiasm of passion, we seem to take part in the interests of others, and imagine ourselves divested of all selfish consideration: but, at bottom, the most generous patriot and most niggardly miser, the bravest hero and most abject coward, have, in every action, an equal regard to their own happiness and welfare. (*Enquiry*: 296)

Hume mentions explicitly Epicurus, Hobbes and Locke as examples of philosophers who defend such accounts of human nature. He could have added his less famous near-contemporaries Archibald Campbell, John Gay and John Clarke. For Hume, such thinkers may still live 'irreproachable lives', in spite of their adherence to a false egoistic psychology. Without really abandoning benevolence and friendship, they are bound to apply some 'philosophical chymistry' to satisfy their obsession with unified philosophical systems. If the first version of the selfish hypothesis suggests that we are motivated by some malicious intention, this second version simply takes us to be mistaken about our deepest motivations. Nevertheless, this second egoistic account of human nature is also clearly 'contrary to common feeling and our most unprejudiced notions' (*Enquiry*: 298). As mentioned above, the desire to 'reduce all the various emotions of the human mind to a perfect simplicity' (*Enquiry*: 299) will lead to a theory with a most serious defect: it forces us into highly complicated and counterintuitive explanations of human behaviour. Ultimately, 'the hypothesis which allows of a disinterested benevolence, distinct from self-love, has really more *simplicity* in it' (*Enquiry*: 301). In other words, the selfish hypothesis has insurmountable epistemological shortcomings.

The most important upshot here is that Hume very perceptively points out that, regarding the question of the moral status of human nature, the two versions of the selfish hypothesis differ enormously. The first forces us into a view of human nature as morally corrupt, whereas the second does not. Hutcheson indiscriminately criticised all versions of the selfish hypothesis as dangerous, since all would keep us from cultivating our natural benevolence. Hume is less critical, and by suggesting that there is a morally neutral version of the selfish hypothesis, he undermines the intimate connection postulated by Hutcheson between asserting the selfish hypothesis and asserting moral corruption. This again points to the limitations of our contemporary notion of egoism in an analysis of eighteenth-century debates on self-love. We need to keep sight of the more fine-grained psychological distinctions to understand their moral corollaries.

Hume on Self-love, Pride and Vanity

After these comments on Hume's discussion of the selfish hypothesis, I want to turn to his approach to the conceptions of self-love, and to his more specific treatment of self-love, pride and vanity. The main point I want to elucidate here is how Hume contributes to the more general tendency in eighteenth-century British moral philosophy to morally rehabilitate self-love and pride. His crucial and most influential point is to make room for a notion of *due* pride or self-esteem, against the more common depiction of pride as a passion opposed to love of God, involving an excessive, unjustified and unduly positive attitude towards ourselves – a depiction nurtured by Augustinian-Calvinist conceptions of *amour-propre*. To some extent, Hume follows Hutcheson's discussion of moral self-approbation, but then goes beyond him. However, Hume also plays with themes from Mandeville and the French Augustinians.[7]

Some initial remarks on terminological issues are apposite. Generally speaking, the English term 'self-love' is vaguer than the term 'pride'. I have argued that 'self-love', in eighteenth-century Britain, refers to a variety of conceptions, for example the basic conception of self-love as self-interested desires or egoism, the more complex conception of self-love as self-esteem or due pride, and the heavily loaded notion of self-love as *amour-propre* or excessive pride – to name only three. Self-love as *amour-propre* is most famously present in Mandeville's clearly defined notion of 'self-liking' in *Part II* of *The Fable of the Bees* (1729). In both editions of *Part I* (1714/1723), Mandeville has a tendency to term this passion 'pride' and, occasionally, 'self-love', but he crucially insists that the person who is subject to it over-values herself, that it engenders competition and conflict, yet that it can be made useful for society.

In contrast to the term 'self-love', 'pride' has a somewhat different history. The term 'pride' is generally less ambiguous than self-love, at least as far as its psychological features are concerned: pride is typically thought to involve some good opinion about oneself, justified or not. Regarding its moral value, pride was commonly treated as a sin, in accordance with the mention in 1 John 2:16 of the 'pride of life'. In the eighteenth century, however, pride became increasingly associated with a possibly innocent and appropriately positive view of oneself. In a still ambiguous context, eighteenth-century philosophers often pointed out that ordinary language may have a distorting effect: Hutcheson had already stressed that in common language, the term 'pride' is generally taken 'in a bad Sense, when one claims that to which he has no Right'. Sometimes, however, it 'denotes Joy upon any apprehended *Right* or *Claim* to Honour' (Hutcheson, *Essay*: 56). True honour exists, for Hutcheson – it is a justified good opinion of ourselves based on our having acted on benevolence. In other words, there is room for *due* pride in Hutcheson. Mandeville, too, reflects upon our common use of language, highlighting that we only give the blameworthy name of 'pride' to the passion that is not well concealed:

> When this Self-liking is excessive, and so openly shewn as to give Offence to others, I know very well it is counted a Vice and call'd Pride: But when it is kept out of Sight, or is so well disguis'd as not to appear in its own Colours, it has no Name, tho' Men act from that and no other Principle. (Mandeville, *Honour*: 3)

Hume shows a similar awareness of the fact that there are social practices that influence our naming of passions. In the *Enquiry, Appendix IV*, 'Of Some Verbal Disputes', he writes: 'The term, pride, is commonly taken in a bad sense; but this sentiment seems indifferent, and may be either good or bad, according as it is well or ill founded, and according to the other circumstances which accompany it' (Hume, *Enquiry*, Appendix IV: 314). Regarding 'well founded' pride, he states that 'the *sentiment* of conscious worth, the self-satisfaction proceeding from a review of a man's own conduct and character [. . .] has no proper name in our language' (*Enquiry*: 314). Note the contrast to Mandeville: the latter had highlighted that pride as 'self-liking' (which is self-love as *amour-propre* or excessive pride), when it is well hidden and gives no offence to others, is not given any name. Still, it is a passion that is ill founded, to use Hume's terminology. Against Mandeville, Hume makes room for *due* pride, which is self-love as self-esteem, arising from 'the endowments of courage and capacity, industry and ingenuity, as well as from any other mental excellencies' (*Enquiry*: 314). According to Hume, and in contrast to Mandeville, it is not well-hidden *excessive* pride that receives no name 'in our language', but *due* pride. And in contrast to Hutcheson, Hume claims that pride can be justified not only on the grounds of our benevolent actions, but also on the grounds of other qualities, which would be non-moral qualities for Hutcheson. In other words, Hume continues the rehabilitation of pride or self-love as self-esteem as a potentially appropriate reaction to our own good qualities or merits, he expands the potential grounds of justification of the passion, and he dissociates it from Mandeville's conception of self-liking, or self-love as *amour-propre*. As we shall see shortly, Smith would continue the rehabilitation of pride or self-love as self-esteem in his own manner, among other things with an attack on Mandeville's reduction to vanity of all self-love as love of praise or desire for esteem.

In the *Treatise*, there is an interesting shift in vocabulary in comparison with the previously discussed authors. For most eighteenth-century British moral philosophers writing before Hume, the term 'self-love' was clearly more central than the term 'pride' – whether self-love was associated with simply, self-interested, 'egoistic' desires, or with more complex psychological phenomena such as pride, vanity and ambition. Maybe the vagueness of the term 'self-love' contributed to its attractiveness. In the *Enquiry*, Hume follows this general trend of using 'self-love' rather than 'pride', but in the *Treatise*, famously, his more central term is pride. This is most obvious in Books II (*Of Passions*) and III (*Of Morals*). In various passages, Hume demonstrates awareness of this terminological issue, and of the potentially problematic vagueness of the term 'self-love'. Still in *Appendix IV* to the *Enquiry*, having stated that 'pride, is commonly taken in a bad sense', he continues as follows: 'The French express this sentiment by the term, *amour propre*, but as they also express self-love as well as vanity by the same term, there arises thence a great confusion in Rochefoucault, and many of their moral writers' (Hume, *Enquiry*: 314). Given the ambiguities of the terms, especially self-love, it is difficult to pin down exactly what Hume means here, but there is another occasion where he demonstrates awareness of terminological ambiguities, namely in his abovementioned discussion of the two versions of the selfish hypothesis in *Appendix II*, 'Of Self-love'. According to him, one version of the selfish hypothesis is based upon a conception of self-love as an innocent, self-interested desire – egoistic self-love. A second version, however, is connected to a conception of self-love as *amour-propre*, which is associated with excessive pride, ambition and vanity (*Enquiry* 9.1: 271). The resulting claims about our being motivated by self-love only are fundamentally different, especially in their moral corollaries.

Hume crucially contributes to a general movement of developing more positive accounts of pride.[8] Hume plays with themes from Mandeville and the French Augustinian moralists, yet instead of adopting their critical view of pride as a vicious even if potentially useful passion, he dissociates the term 'pride' from the conception of self-love as *amour-propre*, attaches it to the conception of self-love as self-esteem or due pride, and highlights the potentially meritorious aspects of pride – not just in terms of its social utility, as in Mandeville, but also in moral terms. In some sense, Hume continues the positive treatment of self-love that one can find in Shaftesbury, Hutcheson, Butler and Campbell: Shaftesbury included the self-affections in the fully virtuous agent's psychological constitution; Hutcheson pointed out self-love's potentially useful roles in the cultivation of virtue, especially in the form of moral self-approbation; Butler treated it as a form of respect for the divinely designed self; and Campbell declared it the very motive for virtuous actions. For Hume, against Mandeville, due pride really exists – it is a form of pride that is something other than an excessive, unjustifiable self-overestimation necessarily leading to competition and conflict, as found in the French Augustinians' *amour-propre* and in Mandeville's self-liking. And like Hutcheson, Hume connects this rehabilitation of pride with a more general moral rehabilitation of human nature against the Calvinist *topos* of the irredeemable corruption of humankind after the Fall. He does not follow Hutcheson in asserting a predominantly positive view of human nature as naturally virtuous, but at least he criticises the view of human nature as morally corrupt. Regarding pride, the contrast with Mandeville is particularly obvious: Mandeville presents pride and self-liking as always excessive, inappropriate and unjustifiable. Under specific circumstances, for example when it is well hidden, this form of excessive self-approbation may turn out to be socially very useful, but even so, it remains a morally corrupt principle in human nature.

One of the most revelatory sections for analysing Hume's approach to pride in the *Treatise* is 'Of Greatness of Mind' (*Treatise* 3.3.2). Hume offers a comparative discussion of 'the passions of *pride* and *humility*' (Hume, *Treatise*: 592). Mikko Tolonen and others have drawn attention to the fact that Hume's analysis of pride shares crucial elements with Mandeville's discussion of self-liking, and with the French Augustinian moralists' analyses of *amour-propre* (Tolonen 2008; 2013). Towards the end of that section, however, Hume makes an important additional move towards rehabilitating this passion. First, Hume reminds us of an idea often discussed by the Augustinians, and calls it 'a trite observation in philosophy' that ''tis our own pride, which makes us so much displeas'd with the pride of other people; and that vanity becomes insupportable to us merely because we are vain' (Hume, *Treatise*: 596). Mandeville, in *Part II* of the *Fable*, made such a claim regarding the passion of self-liking, following the French Augustinian moralists on *amour-propre*. For Hume, this problematic side of pride is rooted in a psychological mechanism involving sympathy and comparison in the person who observes the proud man. In the observer, 'the firm persuasion [the proud man] has of his own merit, takes hold of the imagination, and diminishes us in our own eyes' (*Treatise*: 595). This holds whether the qualities are actually possessed by the proud man or not. Hence, pride in the sense of 'an over-weaning conceit of ourselves, must be vicious; since it causes uneasiness in all men, and presents them every moment with a disagreeable comparison' (*Treatise*: 596). In this form, pride is 'universally blam'd and condemn'd' and associated with the concept of vanity. This certainly looks like a tribute to Mandeville's self-liking and the French Augustinians' *amour-propre*. Hume's debts to Mandeville and Augustinian thinkers are even more striking in his subsequent discussion of 'good-breeding and decency' (*Treatise*: 597). There, he integrates points from Mandeville's analysis of politeness, which for Mandeville mainly consists in concealing the expressive tendencies of one's own self-liking and in supporting the self-liking of others with insincere flattery. The main purpose of politeness, according to Hume, is 'that we shou'd avoid all signs and expressions, which tend directly to show that passion' (*Treatise*: 597). As in Mandeville, politeness in Hume does not consist in suppressing the passion of pride itself, but only in suppressing its expressive tendencies in order to avoid offence and conflict with the pride of others.

However, Hume then substantially diverges from Mandeville and the French Augustinian moralists by making room for a conception of *due* pride – a notion that Hume several times associates with the notion of self-esteem (*Treatise*: 598, 600, 601), thus opposing due pride (that is, self-love as self-esteem) to undue pride or vanity (that is, self-love as *amour-propre* or excessive pride).[9] In the context of his allusions to the Augustinians, Hume makes the un-Augustinian claim that 'nothing can be more laudable, than to have a value for ourselves, where we really have qualities that are valuable' (*Treatise*: 596). Due pride is psychologically beneficial and, it seems, morally valuable since it 'makes us sensible of our own merit, and gives us a confidence and assurance in all our projects and enterprizes' (*Treatise*: 597). If it is well concealed, pride is 'essential to the character of a man of honour' (*Treatise*: 598). Most importantly, against the Augustinian treatment of pride in times of postlapsarian corruption, pride *can* indeed be well founded according to Hume, and if it is also well concealed, it is not only a psychologically necessary, but also a praiseworthy attitude to oneself. It seems that here, Hume presents pride as something that is grounded in an awareness of one's good qualities, which is different from Mandeville's comparative and competitive passion of self-liking. Hume's target in highlighting the positive sides of the passion of pride, against both the Augustinian current and 'common life and conversation' (*Treatise*: 596), is the passion of humility – the prime virtue in the Christian religion, according to Hume (*Treatise*: 600), and the main cause for the bad reputation of pride.

Thus, in the *Treatise*, Hume takes on board several elements of the Augustinian and Mandevillian psychology of self-love as *amour-propre*. Hume highlights why pride can be problematic, and he does this in quite an Augustinian framework. But when Hume points out that pride can indeed be based upon an *appropriate* good opinion of one's own qualities, he rehabilitates pride against the Augustinian critical treatment of the passion of self-love as *amour-propre* or excessive pride, and builds upon a point indicated by Hutcheson. Hutcheson admits pride to be due or appropriate only insofar as it is self-approbation or self-esteem based upon one's moral qualities. Hume, however, extends the field of legitimate grounds to natural qualities. This shows how Hume plays with elements from several different debates to refine his own position.

7.2 SMITH AND THE REHABILITATION OF SELF-LOVE

Smith on the Selfish Hypothesis

The very beginning of *The Theory of Moral Sentiments* (first edition 1759, sixth edition 1790) by Adam Smith (1723–90) can be read as a rejection of the selfish hypothesis, and as announcing Smith's disregard for theories of human nature which insist that we are solely motivated by self-interest. Smith writes:

> How selfish soever man may be supposed, there are evidently some principles in his nature, which interest him in the fortune of others, and render their happiness necessary to him, though he derives nothing from it except the pleasure of seeing it. Of this kind is pity or compassion, the emotion which we feel for the misery of others, when we either see it, or are made to conceive it in a very lively manner. (Smith, *TMS*, I.i.1.1, 2002: 9)

Like his former teacher Hutcheson, Smith presents the passion of pity as a compelling example to convince us of the falsity of the selfish hypothesis. For Hutcheson, pity or compassion was a disinterested 'Determination of our Mind, which strongly proves Benevolence to be natural to us' (Hutcheson, *Inquiry*: 159). Smith does not mention the egoistic analyses of pity by thinkers such as Hobbes, Mandeville and Campbell, and we may thus take him to accept Hutcheson's arguments against the defenders of the selfish hypothesis as valid.

Smith then introduces his account of sympathy, or of 'our fellow-feeling with any passion whatever' (Smith, *TMS*, I.i.1.5, 2002: 13). Besides sympathy being one of the core elements in Smith's moral theory, it is an additional point to convince the reader of the social dimensions of human nature. Smith's account of sympathy differs from what Hutcheson sometimes labelled 'sympathy', namely the public sense or a disinterested 'Determination to be pleased with the *Happiness* of others, and to be uneasy at their *Misery*' (Hutcheson, *Essay*: 17), and it also differs from Hume's account of sympathy as a principle of communication of passions based on 'the conversion of an idea into an impression by the force of imagination' (Hume, *Treatise* 2.3.7: 427). Smith's refined explanation of the mechanisms of the moral sense, which remained for Hutcheson an 'occult quality' (Hutcheson, *Inquiry*: 179), places enormous importance on sympathy and on the spectator's imagination of the wider situation of the observed agent.

In *TMS* VII.iii.1, Smith rejects attempts to reduce moral judgements to self-love or self-interested psychological mechanisms, mentioning Hobbes explicitly. This point also reminds us of Campbell's idea, presented in Chapter 6.2, that our moral approbation of an action depends on our self-love – either we love an agent because she directly gratifies our self-love, or because we imagine ourselves in the position of the person who benefits, and derive pleasure from this imagination. Hutcheson had opposed such ideas with his conception of a disinterested moral sense. Smith explains that thinkers such as Hobbes and Campbell, when they speak about our imagination of being in the other's situation, unknowingly try to give an explanation of the 'indirect sympathy which we feel with the gratitude or resentment of those who received the benefit or suffered the damage resulting from such opposite characters' (Smith, *TMS*, VII.iii.1.3, 2002: 374). Sympathy itself, however, 'cannot, in any sense, be regarded as a selfish principle'. If I sympathise with your sorrows, then

> I consider what I should suffer if I was really you, and I not only change circumstances with you, but I change persons and characters. My grief, therefore, is entirely upon your account, and not in the least upon my own. It is not, therefore, in the least selfish. (Smith, *TMS*, VII.iii.1.4, 2002: 374)

Whether or not Smith's strategy finally succeeds, it is clear that, according to him, there are several fundamentally non-egoistic mechanisms in human psychology that play their roles both in motivation and moral judgement.[10]

For our debates, another difference with Hutcheson is noteworthy in Smith's moral psychology. Like Hutcheson, Smith presupposes the reality of disinterested principles, for example 'generosity, humanity, kindness, compassion, mutual friendship and esteem' (*TMS*, I.ii.4.1, 2002: 47). But like Hume, Smith does not adopt Hutcheson's quite striking optimism about the power of natural benevolence and virtue in human nature. Also, Smith does not accept the fundamental binary distinction between disinterested and self-interested principles that is so essential in Hutcheson.

Rather, Smith often formulates, quite like Hume, more balanced and fine-grained views of our psychologies. He argues, for example, that we should distinguish passions into social, selfish and unsocial ones (*TMS*, I.ii.5, 2002: 49–50), shows at quite some length how we also sympathise with certain selfish passions, and especially argues for a more positive view of self-love against Hutcheson, as we shall see shortly. And when it comes to explaining how we can resist acting upon selfish impulses, Smith insists, somewhat in tension with Hutcheson, that

> it is not the soft power of humanity, it is not that feeble spark of benevolence which Nature has lighted up in the human heart, that is thus capable of counteracting the strongest impulses of self-love. It is a stronger power, a more forcible motive, which exerts itself upon such occasions. It is reason, principle, conscience, the inhabitant of the breast, the man within, the great judge and arbiter of our conduct. (*TMS*, III.iii.4, 2002: 158)

For Smith, the strong 'impulses of self-love' and the 'natural misrepresentations of self-love can be corrected only by the eye of this impartial spectator' (2002: 158).[11] In his account of self-cultivation, Hutcheson had tackled the problem of how to stop passionate self-love. One point was his recommendation of a strengthening of universal benevolence. Smith's solution, which concerns both self-love as a motive and self-love as a possible source of distortion of moral perception, relies on the figure of the impartial spectator, which makes us take into account the perspective of others.

Like Hume before him, Smith spends comparatively little effort on refuting the selfish hypothesis and on arguing for the reality of disinterested benevolence. Again, this was one of Hutcheson's main goals only a few decades earlier, but one gets the impression that for Smith, Hutcheson had established this point, and that there were now other features of our moral psychology to be investigated. But Smith's reduced interest in what was one of Hutcheson's main points does not constitute his most important difference from Hutcheson. Rather, in a similar vein to Hume before him, and in explicit opposition to Hutcheson, Smith suggests a more positive view of the moral value of self-love, especially of self-love as self-esteem and self-love as love of praise. I shall now turn to this theme.

Smith on Hutcheson and Mandeville

In a chapter on Smith's notion of self-interest, Pratap Bhanu Mehta claims that 'for Smith, self-love [. . .] had an appropriate place in the catalogue of human dispositions' (Mehta 2006: 258). I think this broad claim is roughly correct, but considering the present study's emphasis on the variety of conceptions of self-love in eighteenth-century British moral philosophy, I now want to look more precisely into how to understand this point. Smith's moral philosophy and psychology often reflect a moralist's interest in human nature.[12] His analyses in *The Theory of Moral Sentiments* are flavoured with rich descriptions of our moral lives which show his fascination with the classics, but also with the French Augustinian moralists and Mandeville. One domain where Smith's sensibility for the moralists' genre becomes particularly evident is his discussion of the different conceptions of self-love. Like Hutcheson, Smith pays detailed attention to the justifications for and limits of our self-interested pursuit of happiness. This point is most strongly connected to the conception of self-love as egoistic desire, which is central in *The Wealth of Nations*. But he also discusses the notions of self-approbation and due pride (that is, self-love as self-esteem), love of true glory and vanity (as two forms of self-love as love of praise) and undue pride and vanity (in the sense of self-love as *amour-propre*). More so than Hutcheson, Smith has a special interest in the role of vanity in our psychological make-up and social contexts.

Fonna Forman-Barzilai writes in her study of Smith: 'Adam Smith's understanding of self-love is not Hobbesian, but distinctively Stoic in origin' (Forman-Barzilai 2010: 37). I have just suggested that Smith rejects the selfish hypothesis, which can be seen as an anti-Hobbesian and pro-Stoic move, but again, given the variety of conceptions of self-love available to Smith, Forman-Barzilai's statement requires refinement. It seems to me that in Smith's discussion of the different systems of moral philosophy, in Part VII of *The Theory of Moral Sentiments*, he makes two crucial contributions to the debates on self-love, both in the form of critical comments on other philosophers. First, compared to his former teacher Hutcheson, Smith argues for a generally more positive view of egoistic self-love and of self-love as self-esteem. Secondly, Smith attacks Mandeville by insisting on a distinction between appropriate or due pride on the one hand, and undue pride or vanity on the other. As a consequence, Smith argues for a more positive view of self-love as love of praise and rejects both the central place that Mandeville accords to self-love as *amour-propre* in human nature, and the resulting negative moral view of human nature put forward by him. These points emphasise how for Smith, different forms of self-love can have positive values and are not just passions to be overcome in self-cultivation – in spite of the potentially corruptive influence of some forms of self-love in some contexts. Let me first focus on Smith's treatment of Hutcheson, and then look at his discussion of Mandeville.

As far as the question of moral motivation is concerned, Smith famously distinguishes between four different 'systems' of moral philosophy, namely those that make virtue consist in propriety, prudence or benevolence, and lastly the 'licentious' systems. Many of Smith's reflections concern philosophers from classical antiquity, most importantly the Stoics and Epicureans, but Smith also has more recent thinkers in mind – especially Hutcheson.[13] I will here focus on Smith's discussion of those systems that make virtue consist in benevolence, since interestingly, he uses much of this section to argue against Hutcheson for a more positive view of the roles of egoistic self-love, and of self-love as self-esteem in moral motivation. In Smith's presentation, Hutcheson is the most central figure among those philosophers who analyse virtue in terms of benevolence, but he furthermore names the Cambridge Platonists Cudworth, More and Smith, and a rather vague entity called the 'Christian Church'. Now, if according to these thinkers, and especially according to Hutcheson, benevolence is all there is to virtue, then what can we say about the value of self-love? Smith summarises Hutcheson's response, obviously with Hutcheson's moral mathematics in mind. I suggested in Chapter 4 that this is indeed an important part of Hutcheson's answer to the question about the moral value of self-love, but that it is not all he has to say about the fully virtuous agent. I shall return to this point at the end of this section.

Again, most likely with Hutcheson's moral mathematics in mind, Smith presents Hutcheson as having observed 'that whenever in any action, supposed to proceed from benevolent affections, some other motive had been discovered, our sense of the merit of this action was just so far diminished, as this motive was believed to have influenced it' (Smith, *TMS*, VII.ii.3.6, 2002: 356). This is indeed the core message of Hutcheson's formula 'B = (M – I / A)': any contribution by self-love that is necessary to the realisation of a virtuous action diminishes its moral value (Hutcheson, *Inquiry*: 128–9). Benevolence, according to Smith's Hutcheson, is the sole motive that will bestow moral value upon an action – self-love, on the contrary, 'was a principle which could never be virtuous in any degree or in any direction' (Smith, *TMS*, VII.ii.3.12, 2002: 358). For Hutcheson, self-love was either vicious or, at best, depending on the specific circumstances, 'innocent'.

For Smith, still following the formula in Hutcheson's moral mathematics, Hutcheson was so obsessed with presenting benevolence as the sole motive for virtuous actions that even the desire to experience the pleasures of self-approbation (which for Hutcheson are the highest pleasures), produced by the moral sense as a consequence of our virtuous actions, would have to be deducted from the moral value of an action:

> Dr Hutcheson was so far from allowing self-love to be in any case a motive of virtuous actions, that even a regard to the pleasure of self-approbation, to the comfortable applause of our own consciences, according to him, diminished the merit of a benevolent action. (Smith, *TMS*, VII.ii.3.13, 2002: 358)

What Smith has in mind here is the desire to experience self-love as self-esteem or due pride, which is based on a morally virtuous action. At this point, Smith marks his disagreement with Hutcheson. For Smith, self-love as self-esteem – that is, moral self-approbation by our own consciences, consequent upon our virtuous actions and character traits – deserves a more positive treatment than it is given by Hutcheson in his moral philosophy. Smith mentions, first, that 'in the common judgments of mankind', self-love as self-esteem, or 'this regard to the approbation of our own minds', counts as virtuous (2002: 358). Secondly, denying all dimensions of virtue to self-love as self-esteem makes it impossible to explain the fact that we approve of 'inferior virtues' (*TMS*, VII.ii.3.15, 2002: 359) such as prudence and temperance.

But Smith not only makes room for a positive role for self-love as self-esteem, he also extends this to other forms of self-love, which we may subsume under egoistic self-love more generally:

> Regard to our own private happiness and interest, too, appear upon many occasions very laudable principles of action. The habits of oeconomy, industry, discretion, attention, and application of thought, are generally supposed to be cultivated from self-interested motives, and at the same time are apprehended to be very praise-worthy qualities, which deserve the esteem and approbation of every body. (*TMS*, VII.ii.3.16, 2002: 359)

Also, the contraries of these forms of self-love, namely 'carelessness and want of oeconomy', are commonly seen negatively because they demonstrate a 'want of the proper attention to the objects of self-interest' (2002: 359). For Smith, this demonstrates that Hutcheson's approach neglects some important truths about our moral lives, and it allows him then to more effectively contrast Hutcheson's moral philosophy to that of Shaftesbury, where the fully virtuous agent is depicted as one in whom both disinterested *and* self-interested principles are in an appropriate balance or propriety.

In Chapter 4 I suggested that Hutcheson's approach in the moral mathematics is clearly central to his treatment of self-love, benevolence and virtue, but that this does not give us the complete picture of what it is to be a fully virtuous agent. Drawing on Hutcheson's theory of self-cultivation in particular, I highlighted the centrality of the distinction between violent passions and calm affections, and of the question of the scope of emotions such as benevolence and self-love. When it comes to self-cultivation, these are all important factors for Hutcheson, even if they are not included in his rather reductive mathematical model. Most importantly, I drew attention to the passages in Hutcheson in which he presents egoistic self-love in very specific circumstances as not only 'innocent' but even as virtuous. In these passages, Hutcheson is closer to Shaftesbury than in his moral mathematics. It seems that there he allows egoistic self-love to function, to a certain degree, in the make-up of the fully virtuous agent. And against Smith's opposition of Shaftesbury and Hutcheson, one could also stress the fact that Shaftesbury highlights on some occasions that the self-affections are valuable especially insofar as they ultimately make the individual creature more beneficial to the good of the whole. If these points are pertinent, then Smith most likely exaggerates the difference between Hutcheson and Shaftesbury in order to emphasise his own criticisms of Hutcheson, and in order to shed more light on his more positive description of self-love.

Given the generally negative tone of many other eighteenth-century reactions to the 'egoist' Mandeville, it may come as a surprise that Smith actually uses his criticisms of Mandeville to strengthen his moral rehabilitation of self-love. In Smith's criticism of Hutcheson, the focus was on self-love as self-esteem, that is, self-approbation or Hume's *due* pride. In Smith's discussion of Mandeville, he turns his attention to self-love as love of praise, or the desire for approbation and esteem from others. Combining several lines of attack against Mandeville allows Smith to put more flesh on the bones of his positive account of self-love in human motivation.[14] The key elements of his response to Mandeville are a conception of praiseworthiness and a connected distinction between love of virtue (that is, the pure desire to be virtuous – typically found in the wise), love of true glory (that is, self-love as love of praise, in the sense of a desire of *due* praise grounded in the recognition by others of one's virtuous actions and character traits – typically found in ordinary people) and vanity or love of applause (that is, self-love as love of even *unjustified* praise – typically found in the weak and vain).

According to Smith, Mandeville reduces all desire to be praiseworthy – which is, for Smith, at the core of moral motivation – to vanity or 'love of praise and commendation' (Smith, *TMS*, VII.ii.4.7, 2002: 364). Mandeville emphasised the central role of love of praise in the context of his conception of self-love as *amour-propre* or excessive pride: the vexing sentiment that the excessively high value we put on ourselves may in reality be ungrounded can only be remedied by applause from others – whether or not this applause be justified (Mandeville, *Honour*: 7).

Such a desire for praise is what Mandeville calls vanity, and he presents it as the rotten origin of the social practices of flattery and deception, politeness and honour. Crucially, the question of whether or not we are really worthy of the praise we crave plays no role in Mandeville – he rather seems to suggest that we are never worthy of praise.

Smith objects to Mandeville in that he conflates vanity, that is, the desire for unjustified praise, with 'love of true glory', that is, the desire for praise that is justified by our virtuous actions and character traits (Smith, *TMS*, VII.ii.4.8, 2002: 365). In other words, Smith presses a distinction between two versions of self-love as love of praise against Mandeville. What distinguishes the two is the question of whether or not we are, as a matter of fact, praiseworthy, that is, whether we actually possess qualities that merit praise – a question that is not relevant in Mandeville's framework, marked as it is by the Calvinist *topos* of postlapsarian corruption. Smith begins his detailed description of the vain man as follows:

> He is guilty of vanity who desires praise for qualities which are either not praise-worthy in any degree, or not in that degree in which he expects to be praised for them; who sets his character upon the frivolous ornaments of dress and equipage, or upon the equally frivolous accomplishments of ordinary behaviour. (2002: 365)

Remember that for Mandeville – a moralist with the goal of unmasking the hidden rotten motives behind our apparently virtuous actions – love of riches and luxury was just one of many ways in which our sense of what is really praiseworthy can be misled (even if this may have beneficial consequences for society). Mandeville's favourite target was Shaftesbury, whose idea that we are virtuous by nature and could act on naturally virtuous affections Mandeville attacked as deceptive flattery to humankind. Mandeville instead insisted that real moral virtue (as opposed to the social virtues) required self-denial, that is, the voluntary frustration of our passions. Smith also notes that, for Mandeville, it is not the desire for praise but more specifically the desire for *undeserved* praise that motivates us most fundamentally. The fact that Mandeville does not distinguish between due and undue desire for praise makes it possible, according to Smith, for Mandeville to reach his notorious conclusion that what we commonly call 'virtue' or 'public spirit' is in reality nothing but 'the mere offspring of flattery begot upon pride' (Smith, *TMS*, VII.ii.4.7, 2002: 364).

One of the main points in Smith's rejection of Mandeville is that Smith, in a similar vein to Hume, makes room for both a conception of *due* pride, that is, self-love as justified self-esteem, and for a conception of *due* desire for esteem, that is, self-love as love of justified praise. According to Smith, we really can possess and cultivate praiseworthy qualities, most notably the virtues of prudence, justice and beneficence. We are thus not unduly proud if we develop an esteem or approval of ourselves based on those qualities, and we are not vain if we desire to be praised by others for possessing them. The perfection of virtue may be the pure love of virtue, which is completely unconcerned with the opinions of real spectators and free from any desire of praise (with the exception of praise from the impartial spectator). But after all, those agents incorporating the somewhat lower forms of virtue, who are still concerned about the opinions of real spectators, are virtuous agents too.

Smith objects to Mandeville that he has an inflated and vague conception of vanity, and thus for imprecision concerning the different conceptions of self-love. Yet like Hutcheson before him, Smith also opposes Mandeville's claim that genuine moral virtue requires self-denial in the sense of a voluntary frustration of our passions.[15] In this context, Smith identifies two rhetorical moves in Mandeville:

> It was easy for Dr Mandeville to prove, first, that this entire conquest never actually took place among men; and secondly, that, if it was to take place universally, it would be pernicious to society, by putting an end to all industry and commerce, and in a manner to the whole business of human life. By the first of these propositions he seemed to prove that there was no real virtue, and that what pretended to be such, was a mere cheat and imposition upon mankind; and by the second, that private vices were public benefits, since without them no society could prosper or flourish. (Smith, *TMS*, VII.ii.4.12, 2002: 369)

Smith reproaches Mandeville, first, for suggesting a definition of moral virtue (singular) that is impossible for really existing human beings to attain, and secondly, for using this definition in support of both his negative depiction of the social virtues (plural), and the connected conclusion that many vices are useful to the public. But even if Mandeville's psychological statements about flattery and deception 'in some respects bordered upon the truth' (Smith, *TMS*, VII.ii.4.14, 2002: 370), they rely on mistaken psychological and moral assumptions.

Even if Smith remains aware of the problematic potential of self-love in some contexts, we can now see more clearly how self-love can be appropriate to him. Against Mandeville and Hutcheson, Smith argues that several forms of self-love are appropriate ingredients of human nature. First, self-love in the broad sense of egoistic self-love can be appropriate if it does not counteract our due care for the legitimate interests of other people and our own long-term interests – in other words, if it exerts itself in compatibility with the virtue of prudence. This is close to what Hutcheson claimed about self-love as a calm affection, or the calm desire to promote our self-interest. In comparison, however, Smith emphasises more strongly the potentially virtuous aspects of egoistic self-love.

Secondly, self-love in the specific sense of self-esteem or self-approbation can be appropriate if it is based on praiseworthiness, that is, on our possessing qualities that really merit to be esteemed. This is again close to Hutcheson's idea that the moral sense lets the benevolent agent experience moral pleasures upon consideration of her own benevolent motives and character traits. In contrast to Hutcheson, Smith expands the scope beyond mere benevolence to other, lower virtues.

Thirdly, self-love in the specific sense of love of praise, or desire for esteem, can be appropriate, again, if it is connected to praiseworthiness. True, the perfectly virtuous agent will not be concerned with the opinion of others and will only think of the impartial spectator, but the less than perfectly virtuous agent can be incited by her love of praise to cultivate virtue. This is close to Hutcheson's ideas concerning the sense of honour, which makes the agent experience high pleasure upon approval by others, under the condition that the approval concerns her benevolence. Again, Smith expands the scope of potentially praiseworthy features beyond mere benevolence.

It is not surprising that self-love as *amour-propre*, the crucial passion in Mandeville's and Rousseau's narratives of the development of our moral psychologies in society, is not part of Smith's general rehabilitation of self-love as an appropriate human disposition – even if self-love as *amour-propre* might have unintended positive consequences, as famously described in Mandeville. Still, all things considered, and in comparison with his former teacher Hutcheson, Smith significantly extends the rehabilitation of self-love.

7.3 THE SELFISH HYPOTHESIS IN GAY AND ASSOCIATIONIST PSYCHOLOGY

In contrast to Scotland, the selfish hypothesis seems to have been rather tacitly accepted as a useful theory to explain human behaviour in England in the second half of the eighteenth century.[16] Associationist psychology, which went back to John Gay, in particular appreciated the selfish hypothesis as an account of the human mind that offered a unifying principle.

John Gay

In John Clarke of Hull and Archibald Campbell we have seen two authors who attacked Hutcheson by combining the selfish hypothesis with a positive view of human nature. A third influential contemporary English author to use this strategy was John Gay (1699–1745).[17] His *Preliminary Dissertation Concerning the Fundamental Principle of Virtue or Morality* appeared anonymously in Edmund Law's English translation of William King's *Essay on the Origin of Evil* from 1731. Gay is frequently treated as the founder of Associationist psychology and, with David Hartley, Abraham Tucker and others, presented as a precursor of utilitarianism. Gay relies on a Lockean theory of ideas in arguing against ethical rationalism, and he asserts a theological voluntarism. His view of morality is that 'the Will of God is the immediate Criterion of Virtue, and the Happiness of Mankind the Criterion of the Will of God; and therefore the Happiness of Mankind may be said to be the Criterion of Virtue, but *once removed*' (Gay 1731: xix). Promoting the happiness of humankind is in accordance with the will of God, and therefore it is morally virtuous.

Gay's attacks on Hutcheson's claim that moral motivation is disinterested are at the centre of his discussion of self-interest. We have seen Butler attack this Hutchesonian claim as well, but Gay argues against Hutcheson from within the framework of the selfish hypothesis. Gay accepts Hutcheson's anti-rationalism, yet he objects that Hutcheson's account of a disinterested moral sense as a principle of approbation, and of disinterested benevolence as a principle of motivation, 'seems still insufficient, rather cutting the Knot than untying it' (Gay 1731: xiv). Hutcheson relies on occult qualities or instincts, which cannot be further explained. Gay, by contrast, wants to show that both moral motivation and approbation

> are finally resolvable into *Reason* pointing out *private Happiness*, and are conversant only about things apprehended to be means tending to this end; and that whenever this end is not perceiv'd, they are to be accounted for from the *Association of Ideas*, and may properly enough be call'd *Habits*. (1731: xiv)

Focusing on motivation in general, Gay asserts the selfish hypothesis and claims that 'Happiness, private Happiness, is the proper or ultimate End of all our Actions whatever' (1731: xxv). In order to support this claim, Gay relies on Locke's analysis of desire as uneasiness and emphasises the importance of the power of association as a fundamental principle in human psychology, and as the basis for the diversification of our motives. Concerning moral motivation in particular, Gay declares alongside Clarke and Campbell that Hutcheson is mistaken in his assumption that 'Merit is inconsistent with acting upon *private Happiness*, as an ultimate End' (1731: xxv). Even if the ultimate end of every action is the happiness of the agent, the particular ends differ, and it is this difference that constitutes the moral value of the action. The particular end of an action can be, for example, the agent's own happiness, the happiness of others, or to please God.

> Whenever therefore the *particular* End of any Action is the Happiness of another (though the Agent design'd thereby to procure himself Esteem and Favour, and look'd upon that Esteem and Favour as a means of private Happiness) that Action is meritorious. (1731: xxvi)

Thus, even if all our actions are ultimately determined by self-interest, morally virtuous actions are possible under the condition that their particular end is the happiness of others. Within this moral space we are able to make sense of our distinctions between virtue and vice, according to Gay.

David Hartley

After Gay, the selfish hypothesis was revived in the Associationist psychology of David Hartley (1705–57), who in turn influenced, among others, Abraham Tucker, William Paley and Joseph Priestley.[18] Hartley, in his *Observations on Man, his Frame, his Duty, and his Expectations* (1749), defends a necessitarian account of human psychology that rests on the 'Doctrines of *Vibrations* and *Association*' (Hartley 1749: i 5), and that is developed with invocations of Newton, Locke and Gay.[19] As a result of physiological and psychological mechanisms, sensations turn into ideas, and simple ideas are transformed into more complex ones, which results in states of mind such as passions and affections. These can be 'no more than Aggregates of simple Ideas united by Association' which ultimately 'arise thus from Pleasure and Pain' (Hartley 1749: 368–9). Hartley lists seven kinds of pleasures and pains: those of sensation, and the intellectual ones of imagination, ambition, self-interest, sympathy, theopathy and the moral sense. The former, lower kinds are transformed into higher ones by the principle of association. The idea of a hierarchy of pleasures, present in Hutcheson, remains of great importance for subsequent Associationists.

In the framework of Hartley's psychology we can note a shift in attention with regard to the selfish hypothesis. Rather than explicitly insisting on self-interested analyses of all affections, he explores their psychological origin and development from the agent's original experiences of pleasure and pain. In his discussion of the other-directed pleasures and pains of sympathy, for example, Hartley draws attention to their psychological origins in self-interested mechanisms. Compassion, or 'the Uneasiness which a Man feels at the Misery of another' (1749: 474), is generated in children by a process of memory and imagination based on misery they have experienced themselves.

> The same Sources of Compassion remain, though with some Alterations, during our whole Progress through Life; and an attentive Person may plainly discern the constituent Parts of his Compassion, while they are yet the mere internal, and, as one may say, selfish Feelings abovementioned; and before they have put on the Nature of Compassion by Coalescence with the rest. (1749: 475)

While carefully tracing back the selfish origins of other-directed principles, Hartley seems not really interested in repeated assertions of the selfish hypothesis and in explicit analyses of all principles of action in terms of self-interest. Instead, he claims that the doctrine of association proves, for example, 'that there is, and must be, such a Thing as pure disinterested Benevolence' (1749: 474). Similarly, in matters of moral approbation Hartley insists that there is 'disinterested Love and Esteem' (1749: 493), even though in his explanation of the origins of the pleasures and pains of the moral sense, he draws attention to self-interested mechanisms in moral education, to the benefits of virtue and to the importance of the hope of future rewards.

Abraham Tucker

The Light of Nature Pursued (1765–75) by Abraham Tucker (1705–74), published under the pseudonym Edward Search, argues that the moral life requires both reason and revealed religion. It is strongly influenced by Locke, Gay and, especially, Hartley. Without properly discussing the objections from authors such as Shaftesbury, Hutcheson and Butler, Tucker puts forward a moral psychology that rests on the selfish hypothesis, combining it with a view of human nature that emphasises the capacity for forming virtuous habits.[20] The psychological mechanism of association allows for the development and cultivation of virtuous dispositions, which are the source of our highest satisfaction. Tucker's treatment of benevolence is very revealing in this context. The ultimately self-interested aspects of benevolence (which would be Hutchesonian beneficence, that is, doing good to others for ultimately self-interested reasons) are generally hidden to introspection, since 'our ultimate end is very rarely our ultimate point of view' (Tucker 2003: I, ii, 328). As to our reasons for being benevolent, however, 'we must imagine [the wise man] had taken his own heart under examination before, and determined to cherish benevolence there, because of the connection he had observed it to have with [his own] happiness' (2003: 328). This does not mean that benevolence, which Tucker declares to be ultimately self-interested, is selfish in a way that deprives it of merit (2003: 314ff.). Like Hartley, Tucker also extensively discusses the advantages of benevolence and their function in moral education, explaining why the wise man would choose to cultivate benevolence (2003: 328–9).

7.4 TOWARDS THE END OF THE EIGHTEENTH CENTURY

Towards the end of the eighteenth century the selfish hypothesis remained important in England in Associationist psychology, which underlay the works of theological utilitarians such as William Paley and Joseph Priestley.[21] Both had a pronounced interest in bringing Enlightenment values and Christian religion together, and used the doctrine of association of ideas to argue that self-interest properly understood directs us towards virtue and religion. Furthermore, the selfish hypothesis might have a role at the beginning of the utilitarian Jeremy Bentham's *Introduction to the Principles of Morals and Legislation* (1789), where he states: 'Nature has placed mankind under the governance of two sovereign masters, *pain* and *pleasure*' (Bentham 1789: i). But even if this is interpreted as an assertion of the selfish hypothesis, it is important to highlight that Bentham's main interest is to argue for the principle of utility as a criterion of morality that does not focus on the motives for actions but on their consequences for the greatest happiness. The early eighteenth-century question concerning the relation between self-interest and sociability is not the primary focus of his moral philosophy.

In Scotland, the selfish hypothesis remained quite out of fashion. I briefly mentioned Thomas Reid (1710–96) in Chapter 5 on Butler. Again, compared to Hutcheson and Butler as two authors from the first half of the eighteenth century, Reid did not consider refuting the selfish hypothesis as his main task. What mattered more to him was to elaborate the principles of common sense philosophy as a means of opposing Hume's scepticism. In this context, Reid's attention shifted to other aspects of moral philosophy, such as freedom of will and the role of reason in our moral lives. Still, in Reid's *Essays on the Active Powers of Man* (1788), there are several interesting passages for the debates on self-love. One of these is his adopting of a conception of self-love that is evidently inspired by Butler's conception of self-love as respect of self. Many of his arguments against the selfish hypothesis are based on this conception of self-love as a higher-order principle.

Distinguishing between mechanical, animal and rational principles of action, Reid states that the appetites are part of the animal principles requiring 'intention and will in their operation, but not judgment' (Reid 2010: 152). The appetites, 'considered in themselves, are neither social principles of action, nor selfish [. . .] There is no self-love implied in it any more than benevolence' (2010: 95), because there is no concern for any good implied. In reality, it is often the case that 'self-love is sacrificed to appetite' (2010: 95). This point, which relies on a conception of self-love as a higher-order rational principle, Reid sees, like Butler, as contradicting the selfish hypothesis. Reid then argues for the reality of benevolent affections, which presuppose some representation of the good of others. In this context, he looks at the selfish hypothesis in the version of the claim that 'we desire the good of others, only in order to procure some pleasure or good to ourselves' (2010: 110). This was also discussed in Hutcheson as one self-interested analysis of benevolence. Reid produces a theistic teleological argument: we need society to survive, and in order to function in society, we cannot be motivated by rational principles only (such as self-love, as opposed to self-interested desires). Rather, 'our rational principles are aided by principles of an inferior order', such as affections and appetites (2010: 111). Thus, given the workings of our minds in view of our need to live in society, 'the benevolent affections planted in human nature, appear therefore no less necessary for the preservation of the human species, than the appetites of hunger and thirst' (2010: 111). There are various particular benevolent affections, such as parental affections, gratitude, pity, friendship and love between the sexes, which for Reid demonstrate the reality of benevolence in general. Reid states that he is aware that 'there has been much subtile disputation in ancient and modern times' regarding the question of whether these benevolent affections are reducible to self-love, but 'I decline entering into this dispute, till I shall have explained that principle of action which we commonly call *self-love*' (2010: 120).

Reid presents self-love as one of the mind's rational principles, 'which have that name, because they can have no existence in beings not endowed with reason, and, in all their exertions, require, not only intention and will, but judgment or reason' (2010: 152). Like Butler, Reid thus uses a relatively restricted sense of the term 'self-love'. This is different from Hutcheson, for whom self-directed first-order passions and affections could be instances of self-love (in the sense of self-love as egoistic desire). Self-love, for Reid, aims at 'what is good for us upon the whole'. Given the providential ordering of this world, this will ultimately coincide with our moral duty – a claim that reminds us of Butler's claim about the convergence of conscience and self-love (2010: 154). In a similar vein to Butler, Reid treats self-love as a 'leading and governing principle, to which all our animal principles ought to be subordinate' (2010: 156). Self-love 'operates in a calm and cool manner' and it 'implies real judgments in all its operations'. Reid presents the more general idea that the passions thus ought to be 'under the dominion of reason' as directed against Hume's 'contrary maxim' (2010: 157).

Like Butler, Reid conceives self-love as a rational principle, as 'a regard to our good upon the whole', which will ultimately lead 'to the practice of every virtue' (2010: 159). However, Reid specifies that

> a regard to our own good cannot, of itself, produce any benevolent affection. But, if such affections be a part of our constitution, and if the exercise of them make a capital part of our happiness, a regard to our own good ought to lead us to cultivate and exercise them, as every benevolent affection makes the good of others to be our own. (2010: 164)

This point reminds us of Hutcheson's argument that self-love cannot produce benevolence, with the notable difference that, for Hutcheson, self-love is also a first-order principle. Reid points out several 'defects' of self-love, even in the sense of a higher-order principle governing other, non-rational principles with the self-interested general goal of promoting our good on the whole. Self-love requires a reflective and extensive perspective that only few will be able to adopt; it cannot produce on its own the 'noblest kind of virtue, which claims our highest love and esteem' (2010: 165); and it does not increase our chances of happiness to be overly concerned with our own good (2010: 166). Thus, self-love cannot be but one of several rational principles.

In conclusion, I should mention Dugald Stewart's *The Philosophy of the Active and Moral Powers of Man* (1829). In Book 2, *Of our rational and governing principles of action*, Stewart discusses our 'prudential regard to our own happiness, or, what is commonly called by moralists, the principle of self-love' (Stewart 1829: 91). Like Butler and Reid, Stewart juxtaposes particular principles of action to that rational principle of action called 'self-love', which presupposes a capacity 'to form the notion of *happiness*, or what is good for it upon the whole, and to deliberate about the most effectual means of attaining it' (1829: 96). This should not be confounded with 'the word *selfishness*' (1829: 97). Explicitly against the Swiss Protestant theologian Huldrych Zwingli (1484–1531), and against the Augustinians more generally, Stewart argues that self-love is not 'the original or radical sin in our nature' (1829: 98). Self-love is different from ambition and vanity (1829: 93, 95). At the end of his treatment, Stewart quotes Aristotle's discussion of the two sorts of φιλαυτία in *Nicomachean Ethics* IX.8. – the exact passage that Archibald Campbell had quoted about a century earlier in an unsuccessful attempt to shield himself against orthodox criticisms. A lot had happened in between.

7.5 CONCLUSION

This chapter has drawn attention to several important points regarding the development of the debates on self-love in the second half of the eighteenth century. I have suggested that the selfish hypothesis, which was one of the central themes in the debates in the first half of the century, attracted less attention in the second half. On this point, an interesting difference appears between the Scottish and the English context: in Scotland, the selfish hypothesis was generally considered as refuted, and Hutcheson's claim about the reality of disinterested sociable and virtuous principles in human nature was quite generally accepted. From this point of view, Campbell's obsessive insistence on the selfish hypothesis remains an exception in Scotland. In England, however, under the influence of Associationist psychology, the selfish hypothesis was more commonly treated as a useful hypothesis to understand the workings of our minds in a unified framework.

In Scotland, with attention shifting away from the selfish hypothesis, and with a general acceptance of some minimal form of sociability based on benevolence, sympathy or similar principles, new discussions emerged. Already in the first half of the eighteenth century, following previous attempts by, for example, the Cambridge Platonists, there was a widespread tendency to morally rehabilitate human nature against the Calvinist *topos* of postlapsarian corruption, and this partly extended to a rehabilitation of self-love. In the second half of the eighteenth century, and in different ways, authors such as Hume and Smith continue to make room for more positive views of self-love. In some sense, they not only follow Butler, but also Campbell in his treatment of self-love as love of praise, even if they clearly reject Campbell's egoistic psychological framework. Hume argues that pride, or self-love as self-esteem, can be justified and morally praiseworthy. In some sense, this is an extension of Hutcheson's claim that self-approbation by the moral sense, based on our benevolent motives and character traits, can be appropriate. Smith attacks Hutcheson's rather critical view of self-love and furthermore argues in his rejection of Mandeville that self-love as love of praise, or the desire of esteem, can be a virtuous motive. A last point that is relevant to the rehabilitation of self-love is the interest of several later authors in Butler's conception of self-love as respect of self.

NOTES

1. See Hume's famous letter to Hutcheson from 17 September 1739 (Hume 2011: I, 32–5). The comparison between the anatomist's and the painter's approach to moral philosophy, and Hume's more general connections with Mandeville, are discussed in, for example, Gill (2000; 2006: 201–8), Herdt (2008: 221), Tolonen (2013: 147–57) and Harris (2015: 78–85). Gill (2006: 203–5) suggests that Hume did not want to address the question of the moral status of postlapsarian human nature at all, and he draws attention to Hume's refusal in the *Treatise* 'to give God any role in its account of morality and human nature'. This points to a very important difference between the philosophical projects of Hume and his precursors, but at times this difference may be somewhat less profound than often claimed, as the subsequent analyses suggest.
2. I refer the reader to Harris (2015), the intellectual biography of Hume.
3. See, for example, Norton (1982: 147), Gill (2000: 90) and Harris (2015: 71–2, 256).
4. A similar point is again made by Ferguson in the *Essay on the History of Civil Society* (1767), when he differentiates between the approach by the 'vulgar' and the approach by the 'speculative', who try to reduce all benevolence to self-love (Ferguson 1995: 19). But 'if a man of speculation should prove that we are selfish in a sense of his own, it does not follow that we are so in the sense of the vulgar' (1995: 20).
5. Harris (2015: 163) suggests that this essay 'is very hard not to read as a kind of supplement to the *Treatise*. It raised the question that Hume had very carefully *not* raised in his anatomical study of human nature.'
6. On the question of how our 'circles of sympathy' become extended, Smith developed the most complete account during the Scottish Enlightenment, and this has often been linked to the Stoic conception of οἰκείωσις. See most importantly Forman-Barzilai (2010).
7. On Hume's playing with themes from Mandeville and the Augustinians, see, for example, Herdt (2008: 306–21), Taylor (2012; 2015: 134–59), Tolonen (2013: 157–227) and Harris (2015: 102–16).

8. Jennifer Herdt has termed this the 'Bourgeois rehabilitation of pride' (2008: 306). See also Taylor's reflections on Hume's account of pride in Taylor (2015: 140–59).

9. See furthermore Taylor (2015: 140–1) on the differences between Hume on the one hand, and Mandeville and Hobbes on the other.

10. See, for example, Griswold (1999: 126–7).

11. Heath (2013: 250–3) provides an illuminating discussion of Smith's remarks concerning self-love's corrupting influence on moral perception. In this context, Heath emphasises Smith's critical view of self-love as a source of delusion, which is, however, overcome by the impartial spectator. This point is compatible with my highlighting Smith's positive views of self-love in motivational contexts.

12. This is also true for Smith's interest in Rousseau's moral philosophy, where the distinction between *amour-propre* and *amour de soi* played a central role – a point with which Smith famously plays in his *Letter to the Authors of the Edinburgh Review* when he compares Rousseau and Mandeville. For a recent discussion, see Griswold (2018).

13. Smith's interest in the Stoics has attracted the attention of various commentators. Raphael and Macfie comment that 'Smith's ethical doctrines are in fact a combination of Stoic and Christian virtues' (1976: 6). This idea is not entirely off the mark, and merits a more critical discussion. See, for example, Vivenza (2001), Forman-Barzilai (2010) and my brief comments in Maurer (2016c: 254–5; 263–6).

14. On Smith's frequently discussed criticisms of Mandeville, see also Hanley (2009: 92–9), who reads these passages in the light of an 'ascent of self-love in three stages', namely 'the love of praise, the love of true glory, and the love of virtue'. In my reading, Smith does not positively suggest that love of virtue is some kind of self-love, or that it proceeds from self-love, but only that 'self-love may frequently be a virtuous motive of action' (Smith, *TMS*, VII.ii.4.8, 2002: 365). In any case, Hanley is right to point out the crucial role of different forms or stages of self-love in Smith's account of the psychological development of the virtuous agent.

15. Self-command is one of the central themes in Smith's moral theory. Within certain limits, it reminds us of his interest in the Stoics and Aristotle. See Vivenza (2001: 57–61) and Maurer (2016c: 263–6). Especially when it comes to a comparison between Smith and Mandeville, the crucial difference between controlling one's emotions and frustrating them needs to be noted. Philosophers such as Shaftesbury, Hutcheson and Campbell had elaborate theories of how to control, redirect and improve one's emotions, both violent and calm, but Mandeville goes much further when claiming that the passions need to be *frustrated* to make genuine moral virtue possible.

16. Parts of this section are closely based on Maurer (2013a: 304–7).

17. On Gay, see Price (1999). On Gay and the later Associationists as precursors of utilitarianism, see Albee (1990) and Crimmins (1998).

18. Given their shared interest in the selfish hypothesis, it is certainly noteworthy that Hartley supported the publication of Campbell's *Necessity of Revelation* – see Mills (2015: 736).
19. For Hartley in general, see Allen (1999). For a comparative discussion of Hartley, Tucker and Priestley in view of Associationism and the free will debate, see Harris (2005: 155–78).
20. See Harris's *Introduction* in Tucker (2003: I, ix) and Nuovo (1999).
21. Parts of this section are based on Maurer (2013a: 310–11).

8. Conclusion

In this book, I have shed new light on the debates on self-love that occupied a central place in eighteenth-century British moral philosophy. In order to appropriately describe developments throughout the century I have, crucially, not only paid attention to major, canonical philosophers, but I have also discussed lesser-known figures and their contexts, for example Archibald Campbell and his dealings with the Committee for Purity of Doctrine of the Scottish Kirk. This has allowed me to highlight how very different thinkers, major and minor, were in intellectual conversation with each other.

In the first chapter, I distinguished several thematic areas of particular importance for our understanding of the debates, namely, the presence of five specific conceptions of self-love, which have different relations to our present-day notion of egoism; the arguments concerning the selfish hypothesis, or the claim that we are only motivated by (some kind of) self-love; and the connections between the debates on self-love and more general discussions of the moral status of human nature. I have furthermore regularly drawn attention to how the eighteenth-century trend to formulate more positive views of human nature than the pessimistic one suggested by the Calvinist *topos* of postlapsarian corruption often included the development of more or less explicitly positive accounts of self-love.

Crucially, I have drawn attention to the vagueness of the central term of this study, 'self-love'. Present-day commentators, especially in the discipline of philosophy, have a tendency to associate it with our present-day notion of egoism, and thus with the desire to promote one's own well-being or to procure some good to the agent herself. Egoistic desires are typically opposed to altruistic ones, the latter being defined as ultimately aiming at the promotion of the well-being of others, for their own sake. In several eighteenth-century authors, most prominently

Hutcheson, mapping the distinction between self-love (or self-interested desires) and benevolence (or disinterested desires) on to the distinction between egoism and altruism is indeed appropriate. Then again, there are numerous cases where it is not – crucially in the case of Butler, who relies on a very different conception of self-love than Hutcheson, and who accordingly uses very different conceptions of interestedness and disinterestedness. We need to be aware of such differences in order to correctly understand their central claims.

Grasping the more specific meanings of the term 'self-love' is crucial to reconstructing the main arguments in the debates on self-love. Besides egoistic self-love, I have shown that the term 'self-love' often refers to love of praise (or, as it is often called, desire of esteem). Here, a specific good is desired for oneself, a good that requires us to see ourselves as agents in a social context. I have shown how strongly the moral evaluation of that form of self-love varied: it was presented by Mandeville as an unjustified and morally problematic (yet at the same time useful) desire to be flattered in order to secure our shaky belief in our own superiority; Campbell treated it as the motive for morally virtuous actions; Smith argued that insofar as self-love as love of praise was connected to a desire to be praiseworthy, it constituted a central ingredient of the moral lives of ordinary, non-sage moral agents.

A third important conception of self-love, then, is self-love as self-esteem, or *due* pride. Here, the term refers to some positive evaluation of the agent by herself, which can be in principle justified. In the early eighteenth century this conception of self-love was present, for example, in Hutcheson's discussions of the agent's self-approbation by her moral sense, yet it became much more important in Hume's discussion of due pride, and in Smith's distinction between due pride and vanity.

Hume and others noted the comparative scarcity in the early eighteenth century of a conception of pride as a potentially justified positive attitude to oneself. This may be partly due to the then more strongly present Calvinist *topos* of postlapsarian corruption. In this context, love of self was typically presented as opposed to love of God, and pride was typically criticised as an attitude that had degenerated into something vicious. This theological background informs a fourth conception of self-love, self-love as *amour-propre* (or *excessive* pride, as opposed to due pride). Self-love as *amour-propre* had its most prominent and influential presence in Mandeville, in the passion he labels 'self-liking' in *Part II* of *The Fable of the Bees*, and 'pride' or 'self-love' in *Part I*. In the process of overcoming the Calvinist *topos* of postlapsarian corruption, the claim that pride is always unjustified and excessive met with numerous objections, most prominently from Hume and

Smith, who both defended pride against Mandeville's views and thus partly contributed to its moral rehabilitation. They attacked not only Mandeville's descriptive psychology, but also his moral pessimism regarding our psychological make-up.

The fifth conception of self-love, then, is what I have termed self-love as respect of self. This was crucially developed by Butler, in a different interpretation of Aristotle's remarks on φιλαυτία than that of Campbell, and it exerted quite some influence during the second half of the eighteenth century. The idea that we can only speak of an action as 'motivated by self-love' under the condition that it be motivated by a rational higher-order principle, but not if it is motivated by just any egoistic first-order desire, clarifies some of the most important differences between Butler and Hutcheson, including their distinct uses of the adjectives 'interested' and 'disinterested'. For Butler, in stark contrast to Hutcheson, it does not make sense to speak of virtue as 'disinterested', since self-love as respect of self will naturally direct us towards virtue. The conception of self-love as respect of self came to play a special role in its moral rehabilitation against the Augustinian understanding of self-love as opposed to love of God.

Bearing in mind these different conceptions of self-love allows for a much more fine-grained and appropriate description of the debates on self-love than a reconstruction only in terms of the notion of egoism. One of the crucial themes in these debates concerns the arguments for and against the selfish hypothesis, that is, the claim that self-love (in some form or other) is the sole motivational source for our actions. I have shown how central a place the selfish hypothesis occupied, especially in the first half of the century. Shaftesbury, who rejects it, and Mandeville, who can be taken to argue in favour of some version of it, set the stage for these debates. Hutcheson and Butler took positions against the selfish hypothesis, and Campbell, Gay and Clarke defended it, yet in a tone that was very different from Mandeville's. This fact is generally ignored by present-day commentators.

In the early decades of the eighteenth century, numerous arguments for and against different versions of the selfish hypothesis were debated. Often, the conception of self-love that informed these arguments was self-love as egoistic or self-love as hedonistic egoistic desire. Yet one could also construe versions of the selfish hypothesis centring on the conception of self-love as love of praise (or love of esteem), defended in different versions by Mandeville and Campbell, and attacked by Hutcheson and others; as well as versions built on the conceptions of self-love as self-esteem (or due pride) and as *amour-propre* (or excessive pride), suggested, for example, by Mandeville and attacked by Hutcheson. We have also seen

Butler, Hutcheson, Reid and others attacking the claim that self-love as respect of self could be the sole motive for our actions. Especially in the case of Butler, I have pointed to arguments that can only be properly understood and compared to Hutcheson's if we take into account the deep differences between their respective conceptions of self-love.

I have suggested that the selfish hypothesis was somewhat less important in the second half of the eighteenth century than in the first – in tendency, attention shifted to other themes. Here, an interesting difference between the Scottish and the English debates emerges. In the Scottish context, where questions concerning sympathy and sociability became central, the selfish hypothesis was quite commonly treated as having been successfully rejected. In the English context, by contrast, Associationist psychologists were deeply interested in proposing a unifying explanatory principle for the workings of the mind, and they considered the selfish hypothesis more commonly as established.

One particularly important point deserves to be repeated: Hutcheson defended the view that accepting the selfish hypothesis (in any of its versions) would force us into a pessimistic view of the moral status of human nature as incapable of virtue, and would thus keep us from cultivating it. However, authors such as Campbell, Gay, Clarke and the Associationists contradict Hutcheson on this point. They took great pains to make room for a positive account of human nature and for conceptions of moral self-cultivation within the psychological framework of the selfish hypothesis. Hume seems to have seen the controversial nature of Hutcheson's claim that the selfish hypothesis forces us into a pessimistic view of human nature. Hume did not himself adopt the selfish hypothesis, but he drew attention to the fact that there are very different versions of it – some indeed debasing human nature, yet others simply proposing some innocent 'philosophical chymistry', motivated by an obsessive concern with finding one single explanatory principle of human behaviour (Hume, *Enquiry*: 298).

The debates on the moral corollaries of the selfish hypothesis bring us to a more general theme. Following several present-day commentators (for example, Michael Gill and Colin Heydt), I argue that the question of the moral status of human nature was crucial throughout the eighteenth century, and that the period is characterised by the development of more positive views of human nature in comparison to the negative Calvinist view. This latter is deeply marked by the *topos* of irredeemable postlapsarian corruption, and it dominated seventeenth-century moral theology and philosophy (with notable exceptions). According to this view, genuine morality and moral self-cultivation are not within our power – justification is not by works but by grace, to put it in more theological terms. Such claims were opposed in various ways, and sometimes in direct connection with the debates on self-love. Shaftesbury, Hutcheson and Butler insisted that self-love is not the sole principle in human nature, and that there are disinterested principles and a moral faculty, which makes human nature naturally virtuous. Mandeville ridiculed Shaftesbury's position and argued against a connection between virtue and simply acting on natural passions – for Mandeville, genuine moral virtue (singular), as opposed to the social virtues (plural), requires self-denial, that is, the voluntary frustration of our corrupt natural passions. But we are hardly ever (or never) capable of performing self-denial. Nevertheless, the world is providentially ordered so that we can live in a peaceful and flourishing society of hypocrites and flatterers.

Yet arguing for the reality of disinterested benevolent emotions besides self-interested ones was not the sole strategy for morally rehabilitating human nature against grim Augustinian views. There were numerous arguments for the view that self-love, one of the basic motivational principles in human nature, is not corrupt. In some cases, the moral rehabilitation of human nature was thus connected to the rehabilitation of self-love, considered by others as an utterly suspicious feature of postlapsarian human nature. We have seen Shaftesbury, an opponent of the selfish hypothesis, put forward a positive view of self-love as a feature of the fully virtuous agent. With arguably less emphasis, Hutcheson depicted self-love on some occasions as a good feature of human nature – Butler and Smith went much further. Campbell, a staunch defender of the selfish hypothesis, also argues for positive views of self-love: for Campbell, self-love as love of praise (or, in Campbell's own terminology, self-love in the form of 'desire of esteem') is even the motive for morally virtuous actions.

In such debates, the Classics often occupy most interesting roles. This holds particularly for the Stoics, who in their theory of οἰκείωσις (*oikeiôsis*) were often interpreted as defending the reality of some form of disinterested benevolence. Interestingly, in the seventeenth century, when questions about free will and determinism dominated the discussions, it was not uncommon to associate the Stoics with Hobbes. Hutcheson, however, in the vein of Shaftesbury, presented Hobbes alongside the Epicureans as a defender of the selfish hypothesis, and as opposed by the Stoics, Shaftesbury and himself. In other words, Hutcheson used the Stoics in support of his fundamental claim that there is natural benevolence, natural virtue and a moral sense. Yet interestingly enough, Campbell seems to have thought that the Stoics could be used in his favour as well, even if he adopts the selfish hypothesis. When Campbell attacks Hobbes's analysis of sociability as based on mutual fear, and proposes his analysis in terms of love of oneself in others, he often refers to the Stoics. Such points must at least make us hesitate to adopt too readily the rough dichotomy between (neo-)Stoics on the one hand, and (neo-)Epicureans and (neo-)Augustinians on the other.

Some final remarks about method may be apposite. The central goal of the present study was to achieve a better understanding of the debates on self-love in eighteenth-century British moral philosophy. This has required several lines of inquiry, which are more or less common (and, sometimes, more or less valued) in the intellectual enterprises called 'philosophy', 'history of philosophy' and 'intellectual history'. The conceptions of self-love needed to be analysed in greater detail to allow for more accurate reconstructions of the key arguments in the debates – the most prominent examples were the arguments concerning the selfish hypothesis and the moral value of self-love. In addition, the larger aim of this book required on several occasions an examination of sources outside philosophy strictly speaking – the most prominent were theological documents. It also involved studying so-called 'minor' authors, such as Campbell, who have never made it into the reading lists of either philosophy or intellectual history (and probably never will).

What can we learn for the debates on self-love specifically from such excursions into, say, peripheral areas of the history of philosophy? One crucial lesson, I think, is the necessity of reassessing some preconceived ideas about the period. The case of Campbell has demonstrated, for example, that Hutcheson's binary presentation of the relevant positions in the debates on self-love, which to quite some extent still informs our present-day reading, is distorting. Among other reasons, we must hesitate to accept Hutcheson's presentation because Campbell, who was like Hutcheson himself a student of Simson, argues for a very positive view of the moral status of human nature – while endorsing the framework of the selfish hypothesis. Even more so, we must acknowledge that the orthodox Calvinist Committee for Purity of Doctrine attacked Campbell for his positive views of postlapsarian human nature as naturally virtuous, and for his positive views of self-love, but not for his adopting of the selfish hypothesis. Such points suggest that one of the period's most appealing hidden topics was the broader Calvinist *topos* of postlapsarian corruption, much more so than the selfish hypothesis. Hutcheson must have been aware of this, even if he presented himself as primarily concerned with the selfish hypothesis, and his philosophical positions almost got him into problems with the orthodox faction in the Kirk (see Moore 2013).

This suggests that studying so-called 'minor' thinkers and their broader intellectual contexts may make us reconsider our ideas of what was really important in a past philosophical debate. Some will ask whether studying past philosophical debates, let alone *minores*, really counts as 'philosophy'. I shall not attempt to give an answer here, yet I hope that the exploration of the debates on self-love in this book has suggested at least on some occasions that it might be fruitful to look outside the narrow boundaries of what we presently define as the core business of an academic discipline. One of the lessons to be learned by philosophers from past theological debates is that future generations might look back with puzzlement at obsessive attempts to defend one single, orthodox version of an intellectual enterprise. Latitudinarian approaches may prove to be valuable not only in matters of theology.

Bibliography

PRIMARY SOURCES

Abbadie, Jacques (2003 [1692]), *L'art de se connaître soi-même*, Paris: Fayard.

Aristotle (2002), *Nicomachean Ethics*, trans. and ed. Sarah Broadie and Christopher Rowe, Oxford: Oxford University Press.

Bayle, Pierre (2007 [1683]), *Pensées diverses sur la comète*, ed. Joyce and Hubert Bost, Paris: Flammarion.

Bentham, Jeremy (1789), *An Introduction to the Principles of Morals and Legislation*, London.

[Blair, Hugh] (1755), 'Review of *A System of Moral Philosophy*, by Francis Hutcheson', *Edinburgh Review*, 1, 9–23.

Blair, Hugh (1824 [1777]), *Sermons*, 2 vols, Edinburgh: James Shaw.

Boston, Thomas (1787 [1720]), *Human Nature in its Fourfold State*, Falkirk.

Butler, Joseph (2017 [1726]), *Fifteen Sermons Preached at the Rolls Chapel and Other Writings on Ethics*, ed. David McNaughton, Oxford: Oxford University Press.

Calvin, Jean (2008 [1541]), *Institution de la religion chrétienne*, ed. Olivier Millett, 2 vols, Geneva: Droz.

Campbell, Archibald (1733), *An Enquiry into the Original of Moral Virtue*, Edinburgh.

Campbell, Archibald (1735), *Remarks upon some Passages in Books Publish'd by Mr. Archibald Campbell, S.T.P. Professor of Divinity and Ecclesiastical History in the University of St. Andrews, with His Explications on them*, Edinburgh.

Campbell, Archibald (1736a), *Professor Campbell's Further Explications With Respect to Some Articles of the former Charge, Wherein the R. Committee for Purity of Doctrine have Declar'd Themselves not Satisfy'd*, Edinburgh.

Campbell, Archibald (1736b), *The Report of the Committee for Purity of Doctrine, at Edinburgh, March 16, 1736. With Professor Campbell's Remarks upon It. To which is subjoin'd, in the Way of Conclusion, A Short Account of the Orthodoxy of Both Sides*, Edinburgh.

Carmichael, Gershom (2002 [1724]), *Natural Rights on the Threshold of the Scottish Enlightenment: The Writings of Gershom Carmichael*, ed. James Moore and Michael Silverthorne, Indianapolis: Liberty Fund.

Church Law Society (ed.) (1843), *Acts of the General Assembly of the Church of Scotland, 1638–1842*, Edinburgh: The Edinburgh Printing & Publishing Society.

Church of Scotland (ed.) (1728), *The Confession of Faith, The Larger and Shorter Catechisms, with the Scripture-Proofs at large*, Edinburgh.

Clarke, John (1726), *The Foundation of Morality in Theory and Practice Considered*, York.

Cudworth, Ralph (1678), *The True Intellectual System of the Universe*, London.

Dubos, Jean-Baptiste (1770 [1719]), *Réflexions critiques sur la poésie et sur la peinture*, 2 vols, Paris.

Esprit, Jacques (1996 [1679]), *La fausseté des vertus humaines*, ed. Pascal Quignard, Paris: Aubier.

Ferguson, Adam (1995 [1767]), *An Essay on the History of Civil Society*, ed. Fania Oz-Salzberger, Cambridge: Cambridge University Press.

Forbes, Alexander (1734), 'An Essay on Self-love', in *Essays Moral and Philosophical, On Several Subjects*, London.

Gay, John (1731), 'Preliminary Dissertation Concerning the Fundamental Principle of Virtue or Morality', in *An Essay on the Origin of Evil, by Dr. William King*, trans. Edmund Law, London.

Hartley, David (1749), *Observations on Man, his Frame, his Duty, and his Expectations*, 2 vols, London.

Hobbes, Thomas (1991 [1658/1642]), *Man and Citizen (De Homine and De Cive)*, trans. Charles Wood, Thomas Scott-Craig and Bernard Gert, ed. Bernard Gert, Indianapolis: Hackett.

Hobbes, Thomas (1994a [1640]), Human Nature and De Corpore Politico, ed. J. C. A. Gaskin, Oxford: Oxford University Press.

Hobbes, Thomas (1994b [1651]), *Leviathan. With Selected Variants from the Latin Edition of 1668*, trans. Charles Wood, Thomas Scott-Craig and Bernard Gert, ed. Edwin Curley, Indianapolis: Hackett.

Home, Henry, Lord Kames (2005 [1751]), *Essays on the Principles of Morality and Natural Religion*, Indianapolis: Liberty Fund.

Hume, David (1978 [1739/1740]), *A Treatise of Human Nature*, ed. Lewis Selby-Bigge, Oxford: Oxford University Press.

Hume, David (1987), *Essays Moral, Political, and Literary*, ed. Eugene Miller, Indianapolis: Liberty Fund.

Hume, David (1996 [1748/1751]), *Enquiries Concerning Human Understanding and Concerning the Principles of Morals*, ed. Lewis Selby-Bigge and Peter Nidditch, Oxford: Oxford University Press.

Hume, David (2011), *The Letters of David Hume*, ed. John Greig, 2 vols, Oxford: Oxford University Press.

Hutcheson, Francis (1750), *Reflections upon Laughter and Remarks upon the Fable of the Bees*, Glasgow.

Hutcheson, Francis (1755), *A System of Moral Philosophy*, London.

Hutcheson, Francis (2001 [1728]), *An Essay on the Nature and Conduct of the Passions and Affections, with Illustrations on the Moral Sense*, ed. Aaron Garrett, Indianapolis: Liberty Fund.

Hutcheson, Francis (2006 [1730]), 'On the Natural Sociability of Mankind Inaugural Oration', in *Logic, Metaphysics, and the Natural Sociability of Mankind*, ed. James Moore and Michael Silverthorne, Indianapolis: Liberty Fund, 189–216.

Hutcheson, Francis (2008 [1725]), *An Inquiry into the Original of Our Ideas of Beauty and Virtue, in Two Treatises*, ed. William Leidhold, rev. edn, Indianapolis: Liberty Fund.

Innes, Alexander (1728), *Arete-Logia or, An Enquiry Into the Original of Moral Virtue*, London.

La Rochefoucauld, François de (1976 [1665]), *Réflexions ou Sentences et Maximes morales. Suivi de Réflexions diverses et des Maximes de Madame de Sablé*, ed. Jean Lafond, Paris: Gallimard.

Leechman, William (1755), 'Preface', in Francis Hutcheson, *A System of Moral Philosophy*, London.

MacMahon, Thomas O'Brien (1774), *An Essay on the Depravity and Corruption of Human Nature*, London.

Mandeville, Bernard (1732a), *An Enquiry Into the Origin of Honour, and the Usefulness of Christianity in War*, London.

Mandeville, Bernard (1732b), *A Letter to Dion, Occasion'd by his Book Call'd Alciphron, or the Minute Philosopher*, London.

Mandeville, Bernard (1988a [1714/1723]), *The Fable of the Bees, or Private Vices, Publick Benefits*, ed. Frederick Kaye, Indianapolis: Liberty Fund.

Mandeville, Bernard (1988b [1714]), 'An Enquiry Into the Origin of Moral Virtue', in *The Fable of the Bees, or Private Vices, Publick Benefits*, ed. Frederick Kaye, Indianapolis: Liberty Fund, 41–57.

Mandeville, Bernard (1988c [1714]), 'Remarks', in *The Fable of the Bees, or Private Vices, Publick Benefits*, ed. Frederick Kaye, Indianapolis: Liberty Fund, 58–251.

Mandeville, Bernard (1988d [1723]), 'An Essay on Charity, and Charity-Schools', in *The Fable of the Bees, or Private Vices, Publick Benefits*, ed. Frederick Kaye, Indianapolis: Liberty Fund, 253–322.

Mandeville, Bernard (1988e [1723]), 'A Search Into the Nature of Society', in *The Fable of the Bees, or Private Vices, Publick Benefits*, ed. Frederick Kaye, Indianapolis: Liberty Fund, 323–69.

Mandeville, Bernard (1988f [1729]), *The Fable of the Bees. Part II. By the Author of the First*, ed. Frederick Kaye, Indianapolis: Liberty Fund.

Mandeville, Bernard (2006 [1724]), *A Modest Defence of Publick Stews*, ed. Irwin Primer, New York: Palgrave Macmillan.

Moncrieff, Alexander (1735), *An Enquiry into the Principle, Rule and End of Moral Actions*, Edinburgh.

More, Henry (1690), *An Account of Virtue: or, Dr. Henry More's Abridgment of Morals, Put into English*, London [English translation of More's *Enchiridion Ethicum* from 1668].

More, Henry (1756), *An Essay on Disinterested Love, in a Letter to Bishop Stillingfleet*, Glasgow.
Nicole, Pierre (1999 [1675]), 'De la charité et de l'amour-propre', in *Essais de morale*, ed. Laurent Thirouin, Paris: PUF, 381–415.
Pufendorf, Samuel (2003 [1673/1691]), *The Whole Duty of Man, According to the Law of Nature*, ed. Ian Hunter and David Saunders, Indianapolis: Liberty Fund.
Reid, Thomas (2010 [1788]), *Essays on the Active Powers of Man*, ed. Knud Haakonssen and James Harris, Edinburgh: Edinburgh University Press.
Shaftesbury, Anthony Ashley Cooper, 3rd Earl of (1900), *The Life, Unpublished Letters, and Philosophical Regimen of Anthony, Earl of Shaftesbury, Author of the "Characteristics"*, ed. Benjamin Rand, London: Swan Sonnenschein.
Shaftesbury, Anthony Ashley Cooper, 3rd Earl of (1999a [1711]), *Characteristics of Men, Manners, Opinions, Times*, ed. Lawrence Klein, Cambridge: Cambridge University Press.
Shaftesbury, Anthony Ashley Cooper, 3rd Earl of (1999b [1711/1699]), 'An Inquiry Concerning Virtue or Merit', in *Characteristics of Men, Manners, Opinions, Times*, ed. Lawrence Klein, Cambridge: Cambridge University Press, 163–230.
Shaftesbury, Anthony Ashley Cooper, 3rd Earl of (1999c [1711/1709]), 'Sensus Communis, an Essay on the Freedom of Wit and Humour in a Letter to a Friend', in *Characteristics of Men, Manners, Opinions, Times*, ed. Lawrence Klein, Cambridge: Cambridge University Press, 29–69.
Shaftesbury, Anthony Ashley Cooper, 3rd Earl of (1999d [1711/1709]), 'The Moralists, a Philosophical Rhapsody, being a Recital of Certain Conversations on Natural and Moral Subjects', in *Characteristics of Men, Manners, Opinions, Times*, ed. Lawrence Klein, Cambridge: Cambridge University Press, 231–338.
Shaftesbury, Anthony Ashley Cooper, 3rd Earl of (1999e [1711]), 'Miscellaneous Reflections on the Preceding Treatises and Other Critical Subjects', in *Characteristics of Men, Manners, Opinions, Times*, ed. Lawrence Klein, Cambridge: Cambridge University Press, 339–483.
Shaftesbury, Anthony Ashley Cooper, 3rd Earl of (2013 [manuscript, 1706]), *Pathologia, A Theory of the Passions*, trans. and ed. Laurent Jaffro, Christian Maurer and Alain Petit, *History of European Ideas* 39:2, 221–40.
Smith, Adam (2002 [1759/1790]), *The Theory of Moral Sentiments*, ed. Knud Haakonssen, Cambridge: Cambridge University Press.
Stewart, Dugald (1829), *The Philosophy of the Active and Moral Powers of Man*, Cambridge.
Tucker, Abraham (2003 [1768]), *The Light of Nature Pursued*, ed. James Harris, 4 vols, Bristol: Thoemmes Press.

Turnbull, George (2005 [1740]), *The Principles of Moral and Christian Philosophy*, 2 vols, ed. Alexander Broadie, Indianapolis: Liberty Fund.
University Minutes of the University of St. Andrews [manuscript source] (1726–42), vol. 4: University Records, 25 April 1726–8 June 1742.
Witherspoon, John (1763 [1753]), *Ecclesiastical Characteristics: Or, the Arcana of Church Policy. Being an Humble Attempt to open up the Mystery of Moderation*, Edinburgh.

CRITICAL STUDIES

Ahnert, Thomas (2014), *The Moral Culture of the Scottish Enlightenment (1690–1805)*, New Haven, CT: Yale University Press.
Albee, Ernest (1990 [1902]), *A History of English Utilitarianism*, Bristol: Thoemmes Press.
Allen, Richard C. (1999), *David Hartley on Human Nature*, Albany: State University of New York Press.
Annas, Julia (1993), *The Morality of Happiness*, Oxford: Oxford University Press.
Bishop, John (1996), 'Moral Motivation and the Development of Francis Hutcheson's Philosophy', *Journal of the History of Ideas*, 57:2, 277–95.
Blackburn, Simon (2014), *Mirror, Mirror. The Uses and Abuses of Self-Love*, Princeton: Princeton University Press.
Branchi, Andrea (2014), 'Vanity, Virtue and the Duel: The Scottish Response to Mandeville', *Journal of Scottish Philosophy*, 12:1, 71–93.
Broad, C. D. (1971), *Five Types of Ethical Theory*, London: Routledge and Kegan Paul.
Broadie, Alexander (ed.) (2003), *The Cambridge Companion to the Scottish Enlightenment*, Cambridge: Cambridge University Press.
Brooke, Christopher (2012), *Philosophic Pride. Stoicism and Political Thought from Lipsius to Rousseau*, Princeton: Princeton University Press.
Carey, Daniel (2006), *Locke, Shaftesbury, and Hutcheson. Contesting Diversity in the Enlightenment and Beyond*, Cambridge: Cambridge University Press.
Carrive, Paulette (1980), *Bernard Mandeville. Passions, Vices, Vertus*, Paris: Vrin.
Crimmins, James E. (1998), *Utilitarians and Religion*, Bristol: Thoemmes Press.
Cunliffe, Christopher (ed.) (1992), *Joseph Butler's Moral and Religious Thought*, Oxford: Clarendon Press.
Darwall, Stephen (1995), *The British Moralists and the Internal 'Ought': 1640–1740*, Cambridge: Cambridge University Press.
Duncan-Jones, Austin (1952), *Butler's Moral Philosophy*, Harmondsworth: Penguin.

Force, Pierre (2003), *Self-Interest before Adam Smith. A Genealogy of Economic Science*, Cambridge: Cambridge University Press.

Forman-Barzilai, Fonna (2010), *Adam Smith and the Circles of Sympathy. Cosmopolitanism and Moral Theory*, Cambridge: Cambridge University Press.

Frankfurt, Harry (2004), *The Reasons of Love*, Princeton: Princeton University Press.

Frey, Richard G. (1992), 'Butler on Self-Love and Benevolence', in Christopher Cunliffe (ed.), *Joseph Butler's Moral and Religious Thought*, Oxford: Clarendon Press, 243–67.

Garrett, Aaron (2012), 'Joseph Butler's Moral Philosophy', in Edward N. Zalta (ed.), *The Stanford Encyclopedia of Philosophy*, https://plato.stanford.edu/archives/win2014/entries/butler-moral/ (last accessed 24 February 2018).

Garrett, Aaron, and Harris, James (eds) (2015), *Scottish Philosophy in the Eighteenth Century, vol. 1: Morals, Politics, Art, Religion*, Oxford: Oxford University Press.

Garrett, Aaron, and Heydt, Colin (2015), 'Moral Philosophy. Practical and Speculative', in Aaron Garrett and James Harris (eds), *Scottish Philosophy in the Eighteenth Century, vol. 1: Morals, Politics, Art, Religion*, Oxford: Oxford University Press, 77–130.

Gill, Michael B. (2000), 'Hume's Progressive View of Human Nature', *Hume Studies*, 26:1, 87–108.

Gill, Michael B. (2006), *The British Moralists on Human Nature and the Birth of Secular Ethics*, Cambridge: Cambridge University Press.

Gill, Michael B. (2010), 'From Cambridge Platonism to Scottish Sentimentalism', *Journal of Scottish Philosophy*, 8:1, 13–31.

Goldsmith, M. M. (1985), *Private Vices, Public Benefits. Bernard Mandeville's Social and Political Thought*, Cambridge: Cambridge University Press.

Grean, Stanley (1964), 'Self-Interest and Public Interest in Shaftesbury's Philosophy', *Journal of the History of Philosophy*, 11:1, 37–45.

Grean, Stanley (1967), *Shaftesbury's Philosophy of Religion and Ethics. A Study in Enthusiasm*, Athens: Ohio University Press.

Griswold, Charles (1999), *Adam Smith and the Virtues of Enlightenment*, Cambridge: Cambridge University Press.

Griswold, Charles (2018), *Jean-Jacques Rousseau and Adam Smith. A Philosophical Encounter*, New York: Routledge.

Grote, Simon (2006), 'Hutcheson's Divergence from Shaftesbury', *Journal of Scottish Philosophy*, 4:2, 159–72.

Grote, Simon (2010), 'Shaftesbury's Egoistic Hedonism', in Rainer Godel and Insa Kringler (eds), *Aufklärung. Interdisziplinäres Jahrbuch zur Erforschung des 18. Jahrhunderts und seiner Wirkungsgeschichte*, 22, 135–49.

Haakonssen, Knud (1990), 'Natural Law and Moral Realism: The Scottish Synthesis', in Michael A. Stewart (ed.), *Studies in the Philosophy of the Scottish Enlightenment*, Oxford: Clarendon Press, 61–85.

Haakonssen, Knud (1996), *Natural Law and Moral Philosophy. From Grotius to the Scottish Enlightenment*, Cambridge: Cambridge University Press.

Hanley, Ryan (2009), *Adam Smith and the Character of Virtue*, Cambridge: Cambridge University Press.

Harris, James (2003), 'Answering Bayle's Question: Religious Belief in the Moral Philosophy of the Scottish Enlightenment', in Daniel Garber and Steven Nadler (eds), *Oxford Studies in Early Modern Philosophy*, Oxford: Clarendon Press, 229–53.

Harris, James (2005), 'Hume's Use of the Rhetoric of Calvinism', in Marina Frasca-Spada and Peter Kail (eds), *Impressions of Hume*, Oxford: Oxford University Press, 141–59.

Harris, James (2008), 'Religion in Hutcheson's Moral Philosophy', *Journal of the History of Philosophy*, 46:2, 205–22.

Harris, James (ed.) (2013), *The Oxford Handbook of British Philosophy in the Eighteenth Century*, Oxford: Oxford University Press.

Harris, James (2015), *Hume. An Intellectual Biography*, Cambridge: Cambridge University Press.

Heath, Eugene (1998), 'Mandeville's Bewitching Engine of Praise', *History of Philosophy Quarterly*, 15:2, 205–26.

Heath, Eugene (2013), 'Adam Smith and Self-Interest', in Christopher Berry, Maria Paganelli and Craig Smith (eds), *The Oxford Handbook of Adam Smith*, Oxford: Oxford University Press, 241–64.

Henson, Richard (1988), 'Butler on Selfishness and Self-Love', *Philosophy and Phenomenological Research*, 49:1, 31–57.

Herdt, Jennifer (2008), *Putting on Virtue. The Legacy of the Splendid Vices*, Chicago: University of Chicago Press.

Heydt, Colin (2018), *Moral Philosophy in Eighteenth-Century Britain. God, Self, and Other*, Cambridge: Cambridge University Press.

Hirschman, Albert O. (1977), *The Passions and the Interests. Political Arguments for Capitalism before Its Triumph*, Princeton: Princeton University Press.

Hont, Istvan (2006), 'The Early Enlightenment Debate on Commerce and Luxury', in Mark Goldie and Robert Wokler (eds), *The Cambridge History of Eighteenth-Century Political Thought*, Cambridge: Cambridge University Press, 379–418.

Hundert, E. G. (1994), *The Enlightenment's Fable. Bernard Mandeville and the Discovery of Society*, Cambridge: Cambridge University Press.

Hutton, Sarah (2014), 'Intellectual History and the History of Philosophy', *History of European Ideas*, 40:7, 925–37.

Hutton, Sarah (2015), *British Philosophy in the Seventeenth Century*, Oxford: Oxford University Press.

Irwin, Terence (2008), *The Development of Ethics. A Historical and Critical Study, vol. II: From Suarez to Rousseau*, Oxford: Oxford University Press.

Jaffro, Laurent (2000), 'La question du sens moral et le lexique stoïcien. Sur la définition du "sense" comme "affection" dans l'Enquête sur la vertu', in Fabienne Brugère and Michel Malherbe (eds), *Shaftesbury. Philosophie et Politesse. Actes du Colloque (Université de Nantes, 1996)*, Paris: Honoré Champion, 61–78.

Jaffro, Laurent (2008), 'Which Platonism for Which Modernity? A Note on Shaftesbury's Socratic Sea-Cards', in Douglas Hedley and Sarah Hutton (eds), *Platonism at the Origins of Modernity: Studies on Platonism and Early Modern Philosophy*, Dordrecht: Springer, 255–67.

Jaffro, Laurent (2013), 'La mesure du bien. Que calcule le calcul moral de Hutcheson?', *Philosophiques*, 40:1, 197–215.

Jensen, Henning (1971), *Motivation and the Moral Sense in Francis Hutcheson's Ethical Theory*, The Hague: Martinus Nijhoff.

Kavka, Gregory S. (1986), *Hobbesian Moral and Political Theory*, Princeton: Princeton University Press.

Klein, Lawrence (1994), *Shaftesbury and the Culture of Politeness. Moral Discourse and Cultural Politics in Early Eighteenth-Century England*, Cambridge: Cambridge University Press.

Klein, Lawrence (2004), 'Cooper, Anthony Ashley, third earl of Shaftesbury (1671–1713)', in *Oxford Dictionary of National Biography*, Oxford: Oxford University Press, http://www.oxforddnb.com/view/10.1093/ref:odnb/9780198614128.001.0001/odnb-9780198614128-e-6209 (last accessed 24 February 2018).

Lafond, Jean (1996), 'Augustinisme et épicurisme au XVIIe siècle', in Jean Lafond, *L'Homme et son image. Morale et littérature de Montaigne à Mandeville*, Paris: Honoré Champion, 345–68.

Le Brun, Jacques (2002), *Le pur amour de Platon à Lacan*, Paris: Éditions du Seuil.

Leddy, Neven, and Lifschitz, Avi (eds) (2009), *Epicurus in the Enlightenment*, Oxford: Voltaire Foundation.

Lovejoy, Arthur O. (1961), *Reflections on Human Nature*, Baltimore: Johns Hopkins University Press.

Maurer, Christian (2006), 'Two Approaches to Self-Love: Hutcheson and Butler', *European Journal of Analytic Philosophy*, 2:2, 81–96.

Maurer, Christian (2010), 'Hutcheson's Relation to Stoicism in the Light of his Moral Psychology', *Journal of Scottish Philosophy*, 8:1, 33–49.

Maurer, Christian (2012), 'Archibald Campbell's Views of Self-cultivation and Self-denial in Context', *Journal of Scottish Philosophy*, 10:1, 13–27.

Maurer, Christian (2013a), 'Self-interest and Sociability', in James Harris (ed.), *The Oxford Handbook of British Philosophy in the Eighteenth Century*, Oxford: Oxford University Press, 291–314.

Maurer, Christian (2013b), 'Facing the Misery of Others: Pity, Pleasure and Tragedy in Scottish Enlightenment Moral Philosophy', in Tom Jones and Rowan Byoson (eds), *The Poetic Enlightenment. Poetry and Human Science, 1650–1820*, London: Pickering and Chatto, 75–87.

Maurer, Christian (2014), 'What Can an Egoist Say Against an Egoist? On Archibald Campbell's Criticisms of Bernard Mandeville', *Journal of Scottish Philosophy*, 12:1, 1–18.

Maurer, Christian (2015), '"Authors of a yet inferior Kind": Les moralistes augustiniens français, Bernard Mandeville et leurs critiques britanniques sur l'amour-propre', in Béatrice Guion (ed.), *Le Sentiment moral*, Paris: Honoré Champion, 95–110.

Maurer, Christian (2016a), 'Doctrinal Issues Concerning Human Nature and Self-love, and the Case of Archibald Campbell's *Enquiry*', *Intellectual History Review*, 26:3, 355–69.

Maurer, Christian (2016b), 'Archibald Campbell and the Committee for Purity of Doctrine on Natural Reason, Natural Religion, and Revelation', *History of European Ideas*, 42:2, 256–75.

Maurer, Christian (2016c), 'Stoicism and the Scottish Enlightenment', in John Sellars (ed.), *The Routledge Handbook of the Stoic Tradition*, London: Routledge, 254–69.

Maurer, Christian (2016d), '"*A Lapsu Corruptus*": Calvinist Doctrines and Seventeenth-Century Scottish *Theses Ethicæ*', *History of Universities*, 29:2, 188–209.

Maurer, Christian, and Jaffro, Laurent (2013), 'Reading Shaftesbury's *Pathologia*: An Illustration and Defence of the Stoic Account of the Emotions', *History of European Ideas*, 39:2, 207–20.

McNaughton, David (1996), 'British Moralists of the Eighteenth Century: Shaftesbury, Butler and Price', in Stuart Brown (ed.), *British Philosophy and the Age of Enlightenment*, London: Routledge, 203–27.

Mehta, Pratap Bhanu (2006), 'Self-Interest and Other Interests', in Knud Haakonssen (ed.), *The Cambridge Companion to Adam Smith*, Cambridge: Cambridge University Press, 246–69.

Millar, Alan (1988), 'Following Nature', *The Philosophical Quarterly*, 38, 165–85.

Millar, Alan (1992), 'Butler on God and Human Nature', in Christopher Cunliffe (ed.), *Joseph Butler's Moral and Religious Thought*, Oxford: Clarendon Press, 293–315.

Mills, Robin (2015), 'Archibald Campbell's *Necessity of Revelation* (1739) – the Science of Human Nature's First Study of Religion', *History of European Ideas*, 41:6, 728–46.

Monro, Hector (1975), *The Ambivalence of Bernard Mandeville*, Oxford: Clarendon Press.

Moore, James (1990), 'The Two Systems of Francis Hutcheson: On the Origins of the Scottish Enlightenment', in Michael A. Stewart (ed.), *Studies in the Philosophy of the Scottish Enlightenment*, Oxford: Clarendon Press, 37–59.

Moore, James (2013), 'Evangelical Calvinists Versus the Hutcheson Circle: Debating the Faith in Scotland, 1738–1739', in Anne Dunan-Page and Clotilde Prunier (eds), *Debating the Faith: Religion and Letter Writing in Great Britain 1550–1800*, Dordrecht: Springer, 177–93.

Moore, James, and Silverthorne, Michael (1984), 'Natural Sociability and Natural Rights in the Moral Philosophy of Gershom Carmichael', in Vincent Hope (ed.), *Philosophers of the Scottish Enlightenment*, Edinburgh: Edinburgh University Press, 1–12.

Moriarty, Michael (2006), *Fallen Nature, Fallen Selves: Early Modern French Thought II*, Oxford: Oxford University Press.

Moriarty, Michael (2011), *Disguised Vices. Theories of Virtue in Early Modern French Thought*, Oxford: Oxford University Press.

Norton, David Fate (1982), *David Hume. Common-Sense Moralist, Sceptical Metaphysician*, Princeton: Princeton University Press.

Nuovo, Victor (1999), 'Tucker, Abraham (1705–1774)', in John Yolton, John Price and John Stephens (eds), *The Dictionary of Eighteenth-Century British Philosophers*, Bristol: Thoemmes Press, 893–8.

O'Donovan, Oliver (1980), *The Problem of Self-Love in St. Augustine*, New Haven, CT: Yale University Press.

Peltonen, Markku (2003), *The Duel in Early Modern England. Civility, Politeness, and Honour*, Cambridge: Cambridge University Press.

Penelhum, Terence (1985), *Butler*, London: Routledge and Kegan Paul.

Phillips, David (2000), 'Butler and the Nature of Self-Interest', *Philosophy and Phenomenological Research*, 60:2, 347–51.

Pittock, Murray (2006), 'Forbes, Alexander, fourth Lord Forbes of Pitsligo (1678–1762)', in *Oxford Dictionary of National Biography*, Oxford: Oxford University Press, http://www.oxforddnb.com/view/10.1093/ref: odnb/9780198614128.001.0001/odnb-9780198614128-e-9813? rskey=EiGr5w&result=4 (last accessed 24 February 2018).

Price, John (1999), 'Gay, John (1699–1745)', in John Yolton, John Price and John Stephens (eds), *The Dictionary of Eighteenth-Century British Philosophers*, Bristol: Thoemmes Press, 893–8.

Primer, Irwin (2006), *Bernard Mandeville's 'A Modest Defence of Publick Stews'. Prostitution and its Discontents in Early Georgian England*, New York: Palgrave Macmillan.

Raphael, David D., and Macfie, Alec L. (1976), 'Introduction', in Adam Smith, *The Theory of Moral Sentiments*, Oxford: Clarendon Press, 1–52.

Rivers, Isabel (2000), *Reason, Grace, and Sentiment. A Study of the Language of Religion and Ethics in England, 1660–1780. Volume II: Shaftesbury to Hume*, Cambridge: Cambridge University Press.

Roberts, T. A. (1973), *The Concept of Benevolence. Aspects of Eighteenth-Century Moral Philosophy*, Basingstoke: Macmillan.

Robertson, John (2005), *The Case for the Enlightenment. Scotland and Naples 1680–1760*, Cambridge: Cambridge University Press.

Sagar, Paul (2013), 'Sociability, Luxury and Sympathy: The Case of Archibald Campbell', *History of European Ideas*, 39:6, 791–814.

Schrader, Wolfgang H. (1984), *Ethik und Anthropologie in der englischen Aufklärung. Der Wandel der moral-sense-Theorie von Shaftesbury bis Hume*, Hamburg: Felix Meiner.

Scott, William Robert (1900), *Francis Hutcheson. His Life, Teaching and Position in the History of Philosophy*, Cambridge: Cambridge University Press.

Scott-Taggart, Martin (1966), 'Mandeville: Cynic or Fool?', *The Philosophical Quarterly*, 16:1, 221–32.

Scott-Taggart, Martin (1968), 'Butler on Disinterested Actions', *The Philosophical Quarterly*, 18:1, 16–28.

Sellars, John (2006), *Stoicism*, Berkeley: University of California Press.

Sellars, John (2016a), 'Shaftesbury, Stoicism, and Philosophy as a Way of Life', *Sophia*, 55:3, 395–408.

Sellars, John (ed.) (2016b), *The Routledge Handbook of the Stoic Tradition*, London: Routledge.

Shaver, Robert (2014), 'Egoism', in Edward N. Zalta (ed.), *Stanford Encyclopedia of Philosophy*, https://plato.stanford.edu/entries/egoism/ (last accessed 24 February 2018).

Sher, Richard B. (1985), *Church and University in the Scottish Enlightenment. The Moderate Literati of Edinburgh*, Edinburgh: Edinburgh University Press.

Skoczylas, Anne (2008), 'Archibald Campbell's *Enquiry into the Original of Moral Virtue*, Presbyterian Orthodoxy, and the Scottish Enlightenment', *The Scottish Historical Review*, 87:1, 68–100.

Sober, Elliot (1992), 'Hedonism and Butler's Stone', *Ethics*, 103:1, 97–103.

Solomon, Robert C. (1993), *The Passions. Emotions and the Meaning of Life*, Indianapolis: Hackett.

Stewart, Michael A. (1996), 'The Scottish Enlightenment', in Stuart Brown (ed.), *British Philosophy and the Age of Enlightenment*, London: Routledge, 274–308.

Stewart, Robert (1982), 'John Clarke and Francis Hutcheson on Self-Love and Moral Motivation', *Journal of the History of Philosophy*, 20:2, 261–77.

Stiker-Métral, Charles-Olivier (2007), *Narcisse contrarié. L'amour propre dans le discours moral en France (1650–1715)*, Paris: Honoré Champion.

Strasser, Mark (1987), 'Hutcheson on the Higher and Lower Pleasures', *Journal of the History of Philosophy*, 25:4, 517–31.

Sturgeon, Nicholas (1976), 'Nature and Conscience in Butler's Ethics', *The Philosophical Review*, 85:3, 316–56.

Taylor, Jackie (2012), 'Hume on the Dignity of Pride', *Journal of Scottish Philosophy*, 10:1, 29–49.

Taylor, Jackie (2015), *Reflecting Subjects. Passion, Sympathy, and Society in Hume's Philosophy*, Oxford: Oxford University Press.

Tennant, Bob (2011), *Conscience, Consciousness and Ethics in Joseph Butler's Philosophy and Ministry*, Woodbridge: Boydell Press.

Tilley, John (2016), 'Hutcheson's Theological Objection to Egoism', *Journal of Scottish Philosophy*, 14:1, 101–23.

Tilley, John (2018), 'Butler's Stone', *Pacific Philosophical Quarterly*, 99:4, 891–909.

Tolonen, Mikko (2008), 'Politeness, Paris, and the *Treatise*', *Hume Studies*, 34:1, 21–42.

Tolonen, Mikko (2013), *Mandeville and Hume. Anatomists of Civil Society*, Oxford: Voltaire Foundation.

Turco, Luigi (1999), 'Sympathy and Moral Sense: 1725–1740', *British Journal for the History of Philosophy*, 7:1, 79–101.

Turco, Luigi (2003), 'Moral Sense and the Foundations of Morals', in Alexander Broadie (ed.), *The Cambridge Companion to the Scottish Enlightenment*, Cambridge: Cambridge University Press, 136–56.

Vivenza, Gloria (2001), *Adam Smith and the Classics. The Classical Heritage in Adam Smith's Thought*, Oxford: Oxford University Press.

Wilson, Catherine (2008), *Epicureanism at the Origin of Modernity*, Oxford: Oxford University Press.

Wilson, Catherine (2016), 'Political Philosophy in a Lucretian Mode', in David Norbrook, Stephen Harrison and Philip Hardie (eds), *Lucretius and the Early Modern*, Oxford: Oxford University Press, 259–82.

Index

EU Authorised Representative:

Easy Access System Europe Mustamäe tee 50, 10621 Tallinn, Estonia

gpsr.requests@easproject.com

Printed and bound by CPI Group (UK) Ltd, Croydon, CR0 4YY

22/12/2025

02024450-0009